29 95

THE WORLD OF
WORDS

THE WORLD OF
WORDS

VICTOR STEVENSON

Sterling Publishing Co., Inc.
New York

Library of Congress Cataloging-in-Publication Data Available

10 9 8 7 6 5 4 3 2 1

Published 1999 by Sterling Publishing Company, Inc
387 Park Avenue South, New York, N.Y. 10016
Original edition published 1983 by
MacDonald & Co (Publishers) Ltd., London and Sydney
Text 1999 Victor Stevenson
This edition c1983, 1999 Eddison Sadd Editions Limited
Distributed in Canada by Sterling Publishing
c/o Canadian Manda Group, One Atlantic Avenue, Suite 105
Toronto, Ontario, Canada M6K 3E7
Distributed in Great Britain and Europe by Cassell PLC
Wellington House, 125 Strand, London WC2R 0BB, England
Distributed in Australia by Capricorn Link (Australia) Pty Ltd.
P.O. Box 6651, Baulkam Hills, Business Centre, NSW 2153, Australia

The right of Victor Stevenson to be identified as the Author of this Work has been asserted by
him in accordance with the Copyright, Designs and Patents Act 1988.

Printed and bound in the United States of America.

Sterling ISBN   0-8069-3905-2 Trade
                     0-8069-3944-3 Paper

Contents

Foreword

In the beginning was the word. What it was is lost in the black abysm of time, out of reach of all knowledge. But something like two million years ago man-like creatures, walking upright and using patterned tools, began to evolve. At some stage, early man began to communicate by vocal noises more elaborate than the grunts and barks of the fellow-animals over which he was establishing his dominion. The distinctive quality of man is that he is a talking animal. Words are our noblest heritage from those crude beginnings.

Language multiplied and spread across the face of the earth as fruitfully as mankind. What song the Syrens sang, or what name Achilles assumed when he hid himself among women, though puzzling questions, are not beyond all conjecture. We can only guess that hundreds of thousands of languages have been spoken since the beginning from the fact that 2,769 languages (the figure depends a bit on what you count as a language) are spoken around the world today.

There is no class system in the eternal ebb and flow of words. Languages are perfect for the uses of those who speak them. Aleut is exactly suited to the fishy needs of the Aleutian Islanders. Some of the Amerindian languages have grammars of a subtlety that makes French look crude. But we can claim without chauvinism that the languages of Europe, whose extraordinary history is explained and illustrated in this book, are the most influential to have evolved from that ancient Tower of Babel.

This is not because they are the oldest; Chinese is older. It is not because they are the languages of the majority; not quite half the population of the world speak some of the European languages as their first or second languages. It is not even that they are in the process of becoming the world language; though English in fact is. The reason that the languages of Europe are dominant is that Europe was the cradle of modern civilization. Of the numberless words that have been spoken and written since primitive man stopped grunting and started to talk, most of the ones that have changed history, or been handed down as wise, or have founded great religions, or have been remembered or written down as too good to lose, have been in one of the European languages, or their relatives in southern Asia.

The common mother tongue of them all, which is long extinct, but whose existence can be traced from clues in its descendant languages, is called Indo-European. Take that word *mother*. It begins with 'm' and tends to have two syllables in almost all the Indo-European tongues, from Sanskrit *matar* to *meter* in Attic Greek and *mathair* in Gaelic. Think what resonances that word has had down the centuries, from *France, mère des arts, des armes et des loix* to the infernal serpent who deceived 'the mother of mankind'.

The Indo-European mother tongue started to be spoken about 8,000 years ago, probably in the open lands where Europe and Asia meet. Today its descendants are spoken and written at the round earth's imagined corners, from Bengali to Swedish, and from Afrikaans to the Psychobabble of California.

The gloomy bewail the break-up of languages. If they are feeling Doomsday-pessimistic they predict that English too is breaking up, and that by the end of the century a Londoner will be literally unable to understand an Australian speaking Oz and an Indian talking in Bombayspeak. I think that the gloomy are wrong, and that the centripetal forces in language are stronger today than the centrifugal. But even if they are right, break-up and branching-out are natural and healthy processes in language. Latin was a marvellous language, exact, powerful, and flexible. It may have seemed the end of the world when it started to break up. But the Romance languages that sprang from its remains are languages that we can also be proud of.

The history of the growth of the languages of Europe is a story not of decadence but of triumph and great glory. It is of interest not just to etymologists and philologists but to a wide general audience as well. WORDS is a lively and entertaining account which uses a wealth of illustration - photographs, prints and maps - to make its points; after all, 'a picture is worth a thousand words'.

Foreword to the new edition

Words change as fast as we use them. Since this book was first published 16 years ago, many words have come into the English language to fill a gap in the language, and stuck around for long enough to be recorded in new dictionaries. Many of them are specialized, recording the vast changes in science, medicine, computers and the Internet. Similar changes have happened in other European languages, though not as many as in English, which has become the international language for many activities from air traffic control to the world-wide web. Even the vanished voices of so-called dead languages are changing thanks to new discoveries by archaeologists. The vocabulary of Ancient Greek is continually increased and changed by fragments from the papyrus dump at Oxyrhynchus, the modern El Bahnasa in Upper Egypt.

Political earthquakes have shaken languages as well as the world. The Soviet empire has broken up into 15 separate states, and Germany is reasserting itself in Eastern Europe. The Afrikaans language is in retreat, since Apartheid fell in South Africa. From China to Peru, English continues to advance as a second or alternative language for millions. In many branches of science and medicine it has already become the necessary passport. All this means it is a high time for a new edition of WORDS by Victor Stevenson - now retitled THE WORLD OF WORDS. This revised edition brings up to date his charts of the shifting tides of language, and illustrates them with fresh maps and pictures. The WORLD OF WORDS remains the most entertaining and scholarly introduction to the development of language and the words we speak.

Philip Howard

Introduction

"Language is a natural object and its study resembles natural history," observed the Danish scholar Rasmus Rask (1787–1832). A language shares many characteristics with all living things. It evolves from a parent stock and in favourable conditions will spread far from its native soil, generating, as the Latin of Rome did, a family of distinguished offspring. Blended with another (as Anglo-Saxon was blended with Norman French), it may produce a hybrid more vigorous than either of its parents, and displace other less energetic species.

It is also prone to corruption, decay and extinction. Like animals and plants, it has to face competition and undergo changing conditions. If it fails to adapt, it is reduced to insignificance, is given up by those who use it and perishes, for unlike the tangible forms of nature, a language has no life of its own. It exists solely on the lips of its speakers, and its fate is bound up ultimately with the fortunes of those who use it.

The Indo-European language family with which this book is concerned is only one of many throughout the world, each with a story to tell, in which words are tracked like clues across continents and oceans to a conjectural "birthplace" many thousands of miles away. Typical of these is the Austronesian family, one of the largest and most widely scattered.

Its heartland is thought to have been in Malaya and the Indonesian islands, perhaps even having arrived there from Asia. It is the parent of the modern languages of Malaya, Indonesia and the Philippines, is the old language of Taiwan and that of a galaxy of islands spread across the Pacific – the "small islands" of Micronesia, the "dark islands" of Melanesia and the "many islands" of Polynesia. Its outmarkers in Oceania are Hawaii and New Zealand; it was carried to them by navigators whose skill and knowledge of oceanic currents, winds and seasons are one of the wonders of mankind. Their journeys also took them west from Indonesia, across the Indian Ocean, where Malagasy, the language of Madagascar, is a member of the family.

The world's second largest language family is Sino-Tibetan-Burmese, the three principal forms of more than 300 eastern Asian languages. The history of the world would have taken an utterly different course had the Chinese acquired any sort of lasting global empire, as they might have done when their great fleets of trading junks – vessels far larger and more seaworthy than anything in the west at that time – coasted the Indies and Africa in the early years of the fifteenth century. But all these journeys ceased abruptly when, after a few decades, China turned its back on a world in which it had no interest. It was from the west that the great migrations of language took place in modern times, by men looking for a new way to China and the Indies.

The adventurers who carried the European languages to new homes in distant continents between the fifteenth and eighteenth centuries were continuing a process that had began in prehistory. Several thousand years earlier, in the open landscape where Europe meets Asia, there existed a society whose conversation contained the seeds of almost all modern European languages, and many of those in southern Asia.

The dispersal of this mother tongue, or "speech community" of closely related dialects, lasted untold centuries until, in one form or another, its descendants were heard from the Atlantic shores of Europe to the Bay of Bengal. The parent language had vanished and its dialects, separated by time and space, had been transformed into distinctive and disparate language groups. At the dawn of history, those of Europe had begun to assume the identities of Greek and Latin, Celtic and Germanic, Slavonic and Baltic; in the east, the "distant cousins" had diverged into early Iranian forms and Sanskrit, parent of most of India's modern tongues. All memory of that former association had gone, and all common understanding.

History records their subsequent fortunes, which have been mixed, and the influences they have had upon each other, for none has remained "pure" in the face of constant competition and often conflict. The "proto-languages," Italic, Germanic and Slavonic, have created distinctive families of their own and members of two, Italic and Germanic, have shifted their centres of gravity to another continent; there are now far more speakers of Spanish, Portuguese and English in the New World than there are in the Old. Russian, the most widely spoken of the Slavonic languages, has spread, at least in an official capacity, to the borders of China and the Pacific Ocean.

Not all have been as successful. Celtic, which once rivalled the Classical languages of Greece and Rome in the extent of its realms, has been all but abandoned, and is kept alive only on the fringes of the Continent. It has left few marks on its modern contemporaries; in contrast, Greek, the first of European languages to be attested in history, has in its Classical form retained the esteem of posterity, which continues to find it invaluable.

WORDS is a broad-brush portrait of this remarkable family, the growth or decay of its individual members, their rise to eminence and their travails.

V.S. 1998

CHAPTER ONE

Vanished voices

Written records know nothing of the ancient community from whose everyday conversation most of the highly cultivated and individual languages of Europe have descended. What portrait exists of them has been formed from words, often heavily disguised by time, shifts of meaning and grammatical forms, in the modern languages of Europe, southern Asia and – as "expatriates" – in the Americas, Africa and Australia.

Both the community and its language had been dispersed as if by the wind before the beginning of recorded time. For want of a better description, they are called Indo-European, a term coined in 1813 as scholarship unearthed evidence of their existence.

Medieval European scholars were aware of the similarities shared by languages that had long been in contact with each other, as their predecessors of Classical Greece and Rome had remarked upon the common ground shared by their two languages. Even at the level of the market place a medieval Hanseatic trader from Lübeck, travelling between his northern depots and more concerned with a hard bargain than the niceties of conversation, would have noticed how like his Low German dialect was the speech of England, or of Scandinavia. For the most part, however, medieval Christians were content to accept that the Hebrew of the Old Testament was the language of paradise and the subsequent chaos of tongues the result of divine wrath.

Evidence that the languages of Europe had, with few exceptions, evolved in stages from a common source, was found neither in Greece nor Rome, nor anywhere in Europe, but in an ancient and distant language, the Classical Sanskrit of India. Enshrined and unchanged for more than 2,000 years in the ritual speech of its scholars, it was shown to possess massive similarities to Greek and Latin. Only one conclusion could be drawn: all three had come from a common source.

"The Sanskrit language, whatever may be its antiquity, is of a wonderful structure; more perfect than the Greek, more copious than the Latin and more exquisitely refined than either; yet bearing to both of them a stronger affinity, both in the roots of verbs and in the forms of grammar, than could possibly have been produced by accident; so strong that no philologer could examine all three, without believing them to have sprung from a common source which, perhaps, no longer exists …"

Sir William Jones, the British orientalist who made this observation in 1786, went on to suggest that not only Greek and Latin but Gothic [Germanic] and Celtic, as well as Old Persian, might be added to the same family. Jones did not expand on his remarkably accurate hypothesis, but others soon did, to turn what had been largely speculation into a science and to prove, beyond all reasonable doubt, the existence of a primitive or proto-language from which the Indo-European tongues had descended.

Pieced together like fragments of some shattered artifact, words – and even parts of words – common to the languages of Europe, Iran and India build a model of a vanished people and their language, their way of life, and when and where they lived. They were probably not a single ethnic group of people sharing similar physical characteristics, but a mixture of fair- and darker-skinned people, the result of much earlier contacts. During the latter part of the nineteenth century and well into the twentieth, a myth emerged of a super-race, the purely European blue-eyed, blond "Aryan" of superior mental powers and energy. The linguist as much as the anthropologist has proved otherwise; the Sanskrit word *arya*, "of noble birth," provides the source of "Iran" (and, quite possibly, of "Eire").

They lived a part-settled, part-nomadic existence. They had domesticated most of the animals – the cow, the sheep, the goat and the pig – on which their descendants came to rely. They had lately tamed the horse, the motor for their future expansion, and were attended by dogs, the first of all animals to recognize man as a friend. (Few birds have accepted domestication, but the goose was the first to do so – its name is the oldest of all bird names, echoing through most of the Indo-European languages.) They spun and wove cloth from wool – then, as in medieval Europe, a measure of wealth. They worked leather and perhaps some metal, turned pots from clay, cleared the ground and ploughed it, using yoked oxen to pull the hooked branches that were the first ploughs. They planted grain and ground it to produce meal or flour.

Their tribal and family structures were, in primitive form, much as they are in modern society. They had their chiefs and kings, and laws and customs, to govern social behaviour. Marriage was customary, although a man might seize his wife by force or more likely purchase her from her family. There were feuds between

KUON HOUND GHANS GOOSE

More than 5,000 years separate *kuon*★ from 'hound' and *ghans*★ from "goose." The italicized words are those which linguists believe are the ancestral forms from which our modern words have descended.

The dog (an Old English word, of uncertain origin) was the first wild animal to befriend mankind. Following the nomad for scraps of food, the dog's puppies were picked up for children's pets, and it soon joined the human "pack." In return for its welcome, the dog provided guard and help in the hunt – probably teaching hunters about stalking game. The carefully bred hunting hound and retriever of today fulfill the function for which man and his best friend first joined forces.

Among the victims of that early sociable partnership may well have been the goose. Whiffling in from the Arctic, it offered an addition to the larder during the hard months of the winter. The greylag, ancestor of the domestic fowl, is the only species of goose to breed in temperate Europe, providing not only prey for the predator, but also eggs and young for him to collect.

The newly-hatched goslings, "imprinting" the human as foster parent, became part of the family, and the word goose became the first of all bird names in the vocabulary.

★*Kuon:* Gr. *kuon,* Lat. *canis,*
　　　　Ger. *Hund,* Eng. "hound."
★*Ghans:* Gr. *khen,* Lat. *anser,*
　　　　Ger. *Gans,* Eng. "goose."
The Sanskrit word for "goose" *hamsa* is also given to the duck and the swan, which are, like the goose, birds of rivers and marshes.

Jakob Grimm, folklorist and genealogist of Europe's family of languages.

clans, and payment was exacted for wrongs done. Above all there were the gods, clear ancestors of those worshipped not only by Celts, Greeks, Romans and Germanic tribesmen, but also by their distant relatives in south-east Asia, by whatever names they were known.

From their word for "god" or "deity" there emerged the Sanskrit *deva*, the Greek *Zeus*, the Latin *deus*; from their "king" the Sanskrit *raja*, the Latin *rex*, the Irish Celtic *ri*. Family relationships had been established and named – the ancestral Indo-European forms for "father" and "mother" became the Sanskrit *pitar* and *mātar,* Latin *pater* and *mater* and so on, through the family. The apparent difference between the Germanic "father" or *Vater* and the Latin *pater* is explained by a prehistoric phenomenon known as the Germanic sound-shift, in which the letter *p* in the classical languages became *f* or *v* in the long-separated proto-Germanic of the northern lands. There were other consonant changes as well, collectively known as Grimm's Law, after the famous German scholar who first explained them in the nineteenth century.

The homeland

Where the Indo-Europeans lived has been a matter for speculation ever since their existence has been known. Long and bitter debate, often colored by the national prejudices of those engaged in it, has located the homeland variously in Scandinavia, Baltic Russia, Central Europe and the Balkans. One thing is certain above all others: the world of plants and animals with which the old community was familiar was one associated with a northern, colder climate. Spread throughout the old vocabulary are common words for snow and freezing cold, for northern vegetation like the beech, pine, birch and willow, and animals like the bear, wolf and otter; there are none (although many were later borrowed) for the plants and animals of the more exotic climate in which the Indian and Iranian members of the family made their homes.

Common consent now places the original homeland of the Indo-Europeans in eastern Europe, between the Carpathian and Ural mountain ranges, where wide grasslands suited the nomadic pastoralists but where there were also waterways beside which agricultural settlements and homes could be established.

To the north, in the cold birch forests and swamps of the Russian *taiga,* was a scattering of nomadic hunters, ancestors in speech at least of the Finns, Lapps and Hungarians who were in turn to enter Europe. Beyond the Black Sea and the Caucasus, which marked the southern boundaries of Indo-European territory, were the Semitic civilizations of the "fertile crescent," sweeping in an arc from Egypt through the Middle East to the delta of the Tigris and Euphrates rivers. The Indo-Europeans were thus in a transition zone between the ancient way of life of man the hunter and the settled pattern of town and supporting countryside that exists today.

The continent to the west into which the

Indo-Europeans were to spread their parent language offered a greater variety of natural features than anything they were accustomed to. Snow-capped mountain ranges, densely-wooded hills, and plains watered by numberless rivers all crowded into an area which was little more than a sea-frayed appendage to Asia, almost five times its size. Naturalists would describe it as a range of "habitats" in which individual cultures, precursors of Europe's modern linguistic groups and nations, could grow. Above all, it had for the most part a temperate climate, its. western half influenced by maritime winds which spared it the extremes to which more arctic or more tropical realms were exposed. It was fertile soil for a new civilization.

The break-up

That period of pre-history when the Indo-Europeans made up a single, loosely-knit group is thought to have been between 5,000 and 6,000 years ago, 3,000 to 4,000 years BC. The time they began their momentous split-up can only be conjectured, for, like everything else about them, it predates history. A probable time is around the end of the third millennium BC. Two innovations, both of which can be traced to their homeland or close to it, were instrumental. The first was the domestication of the horse, altogether a faster and more serviceable animal than the lumbering ox – which had long been pressed into service as a beast of burden. The other was the wheeled vehicle, which is thought to have been invented in the northern Caucasus.

It was a long time before the efficient trappings of harness were developed to take full advantage of the horse's strength and adaptability, and the saddle was an even later introduction; the horse was at first yoked like the ox and ridden, if at all, bare-backed.

However inefficiently used, the horse and the wheel gave a new mobility and

One of 25,000 clay tablets unearthed at the site of Hattusa, capital of the Hittite empire in Asia Minor. The cuneiform inscriptions show the earliest form of written Indo-European, the oldest, an account of the exploits of a Hittite king, dating from 1,800 BC.

opportunities for expansion to the Indo-Europeans, and began the process by which the old language began to take on new and divergent forms. One of the earliest groups to move encircled the Black Sea and made its home in Asia Minor. These people enter history (and the Bible) as the Hittites and do not stay long; only since the early part of the twentieth century has it been discovered that their language stems from the old Indo-European root. Interestingly, surviving Hittite reliefs show the wheel and the horse combined in the war chariot, the product of a richer and more ambitious society than that represented by the yoked animal of the pastoralist.

Recently discovered texts show that another group reached Chinese Turkestan. Speculation that their presence there hinted at a more easterly homeland for the Indo-European people was quenched by the discovery that their language, called Tocharian and now extinct, contained words of distinctly European origin; their word for "fish," for example, was *laksi*, all but identical to the German word *Lachs,* "salmon," a fish of northern European waters. It is thought possible that the Tocharians came from a home originally in Europe and migrated to eastern Asia, long after the major language groups had reached their permanent settlements. Tocharian became extinct about 1,000 years ago, Hittite probably 1,000 years earlier.

The main eastern and western branches of the family had by now found their way to and settled the land that their descendants now occupy. The Indo-Iranian or Indo-Aryan branch *(see pages 20–24)* reached its vast realms about 2,000 years BC, entering them from the west and north-west by way of the lands surrounding the Caspian Sea.

Into the west

The westward movement of the people who were to become the first "modern Europeans" took them into a gentler climate and an infinitely greener landscape. They rapidly split into different groups, each following its destiny wherever it was to lead them into history *(see map, pages 18–19).* The ancestors of the **Greeks,** the first to be attested in written records, made their way to the Mediterranean peninsula and archipelago (and a pre-Greek culture that left its mark on the language) from which, only briefly, they were to stray. **Italics**, ultimate progenitors of the Latin language and its distinguished descendants, kept company through the Danube plain with the **Celts** (their languages display features that reflect this longer relationship) until they were parted by the Alps; the Celts moved into western Europe, the Italics southward towards the Mediterranean.

Others, attracted by the northern plains and forests and the western Baltic seaboard, enter history as the **Germanic** people, while their eastern neighbours, the **Slavs**, appear to have travelled the least distance from the ancestral estates, perhaps preceded by their near relations, the **Balts**. The modern Baltic languages, Lithuanian and Latvian, possess Indo-European features that have long since vanished from other European languages.

Two other Indo-European languages that flourished in antiquity in central and eastern

THE "EUROPEAN IRANIANS"

Iranian languages are heard today in Iran, Afghanistan, Tajikistan and, as Kurdish, in Turkey and Iraq. They were present and widespread in south-eastern Europe during the lifetime of Herodotus, "The Father of History" (*c.* 484–424 BC), as the languages of the Scythians and related tribes.

The Scythians were formidable warriors, difficult to vanquish in battle, known for attacking then disappearing when attacked. Even their settlements had wheels, "wicker buildings mounted on heavy chariots." They were among the invaders of the Indian subcontinent, and traces of their language have been found in Chinese Turkestan (Sinkiang).

In Europe, they ranged across southern Russia (marked "Scythia" on ancient maps), penetrated into the Danube basin and left a permanent mark on the atlas. The name of the Russian river Don is simply their word "river" and the same element is found also in the Dnieper, Dniester and Danube rivers.

Europe were Illyrian and Thracian. Illyrian was found throughout the region corresponding to what was Yugoslavia, and possibly over a greater area that included something of southern Germany. The Roman conquest of the region began the decline of the language, which nevertheless survived until the Slavonic intrusions from the north. **Albanian**, which is an individual branch of the Indo-European family, may be the last surviving echo of Illyrian.

Thracian, or Thraco-Phrygian, occupied the Balkans east of the Illyrian-speaking regions and north of Greek. Thracians were accounted among the world's most numerous peoples; their language came under early attack from Greek and later from the Latin of the Roman Empire. It may have lasted into the sixth century AD. Phrygian likewise is extinct; it was the language of Homer's Trojans and occupied the western part of Asia Minor after the collapse of the Hittite Empire there.

One last member of the Thraco-Phrygian group, **Armenian**, has survived. Its speakers are thought to have made their way to their present homeland in the Caucasus, destroying what was left of the Hittite Empire on the way. While it lasted, the Hittite language was one of the last survivors of the Indo-European family in the Near East. To the south and east were Semitic speakers, part of a huge family with its generic roots in North Africa – perhaps in the region of the Sahara which, in pre-history, was not the unwelcoming desert it was later to become. Semitic speakers were destined to give the world two of its most widespread religions – Christianity and Islam – and, small but influential, Judaism.

The Babylonians and Assyrians were Semitics. Their languages are now part of ancient history, like Phoenician Punic. Modern Semitic includes Hebrew, Arabic (the official language of a dozen nations) and the widely-used Hausa of West Africa, among many others.

THE FAMILY

The pedigree★ of the Indo-European languages shown here is principally that of the European languages – a chart devoted to the Indo-Aryan group would be quite as complex, the Indian forms alone being as numerous as those of Europe. European languages have had a world-wide impact, while those of the east remain essentially where they were spoken before the modern era. ★*Pedigree,* from French *pied de grue* 'crane's foot'. The bird (Latin *Grus*) was known to the first Indo-Europeans – its name was probably coined by them in imitation of its call.

Greek: an independent and distinguished branch, Greek traces an unbroken descent over 3,000 to 4,000 years but has no "offspring." It flourishes as a nation's tongue and adds "value" to its modern contemporaries.

Hittite and **Tocharian:** two extinct (†) branches of the family. Hittite flourished in Anatolia and Syria until 1,200 BC, Tocharian in central Asia until *c.* 1,000 AD.

Indo-Iranian: the eastern branch of the Indo-European family has two main groups: the **Indo-Aryan** or **Indic languages** descended from Sanskrit (only a few of the major modern languages are shown on the chart); and the **Iranian languages**, modern forms of which include Persian or Farsi, Pushtu, Baluchi, Tajiki and Kurdish.

Albanian: the language of one of the smallest of nations, Albanian (now much influenced by surrounding languages) contains the last vestiges of extinct Illyrian and Thracian which succumbed to the Latin of Rome and later intrusions by Slavonic tribes.

Celtic: once among the most widespread of European languages, Celtic survives as the national language of one country, Ireland, and in Wales, Scotland and Brittany.

Italic: the Italic or 'Romance' languages trace their origins to the Latin of Rome. Where Greek remained confined mainly to Greece, Latin was carried across Europe by the Roman Empire and to the New World by its Portuguese, Spanish and French descendants.

Germanic: the most widely used (through English) group, Germanic has two surviving branches – West (German, Dutch, Frisian and English) and North (Danish, Icelandic, Faeroese, Norwegian and Swedish). The East Germanic (Gothic) branch migrated east to the Black Sea then west with the Ostrogoths and Visigoths, vanishing in the Dark Ages.

Armenian: with its home in the Caucasus since Classical Greece, Armenian traces its roots to the extinct Thraco-Phrygian languages of south-east Europe and Asia Minor. Like Greek and Albanian, Armenian has an independent place in the Indo-European family.

Slavonic: the Slavonic language "exploded" across Europe during the Dark Ages, beyond the Vistula to the Elbe in the west, to the Balkans and the Black Sea in the east. Ten national languages are descended from the old parent.

Baltic: Lithuanian and Latvian survive from the Baltic branch, which occupied an area diminished (it once reached from the Vistula to the Volga) by Slavonic expansion. Old Prussian (extinct) gave way to eastward Germanic expansion.

HITTITE†

VEDIC SANSKRIT

INDO-IRANIAN

BASQUE
MYCENEAN GREEK
ALBANIAN
ARMENIAN

CELTIC

ITALIC

GERMANIC

SLAVONIC

BALTIC

FINNO-UGRIC

Outsiders: the chart includes four European languages that are unrelated to the others, but are described in the book: Basque, which pre-dates all others in Europe, and Finnish, Estonian and Hungarian, which share within the Finno-Ugric group distant origins in north-central Asia.

BC   AD

MODERN LANGUAGES

TOCHARIAN†

ROMANY
HINDI:URDU
PUNJABI
MARATHI
CLASSICAL SANSKRIT   PALI   MIDDLE INDIAN (PRAKRIT)
GUJARATI
BENGALI
ASSAMESE ETC
ÐARDIC (KASHMIRI)
PERSIAN (FARSI)
AVESTAN OLD PERSIAN   PAHLAVI
KURDISH
PUSHTU
BALUCHI
BASQUE
HOMERIC/CLASSICAL GREEK   KOINE
GREEK
ALBANIAN
ARMENIAN

MANX†
GAELIC
IRISH
INSULAR CELTIC
SCOTS GAELIC
BRETON
CORNISH†
LEPONTIC†   OLD BRITISH
WELSH
CONTINENTAL CELTIC†   GAULISH†
FRENCH
CELTIBERIAN†
PROVENÇAL
PORTUGUESE
SPANISH
LATIN
CATALAN
ITALIAN
ROMANSCH
ROMANIAN
ICELANDIC
GOTHIC†
NORWEGIAN
FAEROESE
OLD NORSE
DANISH
SWEDISH
FRISIAN
WEST GERMANIC
DUTCH
ENGLISH
GERMAN
BELARUSIAN
EAST
GREAT RUSSIAN
UKRAINIAN
MACEDONIAN
BULGARIAN
OLD CHURCH SLAVONIC   SOUTH
SERBO-CROAT
SLOVENE
KASHUBIAN
WEST
POLISH
SORB
CZECH, SLOVAK
OLD PRUSSIAN†
LITHUANIAN
LATVIAN
ESTONIAN
FINNISH
HUNGARIAN

VOICES IN A LANDSCAPE

The western world into which the Indo-European tribes began to move, perhaps 5,000 years ago, bore little resemblance to its present appearance. The lowlands were heavily forested and alive with game, but people were few. A start had been made on the clearance of forest lands but little is known of these early Europeans, least of all their languages, unless Basque is one.

The proto-languages from which the modern European tongues are descended began to arrive about 3,000 BC, accompanied by the creak of carts and the lowing of cattle. The tribes had long since begun to split into groups, their dialects drawing further apart as they journeyed through the centuries and across the landscapes. At the dawn of recorded history they were well established in the homelands now associated with them, from the Germanic and Slavonic north to the Italic and Greek south.

3

1 Greek

The first Greeks entered the Balkan peninsula between 3,000 and 2,000 BC. Over the next two millenia they established mainland Europe's first great civilization: Sicily and southern Italy became part of Greater Greece, and Greek cities were established from Massilia (Marseilles) in the west to Byzantium (Istanbul) in the east.

2 Italic

Before the Latium dialect began its march across Europe, Italy was a patchwork of many languages, including Etruscan. From humble beginnings the Latin of Rome was to become, in diverse forms, the language of France, Spain, Portugal and Romania, and ultimately it became an influence on all other European languages.

3 Celtic

The Celts were a power in ancient Europe, their dialects spoken from Ireland and Spain in the west, to Asia Minor in the east, while Latin was just a dialect of Rome. Their spread from a tribal cluster around the headwaters of the Rhine and Danube was equalled only by their diminishing as Rome's power all but obliterated them.

4 Germanic

Travelling through northern Europe, the tribes which became the Germanic people came to their heartland around the western Baltic at the dawn of history. The "folk wanderings" of the early centuries AD carried them west to the British Isles, north to the Scandinavian tundra and south to the Danube and northern Italy.

5 Baltic

Latvia and Lithuania are all that remains of a huge area extending from the Vistula to the Volga (a Baltic name), where the Baltic languages were once heard. Baltic languages are remarkable for their archaisms; they are thought to be closer to the Indo-European parent than any other European language, providing a wealth of clues for the linguist.

6 Slavonic

The heartland of the Slavs is thought to have been in the area of the Pripet marshes, where Belarus now meets the Ukraine. The Slavs' expansion (into history as well as new fields) from the fourth century AD onwards, was sudden and rapid, west to the Elbe, north to the Baltic, south into the Balkans and east towards the Ural Mountains.

7 Illyrian/Albanian

Neighbours to the west of the Thracians, Illyrian speakers occupied the Balkan shores and hinterland of the Adriatic. Mentioned by the Greeks in 500 BC, the Illyrians and their language were subdued by the Romans and the Latin of Rome. Echoes of Illyrian, it is thought, are still to be heard in the *Gheg* and *Tosk* of present-day Albanian.

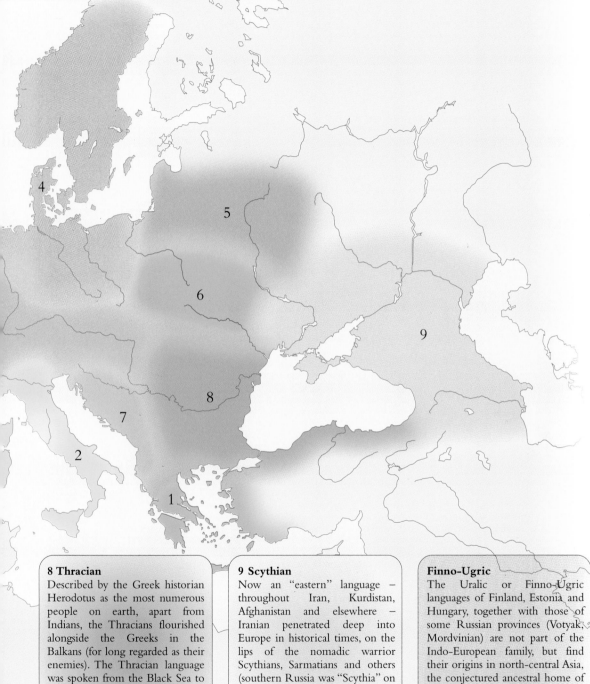

8 Thracian
Described by the Greek historian Herodotus as the most numerous people on earth, apart from Indians, the Thracians flourished alongside the Greeks in the Balkans (for long regarded as their enemies). The Thracian language was spoken from the Black Sea to modern Albania, but fell victim first to Greek, then Latin by the fifth century AD.

9 Scythian
Now an "eastern" language – throughout Iran, Kurdistan, Afghanistan and elsewhere – Iranian penetrated deep into Europe in historical times, on the lips of the nomadic warrior Scythians, Sarmatians and others (southern Russia was "Scythia" on old Greek maps). The language of the raiding Alans still survives today as Ossetic in the

Finno–Ugric
The Uralic or Finno–Ugric languages of Finland, Estonia and Hungary, together with those of some Russian provinces (Votyak, Mordvinian) are not part of the Indo-European family, but find their origins in north-central Asia, the conjectured ancestral home of the Koreans, and possibly the Japanese, who left no trace of their presence on the mainland.

CHAPTER TWO

Distant cousins: the Indo-Aryans

There is a saying in India that every twelve *kos* (about 30 kilometres or 19 miles) the language changes as branches differ on a tree. It is a poetic exaggeration (India is 3,000 kilometres in length from its northernmost point to Cape Comorin in the south, and about the same distance at its widest point) but it is not without some substance in fact and the analogy of tree branches is accurate. There are more than 500 mother tongues spoken in India, Pakistan, Bangladesh and Sri Lanka, and most, apart from the ancient Dravidian languages of the south, are descended from a single illustrious parent "more perfect than the Greek," Sanskrit.

The "perfect parent" arrived in north-west India between 1,000 and 2,000 years BC, settling at first in what is now the Punjab. Its speakers' experience was in some ways similar to that of their distant cousins, the Greeks, who encountered a society more polished than their own when they arrived on the Mediterranean shores. Reaching the River Indus, the Indo-Aryans found the remains of the Dravidian civilization centred around two great cities, Harappa in the north and Mohenjo-Daro to the south. These sophisticated urban centres were solidly built cities, laid out on a grid pattern of streets, with an effective drainage system. This ancient culture, which had

flourished for 1,000 years before the arrival of the invaders from the north, subsequently vanished without trace until its achievements were uncovered by archaeology in the twentieth century.

Once established, the Indo-Aryans carried their language across the rich alluvial plains of the Ganges, shedding their migrant ways and adopting the settled farming techniques of those they had overcome. The older Dravidian languages were confined in the main to the central and southern provinces of the subcontinent where, however, they survive in modern form in Tamil (mostly in the Madras area, and in Sri Lanka), Telugu, Kannada and Malayalam, a variety of Tamil. A number of minor languages descended from the Dravidian.

Sanskrit, the fecund parent of the Indic languages, is important not only for its central role in the culture of the subcontinent but also for the key discovery *(see page 10)* of its kinship with classical Greek and Latin. Like these ancient European tongues, it is still cultivated as a language of learning although at an early date it ceased to be used as an everyday vernacular. After extinct Hittite (cuneiform inscriptions on clay tablets), it was the first Indo-European language to be written down and preserved in the sacred books of India, the Vedas. The first, the Rigveda, an oral tradition of great literary power dating from the latter years of the second millennium BC, is a collection of about 1,000 hymns that in part recall the ancient journeys of the Aryan people and their arrival in India.

The copious literature of the Vedas, in both poetry and prose, covered philosophy, religion,

---

THE INDIAN FAMILY

Hindi/Urdu	Gujarati
Bengali	Marathi
Assamese	Rajasthani
Punjabi	Sinhalese etc.

Sanskrit literature is written in the Devanagari or Nagari alphabet: modern Indian languages still employ it, with some local variations. It may have developed on a model brought back from Mesopotamia by traders, vectors always of new ideas.

medicine and, in the *Sutras*, various aspects of private life. One version of Sanskrit, Pali (meaning "canon law"), is the sacred language of Buddhism. Pali was the first important Prakrit, a series of colloquial dialects that emerged as Sanskrit faded from common use. These form the "Middle Indian" bridge between the parent and the diffuse modern languages, which are spoken by two-thirds of India's population.

Before the arrival of the Portuguese, Dutch and British during the years of European imperial expansion, a huge addition to the old Indian vocabulary was provided by Persian Islamic invaders, who first drove into northern India during the early years of the eighth century. The Islamic moguls dominated the history of India for 1,000 years, and their court language of Persian permeated all aspects of life. Military and administrative, architectural and geographical, and above all religious terms in the modern Indian languages reflect this turbulent passage of history.

The principal language of northern India, where the moguls set up court in Delhi, was Hindi. Blended with the coloring provided by the Persian masters, it forms the basis of modern Hindustani, a common term embracing two communal styles: the High Hindi employed by Hindus and written in Nagari, the Sanskrit alphabet; and Urdu, which is used by the Muslim population and written in the Arabic script. The word *Urdu* finds a relative in English and other European language dictionaries as *horde*, a camp of nomadic warriors.

Today, Hindi is the official state language of India and Urdu effectively that of Pakistan, but in both countries there is a pattern of languages

THE "DISTANT COUSINS" OF THE EUROPEAN LANGUAGES

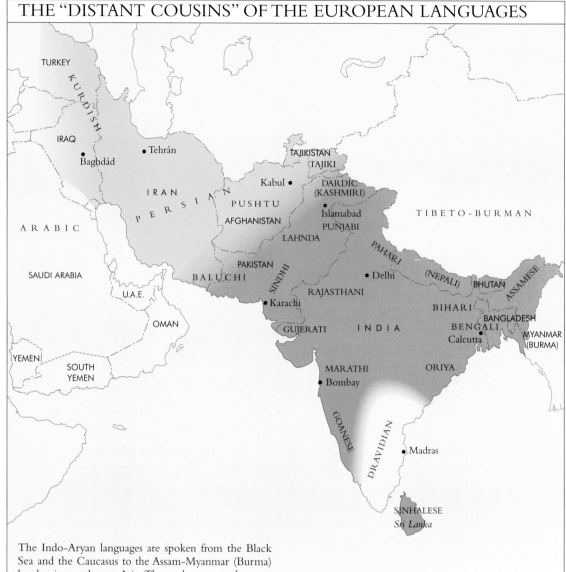

The Indo-Aryan languages are spoken from the Black Sea and the Caucasus to the Assam-Myanmar (Burma) border in south-east Asia. Those shown on the map represent only the principal forms that are spoken over this huge area which has a population far in excess of a billion.

There are scores, if not hundreds, of minor "languages within languages" forming part of the overall Indo-Aryan group, together with a few not part of the family. The most important of these are the Dravidian languages of central southern India. They are survivors from an India far older than that of the conquerors who arrived from western Asia some 3,000 to 4,000 years ago; traces of Dravidian, called Brahui, are still to be found in Baluchistan, far to the north of the present-day Dravidian realms.

Even more ancient than the Dravidian tongues in India are thought to be the Munda languages spoken by several millions in central India. Some believe that Munda may be distantly related to the Mon-Khmer speech of southern Myanmar and Cambodia, which derived its culture from India.

Many colonies of Indians, speaking Hindi or one of the other Indian languages, are to be found in many parts of the world, a result of the Victorian policy of drawing on India for labor in different parts of the empire. In Fiji, the "Little India of the Pacific," Indians outnumber the native Fijians.

admitted as official in the states in which they are spoken. The most widely used is Bengali, which, in addition to being the language of India's largest city, Calcutta, is the official language of the independent state of Bangladesh.

Bengali is adjoined to its south by Oriya, the state language of Orissa, and to the west by the dialects of Bihar. To the north-east its neighbour is Assamese, the most easterly outpost of the Indian languages abutting against the Tibeto-Burman complex.

In the foothills and valleys of Himalayan India, the principal Indo-Aryan languages are classified as Pahari, among which is Nepali. Although Nepali is the state language of Nepal, only about half its inhabitants speak the language and it is a minority tongue in the capital, Katmandu. Other Himalayan languages of the Pahari group are spoken in Gharwal and Kumaon. Dardic, a distinctive language influenced by both Indian and Iranian, is heard in the Vale of Kashmir and in neighboring territories.

The two major language groups of western India are Punjabi and Gujarati. Punjabi is widespread across the border between India and Pakistan and is particularly associated with the Sikhs who make up about half the population of the Indian Punjab. Gujarati, a language spoken by between twenty and thirty million Indians in the lands around the Gulf of Cambay, is very much an emigrant language. Much of Bombay speaks Gujarati, including the small but influential Parsee "Persian" community, and native Gujarati speakers, prominent in matters of commerce, play a

leading role in Indian communities overseas.

Between the Punjab and Gujarat lies the state of Rajasthan. The official language there is Hindi, but it is also home to a pattern of dialects called Rajasthani, which have become scattered by emigration to quite distant parts of India.

The last major state language is the Marathi of Maharashtra, formerly the state of Bombay, its capital city. Some forty million speak Marathi although in Bombay, a typical cosmopolitan seaport, less than half the population are Marathi speakers, the rest coming from Gujarat, the Hindi provinces and the Dravidian south. Akin to Marathi is Konkani or Goanese, concentrated around the old Portuguese enclave of Goa.

Sinhalese, the language of Sri Lanka, is an Indo-Aryan tongue introduced to the island probably in about 500 BC and consolidated with the arrival of Buddhism a couple of hundred years later; the earliest literary compositions of the island are in Sanskrit and the Pali of Buddhism. Sri Lanka has a sizeable minority of Tamil (Dravidian) speakers. The Tamils, representing about twenty per cent of the Sri Lankan population, occupy the north and east of the island.

In Pakistan, the official Urdu, spoken by relatively few Pakistanis, is supplemented by Sindhi and Lahnda, which, with Punjabi (by far the most widespread tongue), represent the westernmost languages of the Indo-Aryan group; their neighbors to the north and west are Baluchi and Pushtu, which are Iranian languages. Dravidian, *Brahui,* survives in the highlands of Baluchistan.

The Iranian group

The modern forms of the Iranian group of languages are Persian, spoken over the greater part of modern Iran; Kurdish, the language of the fiercely independent nomads whose territories include not only Iran, but parts of Iraq, Turkey and Syria; Baluchi; and Pushtu, the language of the Pathans, who make up the larger part of the population of Afghanistan.

At the time of their entry into history, Iranian languages covered a huge expanse of territory from much of Russia and south-eastern Europe to central Asia, as well as the Iranian plateau itself. Slavonic, particularly Russian, contains many "borrowings" from the Iranian languages, most notably of all *bog* "god" – the Indic *bhaga* "provider of goods." That the Iranians were in contact with the Finno-Ugric tribes of the north is evident in at least one Finnic tribal name, the Mordvinians, deriving from the Iranian *mard* "man" and *khvar* "devour" – the "maneaters." The same ancient Iranian "bridge" provides the link between the Finnish *sisar* "sister" and the Sanskrit *svasar*.

The earliest texts are those of the ancient Persian scriptures, the Gathas attributed to Zoroaster (Zarathustra) in the sixth century BC. The language, Avestan, in which they were written, closely resembles that of the Indian Vedas, and was preserved in the sacred literature of the Zoroastrian Parsees who emigrated to India in the face of an expanding Islam.

Old Persian, which arose at the same time as Avestan, was the language of the Achaemenid dynasty, whose expansion was led by Cyrus the Great, founder of an empire that flourished, until it was destroyed by Alexander the Great, from the Greek Aegean to the River Indus. The homeland of the Achaemenids was the modern Iranian province of Fars, hence the modern name for the language, *Farsi*.

The subjection and conversion of Persia by the armies of Islam in the seventh century brought a new, Arabic, element to the resident language, whose effect was comparable with that of Norman French on English (modern Persian has been called "the English of the East," not for any marked resemblance between the languages but for their simplification of old grammatical structures and the absorption by Persian of Arabic terms, as English adopted French and Latin ones). Since the tenth century, Persian, or Farsi, had been written in the Arabic script.

Until it was replaced by Pushtu in 1936, Persian was the state language of Afghanistan and remains the local language of Kabul, the capital. It is also spoken in the (former Soviet, now independent) republic of Tajikistan, where it is known as Tajiki and is the official language. One other distinctive form of Iranian, Ossetic, survives in the central Caucasus. Its speakers are descendants of the Alans who accompanied the Goths and Vandals in their wild sweep through Europe and into Spain during the Dark Ages. One form of Iranian was Sogdian. Long since vanished, it was the tongue of the people of Samarkand, that almost mystical destination for the caravans of Baghdad.

THE IRANIAN FAMILY		
Persian (Farsi)	Tajiki	Pushtu
Kurdish		Baluchi

Gypsy woman and pony: the horse (Romany *grast*, a word borrowed from Armenian) is inseparable from the Gypsy culture of endless mobility.

Romany: the nomad tongue

The last true nomad of the western world is a man of many names. The English call him a gypsy (Egyptian); others have their own distinctive terms for him. To the French he is *bohémien,* to the Italians, Germans and Spanish *zingaro, Zigeuner* and *gitano,* words descending from the Sanskrit *sangkara.* Among his fellows he is a Romany, and Romany, or Rom, is the language he speaks.

There are perhaps a quarter of a million people still using one of a dozen or so dialects of Romany, almost always as an esoteric ingredient of the language of the country in which they are resting. It is now known that it is an Indo-Aryan language and that its origins are in north-western India. Its closest relative appears to be the Dumaki of a tiny caste of metalsmiths and musicians, both pursuits for which the Romany people are famous, living in the Karakoram mountains.

But Romany is the language of wanderers, acquiring something from each of the peoples through whose lands it has passed; while sixty per cent of the British Romany vocabulary derives from its Indo-European source, the remaining forty per cent is made up in approximately equal parts of Iranian, Greek, Balkan Slavonic and English, with a few miscellaneous ingredients gathered, as it were, like herbs by the roadside.

The migration that brought these nomads to Europe from their distant home in northern India is thought to have started about 1,000 years ago. They first appeared in western Europe during the early part of the fifteenth century and were regarded with some awe.

They were clearly not European in appearance, with olive-skin and thick, dark hair ("like a horse's tail" observed a contemporary French writer). More disturbing still was their language, which resembled nothing the Europeans had heard before. A stranger whose language is not understood is one to be suspected, particularly if the womenfolk seem to foretell the future with great accuracy, and all his kind possess the apparent trick of vanishing into thin air overnight.

The gypsies are first recorded in Germany in 1417 and over the next three-quarters of a century appeared in France, Italy, Spain and Russia. Exactly when they arrived in England is not known, but in 1505 the Lord High Treasurer of Scotland paid seven pounds "to the Egyptians by the King's command." It was thus from Egypt, an appropriately exotic source, that the gypsies received the name by which they are known in Britain. Time and students of language were to reveal just how much farther the "Egyptians" had actually travelled.

For centuries it was believed that their language was no more than a secret jargon, drawn like a cloak around their lives to conceal their thoughts and intentions from others. Not until the eighteenth century were the first clues uncovered that showed Romany to have its origins in India. In conversation with students from northern India at Leyden University, a young Hungarian recognized that their language possessed much in common with the gypsy language spoken in his native Hungary. Subsequently, scholarship has proved beyond doubt that Romany began its life in north-west India and has Sanskrit as its ancestor.

The Romany "one" *yekh,* "two" *dui* and "three" *tin* were seen to have their almost identical counterparts in the Sanskrit *eka, dve* and *trini* and the modern Indian *ek, do* and *tin,* and many other basic words remain all but unchanged after 1,000 years of wandering: *pani* "water," *nak* "nose," *churi* "knife" and scores of other words are the same in Romany and Hindustani.

Having established that the gypsies were a fugitive Indian tribe and not, as some would have it, descendants of those who forged the nails for the crucifixion of Christ, scholars were able to trace their route across Asia and Europe. As for the gypsies themselves, they were content to leave their past in dark obscurity: "Where we comes from the dear Lord only knows and He's too high and mighty to tell the likes of us."

Wherever they pitched their tents, the gypsies borrowed words from their hosts. Persian contributed many words including *doshman* "enemy" and *ambrol* "pear;" Armenian gave them *grast* "horse" and *bov* "stove," and Greek provided a fruitful source of new words, including a number of metallurgical terms like *petalo* "horse shoe" (whence the famous gypsy tribal name *Petulengro* "blacksmith").

Romanian, Hungarian and Slavonic languages enriched the Romany dialects that had made their way to Europe by way of the Bosporus. Other gypsies had turned south from the Near East to travel the north coast of Africa, acquiring Arabic additions to their vocabulary. The end of the road for this southern migration was Spain where, in the gypsy dialect known as *Caló,* it has been estimated that there are up to 2,000 words of Arabic origin.

For some the migration continued beyond the shores of Europe: to the United States, Brazil, Australia and New Zealand. But many of the old European groups settled down to a tamer, albeit still nomadic, way of life. Inevitably their language became increasingly influenced by the speech of the country in which they lived. Romany has never had a written form and so has been particularly unstable and vulnerable compared to the literate cultures of Europe. In the late nineteenth century there was still a group of "deep," relatively pure Romany speakers in

Wales, but for the most part, in Britain as elsewhere, Romany became a corrupt language.

A few nouns and verbs might survive, but sentence structure and linking words became those of the adopted country. "Always *jal* by the *divvus*," an English Gypsy might say. "Always go by the day," he means. *Jal* and *divvus* here derive from the Hindustani *jáná* "to go" and the Sanskrit *divasa* "heaven or day." Or he might choose, perhaps for the purpose of confusing outsiders, to use the Romany verb *la* "take." This he could use as a perfectly ordinary English verb: I *lel*, you *lel*, he *lels*. The Spanish gypsy, approaching his language in the same way, will add Spanish verb endings to Romany roots: *lillo, lillas, lilla* "I take, you take, he takes."

"These vagabonds," wrote a fifteenth-century Italian, "are the cleverest thieves in Europe." Whatever the truth of this remark, gypsies have had to live under constant suspicion, and they are international scapegoats, whether for the loss of a ring, the death of a chicken, or at worst, the abduction of a child. Persecuted by the "civilized" races of Europe (the Nazis exterminated 400,000 of them simply for being gypsies), they have preserved their language partly as a deliberate means of self-isolation. It is no wonder that certain Romany words should have found their way into the secret vocabulary of the underworld. From there they have crept into popular slang and then, occasionally, emerged unnoticed into standard usage of the host language.

Spanish has a particularly rich gypsy vocabulary, including *gacho* "beau" or "lover," *sandunga* "elegance" and *canguelo*, a slang term

for "fear." *"C"est bath,"* a French expression meaning "That's first-class," uses a corrupt form of the Romany word *bakht* "good luck." Other Bohemian terms include *rupin* "rich" (from the Romany *rup* "silver," hence Hindustani *rupee*) and *surin* "knife" from *churi*. Old colloquialisms in German include *Kehr* "house" from the Romany *keir*, ultimately a Sanskrit word, and *Grai* "horse."

English displays many colloquialisms of Romany origin, including one of the commonest of all words, "pal," originally *phal* "brother." The "cosh," originally used by gypsies as a stick for dispatching rabbits, has become part of the underworld armory and is particularly to be feared when in the hands of a "rum cove." "Rum" derives ultimately from the gypsy word *rom* "husband" which in time became "queer man" and then the adjective "queer:" "cove" *(kova)* means simply "chap." All are words deriving from Indo-Aryan sources.

The gaily-painted *vardo*, the horse-drawn caravan or "living wagon" of the gypsies, is a rare sight now, seen as often as not parked in the garden of a well-to-do *gorgio*, a "gentile" or non-gypsy, as a plaything for his children. A factory-made family caravan drawn by a motor vehicle has replaced the romantic old wagon that was hand-made to the needs of its occupants. But the wheels and the mobility remain, together with the horizon that has always beckoned the Romany. George Borrow (1803–81) captured the Romany spirit in his *Lavengro:* "There's night and day, brother, both sweet things; sun, moon and stars, brother, all sweet things; there's likewise a wind on the heath. Life is very sweet, brother ..."

CHAPTER THREE

The mystery of Basque

There is no way of knowing how long the Basques have inhabited the southern corner of the Bay of Biscay. *Euskara*, to give their language its own name, was established there long before the Celts and then the Romans came to erase the memory of every other prehistoric tongue. This left Basque the oldest language of Europe; the oldest, that is, in terms of continuous occupation of the lands where it is now spoken. It is tantalizing to reflect that the region of the Basques lies within an area that has revealed some of the earliest records of European civilization in the cave paintings of Lascaux in France and Altamira in Spain, which form out-markers for the territory once occupied by them. But such speculation is dangerous and may turn out to be as extravagant as the once-cherished theory that Basque was the language spoken by all of mankind before the destruction of the Tower of Babel, the "gate of God."

The Basque lands are far smaller today than they were when its people first entered history. The centre of gravity has shifted towards the Biscay coast from the ancient centre of Vascon or Basque culture which, in the seventh century BC, was around the upper reaches of the River Ebro, in the Spanish province of Navarra (Basque *Nafarra*). At their greatest extent, Basque territories ranged on either side of the Pyrenees, along the Biscayan coast from Santander to Bordeaux, and east to Toulouse in France and Saragossa in Spain.

Pressure applied by successive invaders, Roman, Visigoth and Frank among others, caused the once extensive realms of the language to retreat into the fortress of the western Pyrenees, but not without its speakers leaving scars upon those who invested them; the Basques may well have been the "Sarrasins" who mauled Charlemagne's rearguard at the Pass of Roncesvalles in Navarra, the historic engagement (778) celebrated in the epic poem *La Chanson de Roland*.

Part of the English crown from the time of the Plantagenet Henry II (Edward, the Black Prince, fought a campaign through Basque territory), the three northern provinces of Labourd, Basse-Navarre and Soule became part of France at the end of the Hundred Years' War. South of the Spanish border, the Basques came beneath the sway of Castile, although they continued to enjoy a measure of autonomy.

It is by its grammar that Basque distinguishes itself most clearly from the Indo-European family. Attempts to determine through linguistics the true origins of Basque have been signally inconclusive. Some scholars have discerned a living relative in the Caucasus, a traditional haven for wandering peoples and lost languages, while others have argued that Basque is an African language. At the same time, the attractive hypothesis that it is related to ancient Iberian has not borne fruit, for modern Basque, although it appears to consist of a similar range of sounds, has contributed nothing to the deciphering of inscriptions written in the former language of Spain.

Basque vocabulary, as it is today, still gives many insights into the nature of the civilization in which it evolved. It was certainly palaeolithic; the words for essential striking and cutting tools, the pick, the axe, the knife, for example, are all based on the root *aitz*, meaning

The cave drawing of a bison (now long vanished from western Europe) in Altamira, Spain, was the work of paleolithic (Old Stone Age) man. His speech, some aver, was the origin of the mysterious Basque language, which predates all other western European tongues.

stone. As one would expect of a language of such primitive origins, Basque has largely retained its own words for individual objects, while many general terms and almost all abstract concepts have been borrowed from Romance. The social organization of the Basques appears originally to have been on democratic lines, their word for king *errege* being an early borrowing from Latin *regem*. Of subsequent Romance loan-words, many were adopted as a result of the conversion of the Basques to Christianity, which took place around 600 AD, and gained firm hold. Since that time, priests have played a prominent part in the history of the Basques and one of the greatest figures of the Roman Church, Ignatius of Loyola (1491–1556), founder of the Order of Jesuits, was a Basque. Many of the Latinisms adopted by the Basque language are not difficult to recognize, like *eliza* "church" and *gorputz* (from *corpus*, as invoked in the Latin

mass). The Basques did retain some words from their earlier religion: one, *Jinkoa* "God," may have been the exotic source of the English exclamation "By Jingo," and the epithet "jingoism," the nearest English can get in meaning to the French *chauvinisme*.

Basque's influence on Spanish and French outside of Gascony (Gascony, like Biscay, derives from the name of the Vascon people) appears slight when measured in terms of loans. The Spanish word *izquierda* "left," preferred to the Latin *sinister* because of the latter's somewhat unholy connotations, is almost identical to the Basque *ezkerr*, but which came first is a mystery.

As well as placenames, there are some

Basque-Spanish words for geographical features: the Spanish *nava*, a depression in the mountains forming a plain, is a Basque word, describing the terrain of Navarre. Philologists have devoted much research to the similarities between the phonetic system of Basque and that of Spanish, particularly their mutual aversion to Latin *f-*. Castilian eventually replaced *f-* with *h-*, whereas Basque from an early date substituted *b-*, giving such forms as *boronte* from *fronte* "forehead," and *besta* from *festa*. Although nobody has been able to prove

any direct connection between Basque and the other languages of Spain before its Romanization, there do appear to have been tendencies in pronunciation common to the whole peninsula.

Of those counted as speakers of Basque today, some 600,000 in Spain and a further 100,000 in France, not all can be said to be equally proficient; many understand the language, but make little attempt to speak it. The number that write it is even more limited, although this is inevitable in view of the great

BASQUE REALMS

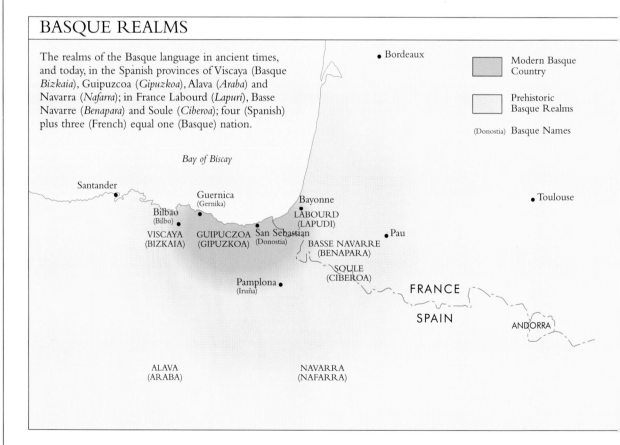

The realms of the Basque language in ancient times, and today, in the Spanish provinces of Viscaya (Basque *Bizkaia*), Guipuzcoa (*Gipuzkoa*), Alava (*Araba*) and Navarra (*Nafarra*); in France Labourd (*Lapuri*), Basse Navarre (*Benapara*) and Soule (*Ciberoa*); four (Spanish) plus three (French) equal one (Basque) nation.

Modern Basque Country

Prehistoric Basque Realms

(Donostia) Basque Names

Bordeaux

Toulouse

Bay of Biscay

Santander

Guernica
(Gernika)

Bayonne
LABOURD
(LAPUDI)

Bilbao
(Bilbo)

VISCAYA
(BIZKAIA)

GUIPUZCOA
(GIPUZKOA)

San Sebastian
(Donostia)

BASSE NAVARRE
(BENAPARA)

Pau

SOULE
(CIBEROA)

Pamplona
(Iruña)

FRANCE

SPAIN

ANDORRA

ALAVA
(ARABA)

NAVARRA
(NAFARRA)

variety of dialects on both sides of the Pyrenees. The most extreme claim of the Basque nationalist, *Zazpiak Bat*, "The seven are one," refers to the four provinces in Spain, plus three in France, where the language is spoken; not many examples of political graffiti are as succinct as "3+4=1" scrawled on Spanish walls.

Few French Basques have allied themselves to the zealous nationalism of their Spanish brothers. In Spain, the Basque provinces make up one of the richer, more industrialized areas of the country, which makes separatism an attractive prospect. In contrast, the Basques of France inhabit a sleepy, rural backwater. Even more important is the fact that the French Basques have never experienced the harsh oppression suffered by the Basques of Spain. In the early years of Franco's regime, anyone caught speaking Basque on the street could be charged with a criminal offence and fined. Even in these more liberal times, the memory of such treatment dies hard and still provides the major impetus of the movement for Basque independence.

The great national barrier of the Pyrenees provided both refuge and bastion for the Basque language as armies and political influences passed to and fro. Their historical role diminished as the fight to save the Basque identity switched to the towns and villages of northern Spain. Its spearhead, ETA (*Euzkadi ta Azkatasuna* "Basque Homeland and Liberty") keeps alive the dream but the Basque language's battle is all but lost. Few now speak it habitually, mostly in the rural areas of Guipuzcoa and Viscaya, and the number is declining, a fate shared by most of Europe's minority tongues. Enough speakers remain to fill the streets of Bilbao and San Sebastian with periodical assertions of their individuality.

CHAPTER FOUR

Greek: from atom to cosmos

The position of Hellenic, or Greek, among modern European languages is unrivalled, either in precedence or illustrious influence. Its history as a language is 1,000 years older than its Classical rival Latin, and it is the first to have a literature of any sort. Unlike Latin, which has an eternal debt to it, it was not the parent of a family of independent tongues and in number of speakers today (between ten and eleven million) it is one of Europe's lesser languages. Yet it continues to work its magic upon all others, particularly in the realms of science.

Greek is heard wherever physicists discuss 1,000 concepts, from the atom to the cosmos or microtechnology to macrobiology, and whenever a doctor diagnoses arthritis or rheumatism. All these terms and many more derive ultimately from the Greek, often with little change; no scientist is unaware of his debt to Greek, but the debt ranges through almost every human activity and interest.

No firm date can be put to the arrival of the first Greek speakers in their new homeland, a rugged landscape consisting almost entirely of coastline and islands; few Greeks today live much more than 100 kilometres from the sea, and most of them live in sight of it. They arrived from the northern Balkans, or perhaps across the Aegean Sea from Anatolia, in a series of waves during the second millennium BC. Unlike most of the other migrant Indo-European groups, the first Greeks encountered a material culture greater than anything they themselves knew. This was the high Minoan civilization centred at Knossos in Crete. The Cretan civilization was not that of an Indo-European people, but their creative influence

colored the whole of eastern Mediterranean life, including that of southern Greece and the Aegean archipelago. It was upon these bedrocks of exquisite culture that the newly arrived Greeks laid the foundations of European civilization.

Although the ancient Greek tongue was replete with words directly descended from its Indo-European parent, it was soon to acquire its first borrowings from the languages spoken by its predecessors in the mainland and archipelago.

The words adopted into Greek from the language of those earlier residents in the Greeks' new-found home are chiefly related to the pastoral/nomadic life once lived there – words like *taurus* "bull" (in Celtic Irish and Welsh it is *tarh* and *tarw*, in Russian *tur*, though the latter refers to the now-extinct aurochs), and its pasture *agros* "field" (Sanskrit *ajras* and English "acre," which originally meant field, rather than a measure of land). The new acquisitions reflect the broadening horizons and interests of the now-settled wanderers, words like *thalassa* "sea" and *nisos* "island," *elaia* "olive," and *chryos* "gold." Up to forty per cent of the modern vocabulary derives from the local pre-Hellenic tongues.

Not later than 1,400 BC, the Greeks devised their first form of writing, now called Linear B (adapting an earlier Minoan form, Linear A, used by the Minoans), which was first deciphered and shown to be Greek as recently as 1952. It was the first attempt at writing a European language and what survives, on clay tablets, appears to consist of business inventories: the bourgeoisie was already on the

Greek villagers: the demotic or "popular" Greek which
they speak is no longer of influence in the outside world,
but it has inherited most of its vocabulary and grammar
from the Greek of Classical Athens.

march. Linear B seems to have gone out of use in the twelfth century BC, after which the Greeks appear to have reverted to illiteracy. But not for long. About the ninth century BC their first and greatest invention appeared – the Greek alphabet, direct ancestor of the Roman, progenitor of the later Cyrillic of the Slavs, and the vehicle for Europe's first literary master-pieces, the *Iliad* and the *Odyssey* of the legendary Homer.

In its early years the language lacked unity. There were four main dialects – Doric, Ionic, Aeolic and Arcado-Cypriot – but within these were the variations of each individual city-state. For a time, different styles of literatures were associated with a different dialect or mixture of dialects. The *Iliad* and *Odyssey* of

Homer, for example, have Aeolic and Ionic characteristics, while lyric poets often favoured the Doric dialect. Tragedians and rhetoricians, however, preferred Attic, the speech of Athens and a subgroup of the Ionic dialect. As the political power of Athens grew, so did the prestige of its language. By the age of Pericles (*c.* 495–429 BC), when democracy was a bold experiment and the Parthenon a gleaming new temple, Attic was on its way to becoming the principal or *Koine* "common" language of Greece. The Greek of today is its descendant.

Like the Parthenon or the practice of democracy, the Attic dialect has changed over the centuries. The grammar and pronunciation have continually evolved. Thousands of new words have entered the vocabulary from Italy,

Rome pays tribute to its master: a detail from Raphael's painting *The School of Athens* in the Vatican shows Plato (427–347 BC) with his pupil Aristotle (*c.* 384–332 BC), "the master of those who know" (Dante).

Turkey, France, England and the United States; corresponding thousands have vanished. The artistic impulse of the language has been crippled by pedantic disputes regarding its purity and by centuries of foreign rule. Yet an extraordinary amount remains untouched by 2,500 years. So conservative is the nature of Greek that a citizen of ancient Athens would be able to read much of what is printed in a modern Athenian newspaper. Some words are entirely unaltered: *adelfós* "brother" and *gráfo* "write" are the same for the student of modern Greek as they were for Pericles. Other words have undergone only a slight change in form: *iméra* "day" and *ipsilós* "high" are recognizable in their modern form of *méra* and *psilós*. Many twentieth-century terms rely upon an Attic vocabulary for their sense: a *kosmonaut*, after all, is not just a Russian spaceman, but an Attic sailor *nautes* of the Attic universe *cosmos.*

In attempting to recreate the glories of their ancient history, the Greek people have encouraged these conservative tendencies. The effects have not been entirely beneficial. As if engulfed in amber, the Greek language has been both preserved and stifled by its exalted past.

In the fourth century BC the dialect of Athens became the most influential language in the western world. Strangely, the man responsible for its sudden prestige was not considered a Greek. King Philip of Macedonia, taking advantage of the chronic disunity among the Greek city-states, conquered the peninsula and established Attic as the official language of his new kingdom. His son, Alexander the Great (356–323 BC) carried Greek with him on his extraordinary expeditions to Asia and Africa. Alexander was dead at the age of thirty-three, and his vast empire soon crumbled, but Greek remained for many centuries the lingua franca of the eastern Mediterranean.

The Greek that was heard throughout the Middle East after the Macedonian conquests was called *he koine dialektos*, the common language. This was no longer the pure Athenian of Pericles or Plato. International currency had simplified its grammar and enriched its vocabulary. The expanding Roman empire inevitably contributed a large share of new words. *Kínsos* "census," *kamísion* "shirt," *kandilábron* "candelabra" and *kenturíon* "centurion" were among the common words introduced from Latin into Koine. But the language of Italy never dominated its eastern empire. Among the slaves and the poor of Rome itself Greek was spoken as frequently as Latin.

Koine did not rely upon outside influences for the source of new words. Greek is a language rich in suffixes: *-tria, -issa, -mos, -ma, -otis, -tirion, -inos, -tos, -tron, -azo* and *-izo* are just a few among the many word endings that were snapped on to old stems, creating a vast new Koine vocabulary. Other words changed their meaning entirely. *Dóma*, once a poetic word for "house," now began to mean "roof"; *stómachos*, once "gullet," slipped down to new lodgings as "stomach"; *opsárion*, formerly an edible delicacy in general, became the word for "fish"; *áriston*, once used to describe breakfast, now meant any meal.

The enormous success of Koine was violently opposed by those who thought that

CONTINUED ON PAGE 38

WELCOME GIFTS FROM THE GREEKS

The debt owed to Greek by other European languages is greater than can ever be repaid. If the Hellenes could call in their verbal loans to the world, science and scholarship generally would be left almost speechless. The debt, however, goes far beyond the terminology of experts, for everyday conversation in a score of languages, and in as many professions from potter to psychiatrist, is alive with Greek words that have been so long assimilated that they are no longer thought of as Greek.

Dozens remain virtually unchanged. *Asbestos* and *acme, basis* and *chaos; character* and *criterion, demon, dogma* and *drama; echo, emphasis* and *enigma; horizon, kudos* and *idea; rhythm* and *scheme, sphere* and *stigma; theatre, theme* and *tyrant* all remain close to their Greek models.

A doctor's handwriting might become even more difficult to decipher if he had to find new words for old-fashioned conditions like *apoplexy*, or fashionable ones like *herpes*. *Arthritis* and *asthma, diarrhoea* and *dysentery* were first described and named by the Greeks. *Epilepsy* and *gangrene, leprosy* and *paralysis, pneumonia, psoriasis, rheumatism, spasm* and *trauma* are found among far more people than ever met a Greek. The more specialized vocabulary of medicine favors Greek above all others, although a better educated public is now aware that cardiac arrest (*cardia* "heart") is heart failure and an analgesic is a pain-killer (*algos* "pain"). The Greek *gaster* "belly" may be afflicted by gastritis, the *hepar, -atos* "liver" with hepatitis and the *phlebs* "vein" with phlebitis. All may require a visit to the pharmacist (*pharmakon* "drug") but a mistakenly prescribed drug may have a narcotic effect (*narke* "numbness"). If it is "toxic," it will have a story to tell. The word originally meant that which pertained to the archer's bow (hence toxophily, or archery), then by extension of meaning to poison on an arrow's tip.

A garden without flowers bearing Greek names would be a dull place. Many are descriptive: clematis (*Klematis*, "climbing plant"); geranium (*geranion*, "cranesbill") and myosotis (*muosotis*, "mouse ear"). Others hint at special properties: narcissus (*narke*, "narcotic," "numbness"); peony (*paion*, "physician"), or have roots in mythology; hebe (Hebe, goddess of youth), hyacinth (Hyakinthos, slain by Apollo).

Many hundreds of words betray their Greek origin in whole or parts, although there may have been some change in meaning. *Aesthesis*, which meant "perception" occurs in anaesthetic; *agros* "field" occurs in agriculture and agronomy; *anemos* "wind" in the device for measuring its speed, the anemometer; *ceramos* "clay" in ceramics; *chroma* "color" in chromatic; *cleptes* "thief" in kleptomania; *comos* "comic" in comedy; *tragoidia* "the song of the goat" in tragedy; *eros* "love" in erotic; *fobos* "fear" in phobia; *gala* "milk" in galaxy (milky way); *gnosis* "knowledge" in agnostic; *helios* "sun" in helium and heliograph; *hiereus* "priest" in archy; *hypocrites* "achiertor" in hypocrite; *mathema* "learning" in mathematics; *mneme* "memory" in mnemonics and amnesia; *planes* "wanderer" in planet; *profetes* "interpreter" in prophet; *strategos* "general" in strategy; *syrinx* "shepherd's pipe" in syringe and *typos* "model" in typical.

Compounds old and new

There are many compounds consisting entirely of Greek elements, some of long standing created by Renaissance scholars, who drew their inspiration from the study of the Classical literature and art of ancient Greece.

Long-standing compounds include anthropology (from *anthropos* "man" and *-logia* "study of," "discourse"); architect (*archi-* "chief" or *arch-* as in "arch-criminal"or "archbishop" and *tecton* "builder"); aristocracy (*aristos* "best" and *cratein* "to rule"); astronomy (*astron* "star" and *nomos* "law"); bibliophile (*biblos* "book" and *filos* "loving"); biography (*bios* "life" and *grafein* "to write"); chronometer (*chronos* "time" and *metron* "measure"); cosmopolitan (*cosmos* "world," "universe" and *polites* "citizen"); democracy (*demos* "people" and *cratein* "to rule"); economy (*oecos* "house" and *nemein* "to manage"); holocaust (*holos* "entire" and *causton* "burned"); hydrophobia (*hydor* "water" and *fobos* "fear"); megalomania (*megalo-* "great" and *mania* "frenzy"); metropolis (*meter, -tros* "mother" and *polis* "city"); microscope (*micro-* "little" and *scopein* "to see"); misogynist (*misein* "to hate," and *gyne* "woman"); monotheism (*monos* "one" and *theos* "god"); neologism (*neo-* "new" and *logia* "study of"); orthodox (*orthos* "correct" and *doxa* "belief"); osteopath (*osteon* "bone" and *pathein* "to suffer"); panacea *pan* "all" and *acos* "remedy"); pandemonium (*pan* "all" and *daemon* "demon"); pedagogue (*paes, paedos* "boy" and *agogos* "leading"); philosopher (*filos* "loving" and *sofia* "wisdom"); polygamy *poly-* "many" and *gamos* "marriage"); protagonist (*proto-* "first" and *agon* "struggle"); protozoa (*proto-*, "first" and *zoon* "animal"); pseudonym *pseudo-* "false" and *onoma* "name"); pyrotechnics (*pyr* "fire" and *technicos* "skilful"); stethoscope (*stethos* "chest" and *scopein* "to see"); technology (*techne* "art," "skill" and *-logia* "study of," "discourse"); telescope (*tele-* "distant" and *scopein* "to see"); thermometer (*thermos* "warm" and *metron* "measure"); tripod (*tri-* "three" and *pous, podos* "foot"); utopia (*u* "not" and *topos* "place"); zoology (*zoon* "animal" and *-logia* "study of").

Astronauts and xenophobes

New coinages arrive almost daily: anti–ballistic missile (*anti* "against" and *ballein* "to throw" added to the Latin *missile*); astronaut (*astron* "star" and *nautes* "sailor"); bionics (*bios* "life" and electronics, originally from *electron* meaning "amber"); cosmodrome (*cosmos* "world," "universe" and *dromos* "racecourse"); cryobiology (*cryos* "frozen" and *biologia* "life study"); ecocatastrophe (*oecos* "house" and *catastrophe* "overturning"); hydronautics (*hydor* "water" and *nautes* "sailor"); Eurocrat (from "Europe" and *cratein* "to rule"); helicopter (*helix* "spiral" and *pteron* "wing"); hyperkinetic (*hyper* "over" and *kineticos* "putting into motion"); hypothermia (*hypo* "under" and *thermos* "warm"); laryngoscope (*larynx, -ngos* "gullet" and *scopein* "to see"); macrobiotic (*macros* "long" and *bios* "life"); megalopolis (*megalo* "great" and *polis* "city"); parameter (*para* "beside" and *metron* "measure"); polytechnic (*poly-* "many" and *technicos* "skilful"); pornography (*porne* "prostitute" and *grafein* "to write"); psychedelic (*psyche* "soul" and *deloun* "to reveal"). The Greeks have words to spare for future developments.

CONTINUED FROM PAGE 35

the language of ancient Athens should not be debased by merchants, soldiers, galley slaves and whores. The Atticists, as they became known, insisted on recreating the Attic dialect in all its obsolete purity. This elite group of literati had no power to influence the language of the millions who spoke Greek, but they did manage to dominate most of what was written. From the first century BC there developed two separate forms of Greek: the Koine of everyday speech and the Attic of schoolrooms and libraries. These two languages only rarely mixed, though on one memorable occasion one of the Greek Fathers of the Church, the great divine John of Chrysostom (*c.* 345–407 AD), was preaching in the learned tongue of the Atticists and an old woman shouted out that she couldn't understand what he was saying. St John wisely continued his sermon in Koine, the Greek of his congregation.

After the collapse of Rome, Greek became the official language of the Byzantine Empire. Constantinople, its embattled capital, suffered invasions both from the east and the west, and the Greek language still reveals the scars of this medieval warfare. In the early years Latin was a natural source of new vocabulary. A Greek could now enter his *spíti* "house," from the Latin *hospitium,* or *paláti* "palace" by way of a *pórta* "door." Later, the merchants of Venice, Genoa, Pisa, Naples and other Italian ports contributed words from their respective dialects. *Grízos* "grey" and *brátso* "arm" reached Greek through the Italian *grigio* and *braccio* in the Middle Ages.

In 1204 the brutal fourth crusade turned Constantinople into a shabby European dependency. The Greek peninsula itself became a confusing patchwork of western colonies, as Venice, Genoa, Burgundy and Catalonia all assisted in dividing a once-proud country. The Greek language suffered a corresponding invasion. Legal French and commercial Italian forced their way into the vocabulary, and the title *misír* (a corruption of *monsieur*) was accorded the new French overlords.

Greek was a language without a state, yet it survived one political outrage after another. An all-accommodating vocabulary, a grammar that bent with each blow but never broke, and a people who were a nation in spirit if not in law, permitted it to weather the repeated indignities of history.

With the fall of Constantinople in 1453, the Byzantine Empire came to a bloody end. Three years later the conquering Turks were in complete control of mainland Greece. For the next 350 years the cradle of democracy was an oppressed colony of the Ottoman Empire.

While the Greek people languished under Turkish rule, their language received a transfusion of new words. *Kafés* "coffee," *piláfi* "pilaf" and *yaoúrti* "yogurt" enriched the Greek menu and subsequently many others; a man could now clothe himself from head (*fési,* "fez") to foot (*papoutsía,* "shoes") in an adopted Turkish wardrobe. This borrowed vocabulary penetrated all aspects of Greek life. The musician with his "lute" *lavoúto,* the traveller with his "trunk" *sentoúki,* and the soldier with his "rifle" *touféki* and "gunpowder" *baroúti,* acquired their equipment from the new masters of Greece.

Throughout these years of Turkish

occupation Greek enjoyed a freedom denied to those who spoke it. New words continued to be formed from resources within the language. One traditional means of word creation that continued to be fruitful was the compound noun in which separate elements were linked by the letter o *ómikron*, as in *merónikhto* "day and night" and *thalassovrákhi* "sea rock." Written and spoken Greek maintained their separate identities. The professional writer used quite a different language when working at his desk than he did when talking at dinner. Only poetry escaped the formal constraints of the literary language.

By the late eighteenth century the grip of the Ottoman Empire was beginning to

weaken. The Greeks, who had never lost their sense of national identity, now became inflamed with the spirit of freedom that was sweeping Europe. Few movements for independence have attracted such international sympathy as the Greek rebellion. Russia, England and France all gave active support, and the Turks eventually capitulated. In 1832, after more than 2,000 years of foreign rule, Greece was a free country once again.

No sooner had the Greeks achieved independence than their language became a political issue. It was easy enough to cease using a few hundred of the more obvious Turkish words, but the problem of establishing a national language proved insurmountable.

GREATER GREECE 800–500 BC

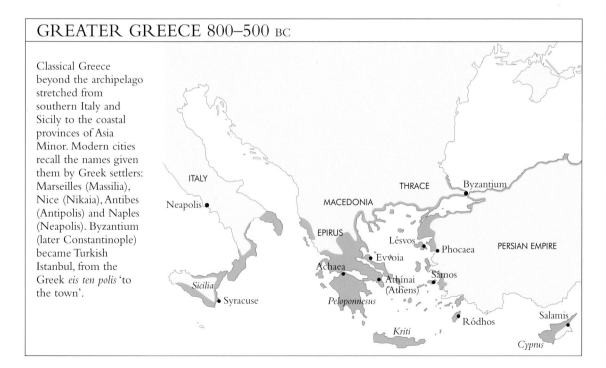

Classical Greece beyond the archipelago stretched from southern Italy and Sicily to the coastal provinces of Asia Minor. Modern cities recall the names given them by Greek settlers: Marseilles (Massilia), Nice (Nikaia), Antibes (Antipolis) and Naples (Neapolis). Byzantium (later Constantinople) became Turkish Istanbul, from the Greek *eis ten polis* 'to the town'.

THE POWERS OF THE PANTHEION

The literature and other arts of the western world would take on a duller sheen without the gods of heroic Greece and their constant intervention in the affairs of men. The first Hellenes (so-called to distinguish themselves from the Pelasgian or pre–Greek occupants of the archipelago) brought their gods with them, and gave them their first home on Olympus, the highest mountain in Thessaly.

These gods made their debut in the western world's first literature, the epic poems of the blind Homer, the *Iliad* and the *Odyssey*. Ever since then, the Greek gods have coloured all the arts when power, beauty and fate have been the inspirations, providing superlatives wherever Homeric qualities needed to be suggested, either in literature or on canvas.

Zeus, the Sky-Father (Greek *Zeu-pater*, Latin *Jupiter*) ruled above all, son of the Titan Cronus and grandson of Uranus, god of the sky born of Chaos. Hera (Roman Juno), the wife of Zeus, was also his sister; their brothers were Poseidon (god of the sea, earthquakes and horses) and Hades, "The Unseen One," god of the underworld, also called Pluto by the Greeks when they would rather not mention Hades.

The offspring of Zeus were legion, by a legion of partners, though his daughter Athene (Roman Minerva), goddess of wisdom, the arts and war, sprang fully armoured from his brow. Another daughter was Aphrodite, goddess of erotic love (Roman Venus). According to some accounts (mythological stories have many versions, embroidered by successive generations of oral tradition), Aphrodite sprang from the foaming sea off Cyprus (*aphros* "foam") and, by Ares, god of war, she produced Eros (love), Deimos (fear) and Phobus (panic).

Ares (Roman Mars) was the only son of Zeus by Hera – there were other mothers for Apollo, Dionysus and Hermes (Mercury). These three brought singular gifts to their devotees. Apollo was the god of light prophecy and music (and mice in Asia Minor where his cult may have existed among the Hittites); Dionysus (Roman Bacchus) was the god of wine and fertility generally, inspiring the "bacchanal;" and Hermes (Mercury) was the messenger of the gods, providing a light in the dark for travellers.

Among all Olympians, Prometheus was held to be the most well-disposed towards mortals, unlike Zeus. For them Prometheus stole the gift of fire, and for his pains he was nailed to a rock for 30,000 years until rescued by Heracles (Hercules). In his vindictive wrath, Zeus also counter-balanced Promethean gifts with Pandora and her dowry, a jar containing all the evils that beset mortals. When she released them, only hope was left behind.

How far back did one have to look before finding a truly "Greek" Greek? The issue was of more than academic interest. What was one to call a fish, for example: *psári* (as it was known to the man in the street), the more academic *opsárion*, or the archaic *ikhthys*?

This linguistic squabble ended in a familiar, unsatisfactory solution: Greece was once again to have two languages. A man could continue speaking what was known as demotic, but as soon as he put pen to paper he would write in *Katharévousa*, the new literary language.

Katharevousa (from *katharós* "pure") was a high-minded attempt to rid Greek of foreign and colloquial influences. The common words for "beer" and "wine" (*bíra* and *krasí*) became *zithos* and *ínos* in Katharevousa, while the *patáta* "potato" was transformed into an exotic *yeómilon*. Scholars rummaged through classical dictionaries to create new Katharevousa words such as *panepistímion* "university," and, a little later, *diastimóplion* "space ship." More surprising are those "Greek" words that were actually created from Greek roots in western Europe and only later adopted by the Greeks. *Atmósféra, atmós,* "air," plus *sféra* "ball," and *fotografía* from the stems for "light" and "write," are characteristic of words that the Greeks had to borrow back from Europe.

The rift between Katharevousa and popular speech reached a violent climax in 1902 when riots broke out in Athens over the publication of a demotic New Testament. Since then the power of Katharevousa has gradually declined, hastened on its way when it was abolished as the official language of the government during the 1970s. Inevitably, foreign words have crept into the vocabulary. The working man, *proletários*, can now sit in the bar watching *futbol*, the most popular *spor* "sport" for Greeks, or the crowning of a beauty queen *mis*.

Although they possessed one of the greatest of ancient empires and founded important cities far beyond Greece – Byzantium (now Istanbul), Marseilles, Naples and Alexandria, among them – the Greeks left few linguistic traces to mark the bounds of their vanished influence. Beyond Greece and the republic of Cyprus no country has Greek, or a language derived from it, as its official language. Most countries of the western world, however, have their Greek speakers, expatriate groups who, like many other Europeans, have sought a new life in new countries with space for them, particularly the United States and Australia (since the end of the Second World War).

Armenian

The source of the Armenian language is not to be found in the republic that now bears its name (sandwiched between Turkey, Azerbaijan, Georgia and Iran) but in the Balkans. It is the independent survivor of three kindred languages of antiquity; the other two, Thracian and Phrygian, disappeared, overcome by either Greek or Latin. The Armenians travelled from south-eastern Europe across the Hellespont and into Asia Minor with the Phrygians (Homer's Trojans), to reach their present homeland at the eastern end of the Black Sea, between the eighth and sixth centuries BC.

For many centuries, the Armenians came under the domination of their southern neighbours, first the Medes, then the Persians.

THE GREEK ALPHABET

Paramount among all alphabets, the Greek alphabet dates from about the tenth century BC. The Greeks took as their model the purely consonantal Semitic of the Phoenicians, adding to it vowels and a chiselled elegance to be inherited by the Romans. Modern Greek capitals are essentially those of the Classical era, the minuscule (lower case) dates from much later, when the stylus on paper or parchment came into use.

α Alpha · β Beta · Γ γ Gamma · δ delta · Ε ε Epsilon · ζ Zeta · η Eta · θ Theta · Ι ι Iota · κ Kappa · λ Lambda · μ Mu · Ν ν Nu · Ξ ξ Xi · Ο Omikron · Π π Pi · Ρ ρ Rho · Σ σ Sigma · Τ τ Tau · Υ υ Upsilon · Φ φ Phi · Χ χ Chi · Ψ ψ Psi · Ω ω Omega

Their language at this time absorbed so much influence from the Iranian that it was for long thought to be merely an aberrant dialect of it. At heart, however, Armenian has been shown to possess a stock of words, albeit much reduced, that demonstrates its independent place in the great family; in words like *hur* "fire" (Greek *pur), mayr* "mother" (Sanskrit *matar*, Latin *mater*) and *dustr* "daughter" (Sanskrit *duhitar*, Lithuanian *dukter*).

Situated at a point where the imperial ambitions of others were in constant confrontation, the Armenians passed through the Middle Ages under foreign rule. At the beginning of the nineteenth century, when Russia annexed Transcaucasia, many Armenians found themselves under the Tsarist regime. They were the lucky ones; those who remained in the lands of the Ottoman Turks were eventually massacred, or driven out, with consequences that have not yet ended.

Present-day Armenian speakers are scattered throughout the world in a diaspora not unlike that of the Jews. Approaching four million live in the former, now independent, republic. There is a significant community in the Lebanon, and all adhere to a Christian Church that was among the first to be founded.

Albanian

Little is known of the origins of Albanian, which was at one time thought to be a form of Greek. Modern evidence points to its being the last and much-altered remnant of the once-widespread but now vanished Illyrian, with traces of the equally extinct Thracian, a language more widespread than Greek in the Classical era. Scholars are not helped by the absence of any Albanian literature before the fifteenth century, although the people themselves were mentioned by Ptolemy 1,500 years earlier.

Historically encroached upon by Slavs from the north and Greeks to the south, the Albanians are traditionally a mountain people. Their language has two main dialects, *Gheg* to the north and *Tosk* to the south, with the capital, Tirana, in the transition zone between the two. It has about five million speakers, two-thirds of whom live in Albania proper, and the rest in the Kosovo province of Serbia, or in Macedonia. There are also traces of Albanian-speaking colonies, refugees from Turkish repression, in southern Italy and Sicily.

It is a language largely of adopted and borrowed words; from the Latin that was once spoken in the Balkans, from Serbian, Macedonian, Greek and – Albania having been part of the Ottoman Empire for nearly 500 years – from Turkish. But ancient traces remain that suggest a migration from the ancient Illyrian north; the Carpathian mountains and the mountains of the Beskid range between Poland and Slovakia have names that can only be explained by the Albanian words *karpë* "rock" and *bjeshkë* "high mountain."

CHAPTER FIVE

Celtic: a ghost of greater times

With Greek and Latin, Celtic is one of the three great languages of European antiquity, an eminence from which it has declined almost to extinction. Latin, its ultimate conqueror throughout mainland Europe, was no more than a local dialect of central Italy at a time when Celtic was commonplace from the Atlantic seaboard to the Danube plain. Today it has no more than a tenuous toehold in the local languages of Wales and Brittany, Ireland and Scotland.

Throughout their history, Celts have all too easily assimilated the languages of others, and their tongue has survived only where it has had the protection of remoteness. During the nineteenth century, millions of native Gaelic speakers emigrated from Ireland to the United States, where their language all but vanished in the great cities. Other Celts, Gaels from the Western Isles of Scotland and Welsh from the Cambrian valleys, also migrated to America, the Gaels to lonely settlements on the Canadian seaboard, the Welsh to Patagonia. Both groups in effect took their isolation with them and have managed to keep their old languages alive to the present day. But the twentieth century is harder to escape than any of its predecessors. The number of Celtic speakers in the Americas has dwindled to a handful as the elderly die and the young, who will always prefer the new to the old, no longer hear the old voices around the home.

THE CELTIC FAMILY		
Welsh	Irish Gaelic	Scottish Gaelic
Cornish (defunct)	Breton	Manx (defunct)

An ancient dominance

Two thousand years ago, the parent language was heard across the breadth of Europe. Its speakers, called *Keltoi* by the Greeks who knew them well, were an energetic, innovative and, for a time, the dominant central European race. They had emerged as a culturally distinct group around 1,000 BC in numbers no greater, probably fewer, than those who speak the modern forms of the language. Their homelands were the hills, valleys and forests of the region which now stretches across the borders of eastern France, northern Switzerland (whose classical name, Helvetia, derives from that of a Celtic people) and south-western Germany.

It was a location ideally suited for expansion. Within the region are the headwaters of three of Europe's greatest rivers, the Danube, Rhine and Rhône; not far away are those of the Seine and Loire, each a natural avenue for campaigning, migration and the spread of language. Many rivers retain in modern form the names used by the Celts – the Rhine, Neckar and Inn in Germany, the Seine and Marne in France, the Thames, Severn, Avon and Tyne in England, the Shannon in Ireland – but many of these names may be even older, borrowed by the Celts from some ancient and forgotten people.

What caused the Celts to stream outward from their homeland was, fairly certainly, a rapid growth of population and the social tensions that emerge when too many people live together. No records exist to indicate a centralized policy of the kind which controlled the growth of Rome's military expansion. By

Irish farmers at market. Persecution and, later, neglect
reduced Irish-speaking parts of Ireland to a few
scattered districts in the west.

the fifth century BC, all France south and west of the Rhine was Celtic-Gaulish speaking, and the language had made its way through the foothills of the eastern Pyrenees to colonize much of Spain in a form which came to be known as Celtiberian.

Caesar later described Gaul as divided into three peoples, each with its own language: the Celtae or Gauls proper, the Belgae (many of whom were to emigrate to Britain) and the Aquitani. The Belgae were certainly Celtic speakers, the Aquitani certainly not. The language of the Aquitani was not Indo-European but was similar to that of the neighbouring Vascones or Basques whose aboriginal tongue, protected by the fastnesses of the Atlantic Pyrenees, resists attempts at assimilation to the present day *(pages 28–31)*.

During the same expansive period (1,000–500 BC) the first Celtic speakers reached the British Isles. Although no date can be put to their arrival, the Goidels or Gaels, ancestors of the modern Irish, are thought to have been the first. How they made their way to the westernmost island is as concealed by time as the date they arrived. Some say they were edged westward from the British mainland by later Celtic arrivals, others, recalling an ancient Gaelic tradition, claim that they came from the Iberian peninsula.

On the continental mainland, Celtic continued to expand. By the fifth century BC it was established in northern Italy. Here it was known as Lepontic, traces of which have survived as inscriptions; the language itself died out early in the modern era. To the north, tribes of Celtic speakers retraced the tracks of their forebears through central Europe, where scores of placenames contain Celtic elements. Some reached the Black Sea while others crossed the Bosporus to settle in Asia Minor. This last group spoke a language akin to that of the Treveri, a Gaulish people remembered many hundreds of miles away in the name of Trier, or Trèves, in the Rhineland. The Greeks called them Galatians and St Paul addressed an epistle to them.

The urbane Hellenes were well aware of the *Keltoi*, whom they regarded as rather superior barbarians, and where they had come from. Impressed by their bravery in combat, Alexander of Macedon confronted a Celtic chieftain with the question: what did the Celts fear most? According to one of Alexander's generals, the Gaul replied "That the sky should fall upon our heads."

So far as their language and their existence as a distinct society were concerned, the worst fears of the Celts were to be realized, but at this time their tide was at its flood, and especially so for the Romans. The Gaulish Celts were warriors of ferocity and skill. Their armies advanced south through Italy, defeating the legions who were still learning their trade. In 390 BC they shattered the gates of Rome itself. Their techniques of warfare went far beyond the *furor*, the yelling, braggartly frenzy by which they summoned up the blood and terrified their opponents. Once the Romans

had got their measure, they were dismissing the *furor* as "the vainglorious bombast of the Celts," but they were not contemptuous of their enemy's technology.

The Celtic mastery of horses was formidable and they were by far the most advanced exponents of wheeled warfare and transport in the west. The Romans admired and learned from them, acquiring for the first time words for their vocabulary which have come down through vernacular Latin into most modern European languages. Almost all Latin words for vehicles are of Celtic origin, including *carrus*, a four-wheeled wagon which the Celts used for baggage and from which have descended our modern cars and "carriages;" and *carpentum*, a two-wheeled vehicle or chariot, from which emerged the Latin *carpentarius*, a wheelwright, and our "carpenter."

From an equally humble source, the Celtic *caballus* "packhorse," there has come the French *cheval* and a whole series of elegant riders, the *chevalier* "cavalier" and "cavalry," the German *Kavalier*, the Spanish *caballero*. In even more commonplace examples, the Romans dropped *feles* for their domesticated "cat" and adopted the Celtic *cattus*, began to wear Celtic *bracae* "breeches," and carry their effects in a *bulga* or leather holdall, hence "bulge."

But for the Latin which adopted them, these Celtic words and a few others (some surviving Celtic words in French, for example, include *charrue* "plough," *arpent* "acre," *lieue* "league" and *alouette* "lark") would have vanished entirely, along with the rest of the language, on the continental mainland. Only placenames would have testified to the range and influence of a once-great people, and there are literally hundreds of those placenames in France alone.

All toponyms containing or which once contained "dun" or "briga" as an element mark Celtic hill settlements or fortresses (Verdun in France, Bregenz in Austria, Brihuela in Spain). Lugdunum, the ancient name for Lyon, contains not only the fortress element but also that of Lug, most powerful of Celtic gods. Lug occurs again in Luguvallum (Carlisle) and elsewhere; Leiden in Holland, Liegnitz in Silesia. German towns and villages with *hal* in their names – Halle, Hallein, Swabisch Hall, Hallstadt – mark the ancient presence of Celts; it was their word for salt and where it was found. Lastly, the people themselves; cities and whole regions bear, in modern form, the names of the old tribes from Paris, the *Parisii*, to Bohemia, the *Boii*.

The rise to greatness of the continental Celts was surpassed by their rate of decline. From the peak in 390 BC their language and culture disintegrated beneath the impact of imperial Rome whose empire ultimately corresponded, and more, with the old Celtic domains from Iberia to Asia Minor. And to the north, where remnants might have survived beyond the Roman boundaries (*limes* "limit") a new and potent force had emerged; the Germanic-speaking peoples.

The last echoes of continental Celtic were heard probably no later than the sixth century AD in the high Swiss valleys. All that was left of the old tongue was now to be found in the British Isles, and in the Breton peninsula, where it was an export from Britain.

Celtic in Britain

The shrieks, maledictions and clatter of weapons that greeted Caesar's first abortive expedition to Britain in 55 BC must have fallen upon ears that were wearily familiar to such sounds. The challenges, the wheeling chariots, the general *furor;* here were the same people, speaking the same language as those the legionnaries had encountered in a dozen campaigns. They were in fact *Belgae,* one of the three tribes into which Caesar had divided Gaul.

The Belgae were latecomers to the British Isles. Other Celts had been arriving in a constant stream for more than 500 years and by the time the Romans arrived had spread their language throughout mainland Britain, smothering what prehistoric tongues might have existed there. An exception was north-western Scotland, where the aboriginal Picts held sway. The Pictish language came to be greatly influenced by Celtic but nothing remains of it apart from some exotic inscriptions as far afield as the Shetlands, and some placenames, among them Fife and Atholl and Caledonia, itself named for one of the principal Pictish tribes.

For the rest of Britain, the Celtic dialects were in universal use and have left clear evidence of their extent, if not in the language then in scores of placenames from Aberdeen (*aber,* as in Welsh today, meant "estuary") to the Scilly Isles; in river names *(page 44)* and other natural features. The west country "combe" or valley is ultimately identical to the Gaulish *cumba* and the Welsh *cwm,* which has entered modern English as mountaineer's parlance;

Traces of a pre-Celtic people: a Pictish inscription from Scotland. Little is known of the Picts or their language, which was absorbed by Celtic, but an old Pictish tribal name survives in "Caledonia" and in a few modern placenames.

there is a "Western Cwm" on the approaches to Everest.

Once it had begun properly, a century after Caesar's incursions, the subjugation of most of Celtic Britain was swift and the language gave way to the rustic Latin of the invaders. There were some uprisings, notably that of Boadicea (or *Boudicca*, Celtic for "Victoria") but in a short while Latin had reduced British over the whole of southern and eastern England and the people were thoroughly Romanized.

The more distant parts of the north and west remained British-speaking. The people of Strathclyde, as it later came to be known, and the rest of the Lowlands were sufficiently thorny a problem for the Romans to shut them out behind Hadrian's Wall, and here the old language kept alive throughout the imperial presence in Britain. Equally successful were the Britons in the mountains of Wales and the craggy moorlands of the Cornish peninsula. Although they were defeated by the Romans they retained their linguistic identity, and on the withdrawal of the legions early in the fifth century a Celtic confederation came into being, stretching through the west from Land's End to the Clyde. Even among the Romanized British the language resurfaced, but not for long. Waiting in the wings were a new people whose language was destined in time to have an all but lethal effect on the Celtic languages. They were the Germanic Angles and Saxons.

Strangers in their own land

"Wales" and the "Welsh" are disparaging terms for a country, a people and its language. The words derive from an ancient Germanic word *wealas* "foreigner," applied by the incoming Anglo-Saxons to the resident British who were henceforth strangers in their own land. The Welsh are not alone as receivers of such cavalier treatment, for speakers of Germanic languages have often used kindred words to describe other people on their own ground. The Norsemen called the French *Valskr* and the Dutch describe their near-neighbours, the French-speaking Walloons of Belgium, as *Waalsch*. The Slavs have a related word, *Vlach,* to describe Romanians, who speak a Latin language.

The Welsh call themselves *Cymry* "fellow-countrymen," their country *Cymru* and their language *Cymraeg*, words related to the Old British *combrogos* "compatriot," recalled in Cambria and in Cumbria, one of the last bastions of Celtic in England. Welsh, which with Gaelic is defined as "insular" Celtic to distinguish it from the continental variety, is nevertheless almost identical to the language of Gaul; its differences from the Celtic of Ireland are signs of a separation more ancient than their division in the British Isles. Where historically Gaelic used the *qu* or *k* sound, the Welsh and the Gauls used *p*, a difference displayed in the words for "son" (Gaelic *mac*, Welsh *map*, now *mab*) and "head" (Gaelic *ceann*, Welsh *pen*) among others.

The Welsh vocabulary as a whole is replete with words which show its antique lineage and its distant cousins. The Welsh *gŵr* "man" equates

THE CELTIC REALMS

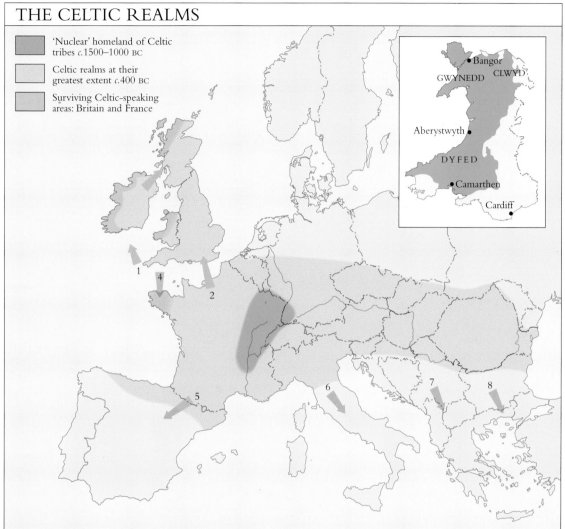

	'Nuclear' homeland of Celtic tribes *c*.1500–1000 BC
	Celtic realms at their greatest extent *c*.400 BC
	Surviving Celtic-speaking areas: Britain and France

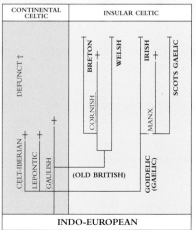

The Celtic languages surviving precariously in the British Isles and Brittany are the last vestiges of a tongue that was once dominant throughout much of Europe. From a heartland in eastern France, Switzerland and Germany, the Celts spread westward to create Gaul, to Ireland (1) where they enter history as the Gaels, and to Britain (2), where the language is still heard in Wales. Later migrations carried Irish Gaelic into Scotland (3), and Old British from Cornwall to Brittany (4). On the continental mainland, they had become a power to be reckoned with; they occupied most of Spain (5), invaded Italy and sacked Rome (6) in 390 BC. Others spread along the Danube, met and fought the Greeks (7), and crossed into Asia Minor, where St Paul knew them as Galatians (8). But their "empire" was amorphous, crumbling once Rome began its march.

"Welsh Wales" (inset): *Cymraeg,* the Celtic language of Wales, has more successfully resisted intrusion by a powerful neighbor than any of the other Celtic tongues.

CONTINENTAL CELTIC	INSULAR CELTIC	
DEFUNCT †	BRETON † / CORNISH †	WELSH
CELT-IBERIAN † / LEPONTIC † / GAULISH †	IRISH / MANX †	SCOTS GAELIC
	(OLD BRITISH)	GOIDELIC (GAELIC)
INDO-EUROPEAN		

CELTS IN AN ALIEN LANDSCAPE
A group of Welsh settlers in Patagonia. In an effort to escape the Anglicization of their language and customs, a party of about 150 made their homes there with the help of the government of Argentina, anxious to populate empty lands. The language survives there, just, on the lips of the older generation, but all are now bilingual and their Celtic culture has become "Hispanicized."

with the Latin *vir*, the Lithuanian *výras* and the English *wer*, as in "werewolf;" *tanau* "thin" with the Sanskrit *tanás* and the Latin *tenuis; rhod* "wheel" with the Latin *rota*, German *Rad* and the Sanskrit *rathas*, literally "chariot" or "wheeled."

Many more, from recognizably Latin, French and English sources, have accrued as a result of historical influences, but the fact that the language as a whole has survived the many inroads made upon it is owed principally to the long period of isolation enjoyed by its speakers. Mountains are uninviting landscapes for invaders, but ideal bases for raiding parties; long after they had consolidated their hold on England, the Anglo-Saxons found it convenient to build an earthwork, Offa's Dyke, to separate the two countries. Beyond it, a nation that was both young and old developed a linguistic culture strong enough to absorb small colonies of Gaels and Norsemen and some English in the north.

At the same time, a rich and lasting literary tradition came into being. The world owes to the Welsh language some of the earliest accounts of the heroic Arthur, the "once and future king" whose spectral image embodies a whole Celtic myth of greatness brought down by treachery but alive, even in death.

The Norman French were more aggressive than the English had been. Within four years of their landing at Hastings they were harassing the Welsh and soon penetrated the coastal lands as far as Pembrokeshire, where they settled some of their English and Flemish retainers. The region was for long known as "Little England beyond Wales" and the Welsh language never returned there. Sentinel castles sprang up and Welsh independence came to an end with the death in 1282 of *Llewellyn ein Llyw Olaf* "Llewellyn, our last prince." The final, ironic blow to a separate existence came when a Welsh family, the Tudors of Anglesey, acquired the English throne. The two countries were drawn into a single political unit with English the language of law and government and of the upper classes.

Condemned to a life "below stairs" and in

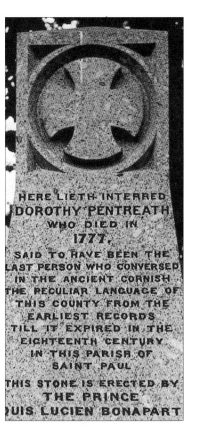

Headstone for a language: a memorial marking the resting place of a dead language in the graveyard of St Paul, Mousehole, in Cornwall. Enthusiasts of the Cornish language keep interest alive in Celtic's last toehold in England.

the fields, Welsh still remained the only tongue of all but a few people in the principality until after the coming of the Industrial Revolution. The raw materials of this apocalyptic change, particularly coal, existed plentifully in the South Wales valleys. With the newly arrived machines and their instructing mechanics, the English language came to the valleys. It replaced Welsh almost completely in the industrial centres and, by the end of the nineteenth century, two-thirds of the population was bilingual. The chapels and hymn books of the nonconformist revival provided one lasting refuge for the language, but otherwise the retreat was general.

One group of people fled the country entirely to keep their language and customs alive. In 1865 a small party led by Michael Jones set up a Welsh-speaking colony along the lower reaches of the Chubut river in Patagonia. Placenames in the modern atlas, Trelew and Puerto Madryn (the settlers' landing place, where Darwin had put ashore from the *Beagle*, thirty years earlier), mark what became a moderately prosperous community.

In rural Wales, the twentieth-century revolution in farming methods has driven to the cities many young people who might have been expected to keep the language alive in the rural heart-lands. The linguistic cohesion which

existed before the Industrial Revolution has gone and at the most recent census there were only 524,600 Welsh speakers, half the number there were at the turn of the century. The number of monolingual Welsh has fallen from fifteen per cent of the population in 1900 to a few thousand now.

The language has regained some ground, in status if not in number of speakers, in recent decades. It is a medium for instruction at primary stage in the schools and now has, in theory at least, equal standing with English in the administration of law and government. Culturally it is a treasured part of national life, which expresses itself each year at the Eisteddfod, and the ancient literary tradition flourishes in its classical form.

The buried language of Kernow

In Cornwall is two speeches: the one is naughtie Englysshe, the other is Cornysshe speche. And there be many men and women the which cannot speake one word of Englysshe, but all Cornysshe. (1542)

The English spoken in Cornwall is no longer naughtier (which in the old sense above meant poorer, or inferior) than anywhere else in Britain, and Cornish as an habitual language has been extinct for 200 years. Its last speaker was an old lady in Mousehole called Dolly

The prehistoric graves and shrines of Brittany are among the most notable in Europe. Words commonly used by antiquarians to describe them (*dolmen* "holestone" and *menhir* "long stone") are of Cornish/Breton origin.

Pentreath, who died in 1777.

Cornish, like Welsh, is the remains of the Old British Celtic. The elements of the name Cornwall (Cornish *Kernow*) derive from a Celtic people, the *Cornouii* and the Germanic *wealas* "foreigner." The Cornish knew the Phoenicians, who came to buy their tin.

Separated from their fellow Celts by the Anglo-Saxon invasions and harassed by Gaelic raiding parties, the Cornish lacked the natural barriers behind which their language might have flourished. Many fled "as from a ravaging flame" across the western approaches to Brittany, where they reintroduced the Celtic language to the continental mainland. In Cornwall itself, the language receded until, in Elizabethan times, it was confined to the uttermost limits of the peninsula, west of Truro.

Antiquarians and others have kept alive a knowledge of Cornish, and in recent times the language has gained a following. Elsewhere there is little trace left of the language except in the placenames where the Celtic past is everywhere recorded, from Penzance (*Pensant* "Holyhead") to Marazion (*Marchas bichan* "Little Market") by way of some of the most obscure Celtic saints: St Breward, St Clether, St Erme, St Pinnock and St Teath.

It is evident, too, in characteristic Cornish surnames; "By *Tre, Pol* and *Pen*, you shall know the Cornishmen"; these elements, contained in names like Trelawny and Trevithick, Poldark and Penrose, are toponymic – *tre* "farmstead," *pol* "pool," *pen* "head" (as in headland). Names

apart, few Cornish words have found a new home in English, quite the commonest being "gull," the seabird, which also found a roost in the French *goéland*.

Breton: an export to France

Whether there were any Celtic speakers in Brittany before the exodus from Cornwall is not known. By the time it happened, between the fifth and seventh centuries, the language had practically disappeared in France. A few traces may have remained, enough perhaps to attract the Cornish fugitives to a place and a people with whom they had something in common, but this is conjecture; modern Breton is clearly descended from Cornish and is thus Celtic of the British variety.

To some Frenchmen in the eighteenth century, the argument would have seemed almost treasonable. They claimed that French itself was derived from "Low Breton," even suggesting that Celtic was the language of Paradise and that Adam and Eve, not to mention the serpent, spoke Low Breton. They were dismissed as "Celtomaniacs" by Voltaire.

Today, Bretons know where their language came from and they have cultural links with their fellow Celts in the British Isles. Between a quarter and a half-million, most of them no longer children, speak *Brezhoneg*, as it is called, on a day-to-day basis and as many more can understand it.

At its greatest extent, Breton was spoken throughout the peninsula, west of a line from

Mont St Michel to the mouth of the Loire. Today, it has retreated inexorably before the advance of French, a fate echoing that of its parent Cornish and for that matter, its other Celtic relative, Gaelic. It is heard as habitual speech only in rural areas and fishing communities where simple conversational needs can be met without recourse to the foreign intruder.

Irish: a rich tradition

For unrecorded centuries the Irish were a secret people in a secret island, remote from the events which were changing forever the fortunes of their Celtic kinsmen in Europe. The spread of Roman influence stopped short before it reached them. The folk wanderings of the Germanic tribes brought the Angles and the Saxons to mainland Britain but left the Irish undisturbed. They were prehistoric, after other *Keltoi* had entered history.

To use a contemporary idiom, there is no

Priceless artefact of Celtic culture, the *Book of Kells* (now in Trinity College, Dublin) was written in Latin and illuminated by Irish monks who developed their own "half uncial" (curved) form of the Roman alphabet. It was reintroduced for public signs, documents and the like, during Ireland's Gaelic Revival.

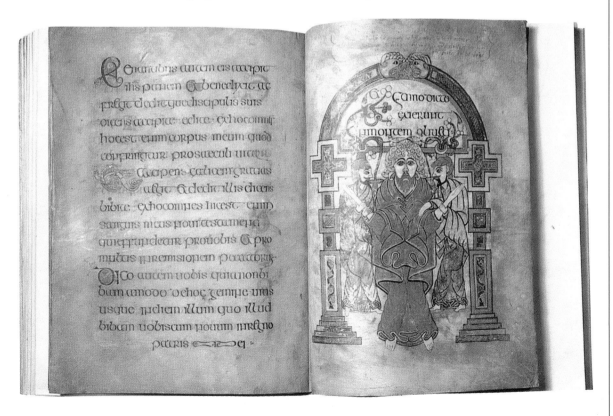

Unlike the Roman-derived Gaelic alphabet, the Ogam alphabet was a purely Irish creation. Its "Morse code" inscriptions of long and short strokes were used almost exclusively to commemorate the famous and the dead. Many examples still exist in Ireland, with a few in Wales, Scotland and the Isle of Man.

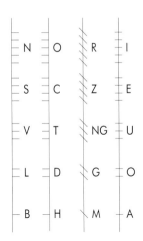

file on these early Gaels. All the evidence is hearsay, but hearsay of an heroic kind in the form of a rich oral tradition that had to wait many centuries before it was written down. This word-of-mouth history (doubtless illuminated from time to time with "new facts" by its bardic keepers to retain the interest of their eager audiences, who had heard it all before) spoke of a society sharing, however distantly, the heroes, customs and myths of their Indo-European relatives.

Their language, nowadays greatly altered by time and outside influences, was similarly archaic. The Gaels' use of the *qu* or *k* sound, where the Britons and Gauls used *p* *(see page 48)* is the older, the *p* being a late innovation among the continental Celts. The Gaelic usage reflects the earlier days of Celtic when, it is believed, its speakers travelled to their European homes in company with those speaking the proto-Italic tongues and before either had acquired a clear identity (Latin *equus* "horse," Old Irish *ech*, Gaulish *epos*).

The victims, later in their history, of invasion and oppression, the Irish enter British history as confident raiders and settlers of neighbouring shores. More than the Anglo-Saxons, they were responsible for driving many of the inhabitants of Cornwall to Brittany and in the north gained a substantial and lasting foothold where their language, as Scottish Gaelic, flourished and still lives.

One small raiding party, landing in Wales, changed the face of Irish history. Among the captives they took back as slaves was a youth called Patrick. After years of captivity he escaped but returned to spread the Christian faith among the pagan Gaels. By the time of his death (about 460 AD), Christianity had taken firm hold and in less than a century, Ireland had 100 bishops, almost as many monasteries and a devotion to the faith only now weakening in its ancient fervour.

Christianity brought to Gaelic a first infusion of foreign words, the Latin of the Church. There emerged also the first written form, at the beginning using the Roman alphabet which became modified into an

The *Gaeltacht*: the counties of Connemara, Mayo, Galway, Kerry and Cork keep the last traces of habitual Irish speech.

Principal Irish-speaking areas

English/Irish

English

ornate and distinctive form of its own, still commonly used in Ireland for public signs and street names and folksy teacloths. Now spoken of no longer as Gaelic but as Classical Old Irish, the language appears in manuscripts which have been preserved on the continent where Irish missionaries, steeped in the monastic tradition and truculent in their zeal (one is said to have frightened the very bears of the forest), played an important part in the founding of many great religious houses.

In Ireland, this was the "golden age of saints and scholars" and its clergy could boast "Paganism has been destroyed, though it was splendid and widespread," a nod to the past, which they could now commit to paper. But the old habits die hard. The numerous *taoiseacha* (chiefs and leaders; the title has been reintroduced for Irish prime ministers) might worship regularly, but they were in no hurry to give up their antique customs of raid and counter-raid. One at least was both king and bishop. Much later, an Irish abbot in Wales carried only a spear as his badge of office, which may help to explain why the early Church in Ireland had scores of saints but no martyrs.

This remarkable period in Irish history was hastened to its close by the arrival of a new and terrible force, the Norse-speaking Vikings. Religious houses were a favourite target for Viking pillage and rapine, and in Ireland the Norsemen must have felt like sweepstake winners. A common prayer of the time, "May God protect us from the fury of the Norsemen," had a special meaning for the islanders.

The Vikings left a permanent mark on the Irish language which shed many of its archaic forms and acquired numerous terms of Norse origin. These were largely to do with the sea and commerce; the Norsemen were traders as well as pirates and they founded the mercantile centres of Dublin, Cork, Limerick, Waterford and Wexford, among others. In exchange for the golden artefacts they had looted from the monasteries, they left words like the peculiarly apt *mal* "tax" and *pinginn* "penny."

The turning point in the history of Ireland and its language was the visit in 1171 of the English King, Henry II, and the beginning of Norman domination. At the outset there was widespread linguistic diversity, with the Anglo-Norman of the conquerors and the English, and sometimes Flemish of their retainers, being spoken in addition to the native Irish. New words and idioms flooded into the resident language, many with the heavy tread of the law and military about them: like *constabla*, "constable," *doinsiún* "dungeon," but other more elegant terms; *clairéad* "claret" and *gúna* "gown."

Within a few generations the newcomers were thoroughly Gaelicized and had become *Hibernis ipsis Hiberniores*, "more Irish than the Irish themselves." English was heard mainly in the vicinity of Dublin, "Within the Pale," as it was called, giving English a new expression.

With the arrival of the Tudors on the throne of England, a period of savage repression began that was to last for centuries. The Tudors began at the top, bringing the old families of Ireland to heel, Norman and old Gael alike. The Cromwellian assault upon everything Irish, the campaign of William of Orange, the enactment of the penal laws of 1695 designed, but with no ultimate success, to extinguish the Catholic faith, had the cumulative effect of eliminating the Irish-speaking aristocracy and destroying their cultural institutions.

By the eighteenth century, English had become almost entirely the language of the cultivated classes but Irish remained the language of the rural population and the working class generally. Tragedy of horrible proportions awaited them. The failure of the potato crop on which the peasant population subsisted caused the deaths from 1848 onward of upwards of a million people, almost all of them Irish-speaking.

There followed a rapid shift to English among the survivors, and massive emigration to the United States. When the position stabilized early in the twentieth century, Irish remained as a community language only in small, isolated pockets, all but a few of them on the western seaboard. These regions, called the *Gaeltacht*, have a population of 77,000, scarcely 15,000 of whom use Irish habitually.

The heart-rending consequences of the Great Famine for the Irish and their language had its reaction in the course of time. As the nineteenth century drew to its close, revealing just how much the language had gone out of use, societies like the Gaelic League came into being to reverse the trend and, more in line with nationalist movements throughout Europe, to treat the language as a hallmark of nationhood. When the Irish Free State was established in 1922, Irish was designated as the national language, taking precedence over English, the second official language of the country. All children are now taught it and most people support its maintenance, but not to the degree of using it at all.

In 1969, the writer and intellectual Máirtín O Cadhain summed it up: "The sky over Irish has again become darker and more threatening." He paraphrases the 2,000-year-old fear, first expressed by a Celt to Alexander the Great: "That the sky should fall on our heads."

No great number of Irish words has passed into the English vocabulary although telephone directories have page after page of "O"s (grandsons of) and "Mac"s (sons of, but most of these are of Scottish Gaelic origin). Some, like bog (*bog* "soft") and smithereens (*smidrini* "small pieces"), have been quite absorbed, but others like shamrock (*seamrog* "clover"), keen (*caoineadh* "lament"), and leprechaun (*leipreachan* "small body"), remain transparently Irish.

One other word from Irish has entered everyday English usage – one peculiarly apt in the light of relations between the two nations; "bother" (*bodhar* "deaf," "vexed").

Scottish Gaelic and Manx

The Irish came to Scotland as *Scoti*, an Ulster people whose name now serves for all the North British, in the fifth century. Taking possession first of Argyll, they advanced their

SCOTTISH GAELIC

Scottish Gaelic *(green)*, carried to north Britain by invaders from Ireland, refuses to perish in the Western Isles of Scotland.

Outer Hebrides

Skye

Inverness

Glasgow

Islay

Edinburgh

culture and language over the greater part of the northern territories, swallowing up the Pictish of the Highlands and, in the south-west, the old Celtic-speaking kingdom of Strathclyde. The Vikings arrived later to establish the Norse tongue in the northernmost regions and in the Western Isles. Gaelic reached its peak in Scotland in the eleventh and twelfth centuries, but by this time the Sassenach of Lothian and Northumbria was ready to begin its march.

It spread through the lowlands and along the east coast as far north as Inverness and by the end of the Elizabethan era had penned Gaelic into the Western Highlands and Isles. There it has survived, despite the Highland clearances of the eighteenth and nineteenth centuries – a tragedy on a par, though not involving anything like the numbers, with that of the Irish famine.

Manx, the language of the Isle of Man, is close to Scottish Gaelic and was spoken by most of the population of the island as late as the seventeenth century. It was no better than moribund by the end of the nineteenth century and its last speakers, old folk who had long given up using it, were dead by the 1960s.

In literature and speech, Scottish Gaelic continues at least as vigorously as Irish, mostly in the Outer Isles, with the greatest concentration in Lewis, but like other forms of Celtic, it has its active supporters.

The harsh economic deprivation that accompanied the Highland clearances drove many people to a new life across the Atlantic, where a colony of Gaelic speakers was set up on Cape Breton Island, Nova Scotia. At the turn of the century, three-quarters of Cape Breton's population of 100,000 could speak Gaelic (the first all-Gaelic newspaper, *Mac Talla*, was published there for a few years) but there are now only a few who can.

The Scottish Gaelic words that have entered English mostly have to do with the landscape and Scotland would be difficult to describe without them; loch and ben (*beinn* "head"), gillie (*gille* "servant"), ptarmigan (*tarmachan*, meaning, literally, "croaker") and capercaillie ("woodhorse") are familiar to an English speaker. So are clan (*clann* "offspring"), claymore (*claidheamh mor* "great sword") and slogan (*sluagh ghairm* "war cry"). But none is heard more often, where English is spoken, than *uisce*, properly *uisce beatha* "water of life". Even the Japanese call it whisky.

Celtic twilight: Loch Shiel from Glenfinnan, a landscape lost for words without "The Gaelic." The old language lives on in unchanging natural features like "loch" and "glen," "cairn" and "crag."

CHAPTER SIX

The legacy of Latium

Romans put an exact year, 753 BC, to the legendary founding of their city by Romulus. It will serve as a birth date, too, for a language whose descendants, the Romance tongues of Italy, France, Spain, Portugal and Romania, are now spoken by 400 million people, in Europe and far beyond it.

The Latins who made their home, Latium, along the River Tiber were one of a group of related people who had migrated to Italy around 1,200 BC, some six centuries before the name of Rome had begun to instil fear or respect in even her closest neighbors. The Italic tribes of which the Latins were part had belonged to the widespread Bronze Age culture that flourished in central Europe, along the banks of the Danube. They were related to the Celts whose own expansion began from the same area. Linguistic evidence points to more than one migration southward through the Alpine passes, for the Italic speakers comprised two distinct groups: Latin and a few related dialects to the west of the peninsula and a much larger eastern group, known as Osco-Umbrian. The Umbrian language is attested only in one spectacular find, a series of inscriptions on bronze tablets from Gubbio, but it is thought to have been spoken over a large area to the north-east of Latium. The better-known Oscan was the language of many southern tribes, including the Volsci and the Samnites, both formidable rivals of Rome in

her early struggles for local supremacy.

What motive brought the Italic people south to their new homeland? A clue lies in its Oscan name *Viteliù* from which the modern *Italia* ultimately derives. *Viteliù* means a "land rich in cattle." Tastes, like words, have sometimes changed little in 3,000 years; *vitello*, or "veal," remains the favorite meat of Italians.

After displacing the scanty prehistoric populations to pockets along the coast as far south as Sicily, the Italic speakers had for a time to give way to more advanced civilizations: first to the enigmatic Etruscans, a non-Indo-European people, in the north-west and later to Greek colonists in the south. The Etruscans flourished in what is now Tuscany and Lazio from 800 to 500 BC. Although they are remembered for their consuming interest in religion and death, in life they were enterprising traders.

While their language has remained a perpetual mystery, the Etruscans' greatest legacy to their neighbors and to posterity was the art of writing. The Etruscan script, based on an early form of the Greek alphabet, was modified to suit the needs of Oscan, Umbrian and above all, of Latin. Thus the Roman alphabet, the most widely used system of writing in the world, is owed at least in part to a people whose own language is not understood.

After the expulsion of Etruscan rule about 500 BC, the young Roman republic was a member of the loosely federated Latin League, but by the fourth century BC, the institutions and laws of Rome came to dominate the surrounding regions. Their durability is reflected in later civilizations which, when

THE LATIN FAMILY		
French	Spanish	Romansch
Italian	Portuguese	Romanian

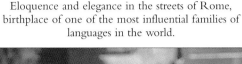

Eloquence and elegance in the streets of Rome,
birthplace of one of the most influential families of
languages in the world.

seeking names for new forms of government, seldom looked beyond Latin. No language has produced a better name for the non-monarchic state than *Res Publica*, the public concern.

The constitutions of most modern republics are upheld as in Rome by the Senate, *senatus* derived from *senex*, an old man. Other Roman offices and officers have changed their function over the centuries. The extraordinary powers of the *dictator*, a temporary appointment in times of crisis, often caused alarm but the word did not have its pejorative twentieth-century meaning. Instead, republics are governed by presidents, although the *praesidens* was not an important Roman office; it was usually applied to the man in charge of a small colony, while the *praesidium*, now used to describe a body of men controlling the destinies of a super power, was originally the small garrison of Roman citizens that helped him control the colony .

Colonia was the name given to the earliest settlements of Romans on conquered lands within Italy, especially along the coast. Modern Italians use it to describe a seaside holiday camp. The modern colony, an overseas dependency, was to the Romans a *provincia*. The first of these were Sicily, Corsica and Sardinia in the third century BC, to which were soon to be added part of France, Spain and North Africa.

The greatest influence upon the increasingly influential Latin of Rome was that of Greece, many of whose people had settled in southern Italy, and whose language still exists there in a form known as Italiot Greek. The Romans, concerned mainly with the business of conquest and administration, took their pleasures and their learning from the Hellenic culture, borrowing hundreds of terms in the fields of food, architecture, literature, science and philosophy. From Greece, cooks brought the word *butyrum* "butter," actors fetched the *scena* on which to perform *tragoedia* and *comoedia* while architects copied Greek designs for the *theatrum* itself. Townspeople in modern Italy, France and Spain do not assemble in a Roman forum but in a Greek *platea*, transformed into the ubiquitous *piazza, place* and *plaza*.

The eventual domination of Greece by Rome only accelerated the flow of Greek vocabulary and customs, but Latin never ousted the older, richer language from the eastern Mediterranean. It was to the west that Latin began its lasting travels.

The two Latins

Early in its history, long before the legions had achieved their greatest conquests, the old language of Latium had taken on two distinctive personalities, the one *urbanus* or

THE LATIN FAMILY

The Romance (Italic) languages descended from the Latin of Rome fall into four groups: Iberian, Gallic, Italian and Balkan. They include five of Europe's official languages: Italian, French, Spanish, Portuguese and Romanian. In addition to Spanish and Portuguese, the Iberian group includes also Galician (from which Portuguese has descended) and Catalan, which forms a linguistic "bridge" between the formal Castilian Spanish and the Provençal or *langue d'oc* of southern France. The Gallic consists of French and Provençal, the latter now a dialect. The Italian group includes, in addition to Italian: Sard (Sardinia); Corsu (Corsica) and the Romansch of Switzerland. Romanian dialects represent the Balkan group.

cultured, the other *rusticus* or common. They are now known as Classical and Vulgar Latin.

The first was the language of literature and oratory and was modelled on that of Rome's cultural mentor, Greece. Reading and playgoing were among the diversions imported from the older culture, and at first Roman authors simply imitated Greek models. A Latin style emerged that was both formal and polished and was used for oratory in the Senate

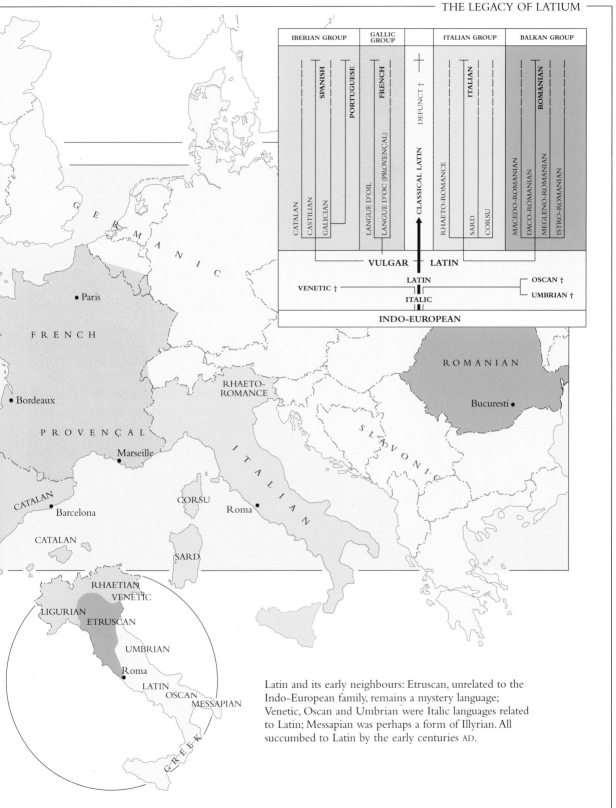

IBERIAN GROUP			GALLIC GROUP			ITALIAN GROUP			BALKAN GROUP			
SPANISH		**PORTUGUESE**	**FRENCH**		DEFUNCT †	**ITALIAN**			**ROMANIAN**			
CATALAN	CASTILIAN	GALICIAN	LANGUE D'OIL	LANGUE D'OC (PROVENÇAL)	CLASSICAL LATIN	RHAETO-ROMANCE	SARD	CORSU	MACEDO-ROMANIAN	DACO-ROMANIAN	MEGLENO-ROMANIAN	ISTRO-ROMANIAN

VULGAR — LATIN

VENETIC † — **LATIN** — OSCAN †

ITALIC — UMBRIAN †

INDO-EUROPEAN

Latin and its early neighbours: Etruscan, unrelated to the Indo-European family, remains a mystery language; Venetic, Oscan and Umbrian were Italic languages related to Latin; Messapian was perhaps a form of Illyrian. All succumbed to Latin by the early centuries AD.

and the courts of law. Under the Republic, eloquence was rewarded with the highest honors; it was through his advocacy rather than his military prowess that Julius Caesar rose to political prominence.

Couched in this Classical language, the laws of Rome became the cement which bound a great empire together. It was the ambition of every provincial subject to enjoy the full legal rights of a Roman citizen and the principles of Roman Law live on to a greater or lesser extent in most of the world's legal systems. Classical Latin phrases such as *de iure, ipso facto* and *in perpetuum* still illuminate the speeches of learned counsel. Justice and injustice, legality and illegality, together with many other concepts based on *ius* and *lex* (the two Latin words for law) have had a very long life, and no better principles by which to regulate social behavior have appeared to supersede them.

But the polished discourse of advocates and authors suffered from a surfeit of complexities and its meaning was elusive to all but those who were masters of it. The order of words in a sentence could be varied for reasons of emphasis and nuances of style and the sense could remain unclear until the sentence was completed. It was not a language for everyday conversation and by the time it had reached its "golden" period in the first century BC (the age of Virgil, Livy and Cicero) it had become incomprehensible to the man in the Roman street. It was his racy speech (and often his slang; the French word *tête* "head," for example, derives from the Latin *testa*, an earthenware pot) which was carried across the Empire to give birth to an entire family of modern languages.

Although a splendid library of great works in Classical Latin survived to inspire countless generations of scholars, very few Roman authors of the Golden Age ever paid more than passing attention to the everyday speech of the people, or gave any sort of account of the chasm that had opened up in Latin. It was left in the main to commoner folk and their casual mistakes to provide most of the clues that marked the development of the Vulgar language and the speech of those who were to inherit it.

Some of the finest of these exist in the graffiti on the walls of Pompeii – shopping lists and assorted scribblings preserved miraculously by lava of Vesuvius after the volcano erupted and buried the town and its inhabitants in 79 AD. For example, the word *locus* "place" is seen to have become *logus* and so, in pronunciation, well on its way to the modern Italian *luogo*, Spanish *lugar*.

Vulgar Latin inscriptions appear not only at Pompeii but throughout the empire where Roman remains survive or have been uncovered by excavation. At the end of the third century AD, the existence of the common language is acknowledged in texts, among them a spelling guide for scribes, the "Appendix of Probius," giving correct and incorrect forms of words; the "correct" usually referring to the written form, the "incorrect" to the spoken.

Among an overwhelmingly illiterate populace, it is the spoken form that governs, and thus the language of the common Roman rather than that of the orator or author provided the basis, or proto-Romance parent, for the modern Romance languages of Italy, France, Spain, Portugal and Romania.

For several centuries, the two forms of Latin coexisted side by side. The Classical form persisted as the language of worship, scholarship and of international dealings well into modern times, but it had long since ceased to be the vernacular of the people who had created it.

Although it had acquired the shroud of a dead language, it continued to speak in the "cold cloister" where the early monastics pored over, copied and translated old documents. They were keeping alive the culture and learning of a young but threatened civilization throughout Europe's Dark Ages.

The Roman road

After the defeats of Carthage and Macedon, Rome dominated the Mediterranean. Its enemies were rarely organized enough to hinder imperial expansion; the Celts of Spain were subdued, while those in the south of Gaul, already urbanized by Greek and Carthaginian traders, came under the rule of Rome. This large area was dubbed *Provincia (Gallia Narbonensis)*, hence the present-day Provence. For a while this stretch of desirable coastline was prey to marauding Gallic and Germanic tribes from the north, but once the conquest of Gaul had been completed by Caesar, and Augustus had quelled the last remnants of opposition in Spain, the western half of the Empire was secure.

For the first two centuries AD, the *Pax Romana* worked well. The currency was stable and new towns grew apace from the profits of increased trade. Wealthy Gauls and Iberians aped their masters and adopted their language,

endowed their *municipiae* with baths, theatres and other public works, all in the Roman style. And joining them all, where once the only means of communication had been forest tracks, there were paved roads. The traveller's fear was no longer of bears and wolves, but of meeting the imperial tax collector.

From the Firth of Forth in northern Britain to the Strait of Gibraltar, from Cape Finisterre to eastern Asia Minor, Roman engineers spun a web of finely constructed highways that were not only arteries for the rapid deployment of troops (who helped to build them between military engagements) to trouble spots, but were vital to trade. The empire was self-sufficient in most of its essential needs and what one region could not supply, another could. The Mediterranean itself was a criss-crossing pattern of trade routes. From Ostia, Rome's port, a well-handled merchant-man could make a passage to Gades (Cadiz) in Spain in about nine days, and took about the same time to reach Alexandria in Egypt.

As the power of Rome began to wane, the timely arrival of Christianity in the west was able to reinforce the trend towards national linguistic communities. Vulgar Latin is thought of as the language of early Christianity; the writings of the Church Fathers, particularly St Augustine and St Jerome, are cited as typical examples, and the word "Vulgate" is still used to describe St Jerome's translation of the Bible. While their writings were far from Classical, being intended to reach a wide audience through a straightforward style, in its fundamental correctness their language was still Latin. It bore little resemblance to the evolving

CONTINUED ON PAGE 66

AN ALPHABET FOR THE WORLD

The twenty-six clear-cut characters of the Roman alphabet can be used to commit to paper almost every language in the world: in comparison, Chinese has 45,000 symbols; an educated Chinese uses about 6,000, but the "man in the street" gets by with 1,500.

The Roman alphabet was not "invented" by the Romans, but was the culmination of a process that had begun in the Semitic lands bordering the eastern Mediterranean. The Romans took their inspiration from the alphabet of their erstwhile masters, the Etruscans (who had taken theirs from the Greek alphabet), refining it into a Classical clarity that has never since been improved upon.

The letter **A** tells the story in summary: originally (in Egyptian) the drawing of an ox's head, it was modified by the Phoenicians into the symbol *aleph,* Semitic "ox." Turned on its end by the Greeks, it became their *alpha*, was adopted by the Etruscans, and then by the Romans. *Alpha* with *beta*, the second letter of the Greek alphabet, makes up the word "alphabet."

The oldest surviving text in Roman dates from about the sixth century BC, an inscription from the Roman Forum. From the first century BC, Latin inscriptions throughout Europe had become too numerous to count. All were in "capitals" – the minuscule or lower case was developed later in a series of "national hands."

▲ Greek A (tenth century BC)

◄ From Semitic *yodh* or "hand;" Greek *iota;* used by Romans to denote a vowel *i* and consonant *y*

► Middle Ages addition to alphabet to differentiate *i* from *y;* from the same source as *i*

▲ Semitic *kaph* "hand held sideways;" became Greek *kappa;* Romans preferred *qu* to represent sound

◄ Originally Semitic *lamed* which meant "ox goad;" became Greek *lambda* and finally Roman *L*

◄ Adopted as *sigma* by Greeks from Semitic *shin;* at first angular, taken by Romans in rounded form

◄ Semitic *resh,* became Greek *rho* and passing through Etruscan to adopt modern form

▲ Changed little in shape since it was Semitic *quoph* "knot;" Greeks used it as a symbol for 90

◄ *Tau,* last letter in Semitic alphabet, virtually a "'signing-off'" cross. Retained almost unchanged

► Adopted by Romans from Greek; a "redundant" letter as easily expressed by *cs* or *ks*

◄ Unknown in Semitic, it was taken from Greek alphabet by Romans for use in borrowed words

▼ Originally Semitic vowel *he* "window" became Greek *epsilon* and passed unchanged into Roman

d
The sign *daleth* meaning "door" in Semitic, turned into familiar triangle "delta" by the Greeks

◀ Began as North Semitic *Beth,* meaning "house;" taken by Greek to form their *beta*

▶ Semitic *vau* "hook" became Greek *phi.* Original *w* sound altered to *f* by Etruscans and Romans

c
Originally *g* sound in Semitic, was changed to *k* sound by Etruscans and adopted by Romans

◀ Originally Semitic sign *gimel,* "camel," became Greek *gamma.* Altered in Rome from *c* to G

◀ Eighth letter since earliest times; originally Semitic *heth* or *kheth,* a word meaning "fence"

o
At first not a vowel, but a Semitic consonant *ayin* "eye;" became Greek forms *omicron* and *omega*

▶ Semitic *pe* or "mouth." Took many forms as Greek *pi* and changed to *P* by Romans

▲ Semitic *mem,* wavy line signifying "waters;" thence into Greek as *mu* and taken over by Romans

▲ Originally Semitic *nun,* a symbol for "fish," then Greek *nu,* then adopted by the Latin alphabet

◀ Originally Greek *upsilon;* always written as *V* by Romans, having both *U* and *V* sounds

▶ Same history as *U,* not used independently to indicate consonant sound until modern times

◀ Semitic *zayin* in origin, became Greek *zeta.* Used, like *y,* by Romans for borrowed Greek words

▲ Invented by Normans to indicate English sound "double u" for which they had no use in French

CONTINUED FROM PAGE 63

habits of speech among the populace. Like the common Romans, Gauls and Iberians were going about the transformation of their languages in their own down-to-earth way.

One feature of "Christian Latin" was a further importation of Greek words. Christ's pun on the name of St Peter: "Thou art Peter: upon this rock I shall build my Church," was meaningless if "rock" or "stone" was translated as the old Latin *lapis*. Translators used the already current Greek word *petros* (*petra* in modern Greek). More significantly, the word that took root for a place of worship was not the Latin *basilica* but the Greek *ecclesia* from which have come the French *église* and Spanish *iglesia*.

Thus from North Africa through Italy, Spain and France to Britain, when a man wrote or worshipped he used Latin, but the language a child learned from his parents was already something different. It contained the seeds from which were to spring the modern Romance languages. Anglo-Saxon was soon to exclude Britain from the family while Arabic did the same for the old North African provinces, but in Italy, France and Spain, Latin had driven down immovable roots. Despite the incursions of Franks, Goths, Lombards and Vandals during the Dark Ages, it was never displaced, only transformed.

Once the violent centuries had come to an end, the implanted Latin of the Empire had become a series of separate speech communities in Italy, the Iberian peninsula, and in northern and southern France (Provence). They had left the Roman cradle and taken on the characteristics of individual and mutually incomprehensible tongues. By the ninth century, French had emerged as a literary as well as a spoken language in the Oaths of Strasbourg (842), which were publicly sworn by Louis and Charles, grandsons of Charlemagne. One brother took the Oath in Frankish German, the other in French, so as to be understood by all their vassals. In the tenth century the first written traces of Italian appear and in the eleventh, Spanish.

There were, in wilder, less accessible regions of the Empire to the north and east of Italy, a few more areas where Latin managed to survive. The most remarkable, and distant, of these was Dacia, conquered and colonized by the emperor Trajan as a bulwark of the Empire to the north of the Danube. Even though the territory was abandoned by the legions after fewer than two centuries, the Latin of the settlers lived on to become the national language and dialects of present-day Romania. The survival of Romanian Romance far from the main body of Latin-derived languages is remarkable in the light of their later history, in which their language resisted assaults from Germanic, Slavonic and Magyar invasions.

South of the Danube also, a Latin language, Romansch, has held fast in the eastern Alps, in the Old Roman province of Rhaetia, and survives in the fast-disappearing "Ladin" of the Dolomites and Friulian, now much corrupted by Venetian Italian. On the far side of the Adriatic, a Latin form known as Dalmatian was recalled at the end of the last century by a somewhat unreliable source, a deaf and toothless old man who remembered it spoken by his parents. Dalmatian came to a violent end when the old man was killed in a mine explosion.

FRENCH: DISTINGUISHED HEIR TO LATIN

It is an irony of history that one of Europe's proudest nations, the French, should take their name from an alien people, the Germanic Franks. At heart the French are Gallic Celts and their language the most distinguished offspring of Latin. It is spoken as a first language by around seventy million people on the European mainland, and in French overseas departments and territories from the West Indies to Oceania, where it has an official role alongside local vernaculars.

For the greater part of modern history, French has been the lingua franca of international affairs and in all matters of discernment, heard not only in the chanceries but also in the *salons* where the well bred and elegant met; until the Revolution, the entire Russian court preferred the cultured harmonies of French to the "barbarous" Slavonic of their subjects.

The claim of French to be the successor of Latin as the pre-eminent language of Europe is impossible to refute, for it was Charlemagne, the King of the Franks, who renewed the values of the fragmented Roman world. Although the Franks were a Germanic people, the conversion of Charlemagne's ancestor, Clovis, in 496, ensured that religion, scholarship and all matters of state were to be carried on in Latin, as before. It was thus determined that *la langue française* should not be the Germanic of those whose name it bore but a daughter of the language of Rome.

The Franks were one of the Germanic tribes that had long troubled the frontiers of Rome's northern dominions. At times they had sought protection within the pale of the Empire, at others they had harried it or been driven beyond it. The Gauls, accustomed to Roman civilities, were not anxious to communicate with their rough neighbors, and it is no surprise that one of the earliest Germanic words to pass into the Vulgar Latin of the Gauls should be *werra*, the French *guerre* "war," German *Wehr*, as in *Wehrmacht*.

Germanic loanwords, recognizable in their Old French forms, have now been so well assimilated that their origins are all but impossible to discern. *Fauteuil* "armchair," was once *faldestol*, literally "folding stool," the king's deckchair for relaxing in after battle. Similarly, one cannot imagine more French-sounding words than *garder* "to guard" and *regarder* but these too, apart from the much later Latin prefix *re-*, were Germanic borrowings from the same root as the English word; as in *guerre*, the Germanic *w* regularly appears in French as *g* or *gu*. Indeed, the French dictionary includes a mere handful of words beginning with *w* and all are of foreign origin.

The *Chansons de Geste*, the epic poems of Roland, Oliver and other Frankish paladins, did much to give the French a national linguistic identity. Although the first manuscripts of any length in French date from the twelfth century, they belong to a much older oral tradition, in which the trappings of medieval warfare have a strong Germanic flavor. Many borrowings, like *bannière*, "guide," the violent *briser* "to smash" and the acquisitive *butin* "loot" are still functional today, while others like *gonfalon* "pennant," *baudrier* "crossbelt" and *haubert* "coat of mail" are laid up in the museum like the objects they describe.

THE KINGDOM OF THE FRANKS

Charlemagne, "Charles the Great" (742–814) was the first great European. When he died, his Frankish kingdom rivalled that of the Roman Empire in size, and was its historical successor in western Europe. The whole of France (excluding Brittany), the Low Countries, Germany east to the Elbe, Bavaria and northern Italy comprised a single Christian entity with "marches" or spheres of influence beyond it. Although the Frankish kingdom was achieved by force of arms (his own, and generations of predecessors'), Charlemagne was far more than an empire builder; he was a patron of the arts and sciences and of learning generally, attracting to his glittering court at Aachen (Aix-la-Chapelle) the best brains of the age. Among them was the English monk, Alcuin of York, who became his principal religious adviser. Aachen, where

Charlemagne's remains rest in the splendid Romanesque chapel modelled on the sixth-century church at Ravenna in Italy, came to be known as the "Second Rome" and embassies arrived there from as far afield as Baghdad, where the court of the legendary Haroun-al-Raschid was more splendid than anything in western Europe.

Among the exotic gifts sent to Charlemagne by the Caliph of the Arabian Nights was an elephant which for years accompanied him on his campaigns, to the delight of his allies and the consternation of his enemies (the great beast had been in France before, with the armies of Hannibal).

The great kingdom did not long outlive its greatest ruler, dissolving within a century of his death, but the foundations of France's subsequent greatness had been laid. For the next 1,000 years, its language ruled the affairs of Europe, heir in every way to Latin.

Equally Germanic is the vocabulary of the new social order introduced by the Franks. The feudal *fief* was originally the same word as the modern German *Vieh,* meaning cattle, while the overlord of the *fief,* the *baron,* derived from a Germanic word that passed into Latin as *baro,* a warrior or freeman. The baron's officials, the *héraut,* the *chambellan,* the *sénéschal* and the *maréchal,* have enjoyed varied careers over the centuries. Heralds are now used metaphorically rather than literally, while the employment prospects for chamberlains and seneschals are even more gloomy. The *maréchal,* on the other hand, rose from the stables where he looked after the horses (his title contains the English word "mare") to command the armies of Napoleon and to appear, thousands of miles away, in the mythology of the American West in his Anglicized form, "marshal."

If all this gives the impression that the

Franks were just flag-waving bullyboys smelling of the byre and midden, it should be remembered that *trève*, a "truce," is also a Germanic loanword. At a more placid level, modern French owes to the Franks many words still in use. The verb *gagner* "to earn," which affects every modern Frenchman in its sense of making money, was originally a Germanic term meaning to go out into the fields to gather food. There were other civilized gifts like *salle* "hall," *jardin* "garden" and that welcoming feature of French life, *auberge* "inn."

Langue d'oïl, langue d'oc

Except for periods of military campaigning, as when Charles Martel defeated the Saracens at Tours in 732 and Pepin and Charlemagne marched to subdue the Lombards in Italy, Frankish domination was usually restricted to the north of France. This led to the development of two distinct languages, the *langue d'oïl* in the north and the *langue d'oc* in the south. *Oïl* and *oc* were the words for "yes" (now *oui*) in the respective areas, both being pared-down versions of the Latin phrase *hoc illud* "that's it." The political independence of the southern nobles, who were theoretically at least vassals of the King of France, was a major factor in the remarkable literary flourishing of the *langue d'oc* in the lyrics of the troubadours from the eleventh to the thirteenth centuries *(see pages 74–5)*.

While this carefree culture was evolving in the south, the feeble successors of Charlemagne had to face the constant threat of raids by the formidable Norsemen. Charles the Simple (893–923) decided that the only solution was to offer the Viking chief Rollo a dukedom and allow his followers to settle there. Norsemen became Normans, and within the space of the tenth century learned to speak French as well as any Frank.

The Vikings were not in the habit of taking their wives along with them. The second generation of Normans mostly had French-speaking mothers but, brought up to the sea, held on to their old Norse nautical expressions. Among the few that have survived in modern French include *havre* "haven" or "harbor," as in Le Havre, *vague* in place of the Latin *onde* "wave," and *équipe*, now applied to a football team and motor-racing stable, as well as to a ship's crew. The handy Germanic words for the points of the compass (*nord, sud, est, ouest*), borrowed about this time, appear to have come from Anglo-Saxon sailors rather than Vikings, as does *bateau*, originally *batel*, from the same word as boat.

Having adopted the French language with alacrity, the Normans were highly effective agents in making it heard beyond France, most importantly installing it as the language of the ruling classes in England. They became excellent scholars and many of the best Old French manuscripts, including the *Song of Roland*, are in a Norman or Anglo-Norman hand.

Northern France now had three major dialects, those of Normandy, Picardy and the Île-de-France. When the University of Paris was founded at the beginning of the thirteenth century, there grew up a tradition of "four nations" among its students: the Gallicani (Gauls), Picardi, Normanni and Angli. The Gallicani came to dominate the institution, especially when their most famous college, the Sorbonne, became the center of medieval scholasticism. Politically, also, the influence of Paris became dominant. Once the crusade against the Albigensian heresy put an end to the power of the lords of the Languedoc, the language of literature and law came to be based throughout the country on the Parisian dialect.

In the new spirit of learning, the scholars of Paris began to look closely at their own language, as they continue to do to this day. They compared French to its parent Latin and found wholesale changes in pronunciation had taken place. It was not surprising, after 1,000 years of everyday, untutored talk. Among the commonest of words, the Latin *ego* "I" had passed through the forms *eo, io* and *jo* before settling on the modern French *je*. The hard Latin *c* had often altered to *ch* (Latin *canis* "dog" became French *chien*) and the hard *g* often became *j*. Picards and Normans, however, continued to use the hard *g*, and so the English eat "gammon" instead of *jambon*.

A single Latin word might have numerous offspring. *Senior* has at various times given *sire, seigneur* and the antique form *sieur*, which still goes strong as the respectful mode of address in *monsieur*. Grammar was an equally haphazard affair at this time, but the modern word order was taking shape.

Many thirteenth and fourteenth-century scholars spent their lives translating from Latin. A Latin *auteur* (from *auctor*) was not simply an author: the word still meant "authority," and what he wrote was sacred. If a translator could not find a suitable French equivalent for a Latin word he simply Gallicized the Latin as far as was necessary to make it appear French. These "learned" borrowings have always been the richest source of a new vocabulary in all the Romance languages. Sometimes they were borrowed independently into Italian, Spanish and Portuguese; if not, they could speedily be transferred from one Romance language to another and into English which, thanks to its absorption of Norman French, accommodated these new words with ease.

Old French words were often replaced by a new "learned" form, *crucifier* being preferred to the picturesque *cloufichier*, a popular distortion which gave the word the added sense of driving in nails. Other words took on a new meaning once a new alternative had entered the language. *Nager* now means "to swim" where once it had meant "to sail" until replaced by *naviguer*, the learned form of the Latin parent *navigare*.

Old French gave way to Middle French in the early fourteenth century. It was a good time neither for the country nor the language. The Sorbonne, hitherto Europe's cultural arbiter, tended to produce more and more footling commentaries on fustian dogma, giving Scholasticism the bad name it possessed thereafter. When French fortunes revived late in the fifteenth century, inquiring minds turned instead to Italy where the Renaissance was producing new inventions and concepts, all of which required new names.

Among the earliest Italian loanwords to enter French were the eminently practical *canon* and *banque*, warfare and raising money to pay for it still being among the chief preoccupations of the kings of France. Italian

Birthplace of William the Conqueror, Falaise Castle reveals the Norse origins of its builders in its name. *Falaise* "cliff" (describing the rock on which it stands) derives from the same Old Norse source as the English lakeland "fell."

DIALECTS OF FRENCH

Boulogne

PICARDY

Le Havre

Bayeux

NORMANDY

ÎLE DE FRANCE

Falaise

Paris

Three major dialects – those of Normandy, Picardy and the Île de France, centred on Paris – were spoken in northern France during the early Middle Ages. At first the least prestigious of the three, the *Francien* of the Île de France came in time to dominance and by the sixteenth century was established as the official language of France.

influence upon French life and language reached its peak during the mid-sixteenth century during the regency of the Italian Catherine de Medici. Many of the loanwords of this period were musical, architectural and artistic terms which now have a worldwide currency. At the same time, French armies were reorganized on Italian models, entailing the adoption of new ranks, *colonel* and *caporal*, and new military formations, *infanterie* and *cavalerie*. To ride a horse to war, it was no longer necessary to be a *chevalier;* a soldier could enlist as a *cavalier* "cavalryman."

Fashions in food and dress were also strongly influenced by Italy and the French have their Italian queen to thank for their reputation in these matters ever since. Exotic foods like *sorbet* and *artichaud* (both originally Arabic words) came to French from the Italian as did more homely fare like *marrons* "sweet chestnuts" and *saucissons* "sausages."

The names of clothes in France have changed almost as often as fashions themselves. Frenchmen's legs have been clad at various times in Celtic *braies*, Latin *chausses* and Frankish *houseaux*. In the end it was the comical Venetian *pantalon* that became the modern French for trousers. *Costume* is also of Italian origin although the Germanic *robe* had found its way into the *garderobe* "wardrobe" at a very early date.

Italy was the major but not the only source of new words during this chaotic period of European history. From their voyages of discovery and conquest, the Spanish landed cargoes of strange new fruits and vegetables like *tomates, tabac* and *chocolat,* while Spanish soldiers, active on French soil during the Religious Wars, introduced *camarade* (originally a room-mate) and several military terms, including *la diane*, the gun or bugle-call that wakes French troops in the morning, and for which English-speaking armies use the French word *reveille*. The French Protestants during the same wars came to be known as *Huguenots*, a word said to derive by roundabout process from *Eidgenosse*, a member of the Swiss confederacy.

The greatest single influence on all European languages during the sixteenth century was the introduction of the printing press, although its initial effect on French was one of confusion rather than clarification. Sixteenth-century spellings are as erratic as those of the medieval scribes, and the fact that many of the printers were Dutch or Italian did not add to their consistency. The diacritic mark of the scribes to indicate a "missîg" letter was adopted indiscriminately by printers to fit their type to the line. It was some time before it was restricted to its present *rôle* (from *roule* or *rolle*, the roll of paper on which an actor's part was written) as the circumflex, which indicates a missing letter (usually *s*) that has fallen silent, as in *mâtelot*, or his *maîtresse*. Another useful device taken up by the printers was the çedilla *ç* as in *garçon*. Before, they had used two letters, *ce*, to indicate a soft *c* before *o* or *a*.

Despite its antique appearance on the page, the spoken language of the cultured Parisian of the late sixteenth century would be understandable today. Some vowel sounds might be unfamiliar and here and there he would use a medievalism or two, but otherwise

Medieval Paris, with its teeming streets and illustrious university, the Sorbonne – founded in 1150 and one of the oldest in the world – was a magnet for students from all over Europe. Its pre-eminence as a center of culture ensured the central role that French was to play in European history throughout modern times.

there would be few difficulties, for it was his language that was to be taken as the standard for classical French and as the model for future generations.

Modern French

While Louis XIV and Richelieu raised the political and cultural prestige of France to new heights in the seventeenth century, the task of ennobling the language remained in the hands of poets. Malherbe, the proverbial herald of French Classicism, took current usage as his model but advocated the exclusion of the colloquial, the archaic and the provincial, for which he coined the expression "dégasconner la langue." If Gascon remains to this day the most vigorous of French regional dialects, Malherbe otherwise had his way and there emerged an educated, literary language such as Dante and Petrarch had given to Italy.

The care and maintenance of this precious creation was handed in 1635 to the Académie française, which guards it tenaciously to this day. A conservative and slow-moving body, the Académie finally produced its first dictionary in 1694. It favored etymological rather than phonetic spellings, and *français* was still spelt *françois*, *école* "school" as *escole*. Not until the nineteenth century was the *o* changed to *a*, to reflect the way it was pronounced, and *françois* to become *français*.

In matters of vocabulary, the Académie was equally slow to admit change. Even technical terms used by artisans in their workshops were excluded from the dictionary as being too vulgar. It is interesting to reflect that in contemporary English the artisan too has been forced to share his workshop with a motley crew of actors, ballet dancers and others.

It was left to eighteenth-century encyclopedists like Diderot and d'Alembert to catalogue this fertile source of new expressions, although for reactionary academicians such respect paid to simple craftsmen was little short of subversive. The elegant clarity of French was, however, an important factor in its becoming the language of peace treaties, international congresses and diplomatic negotiations of all kinds, as it remains to this day. A third of the delegations to the United Nations still use it. Admiration for French thought, literature, art, furnishings, dress and food also added prestige, quite apart from France's dominant political role in Europe.

Imaginative use of their own language and of Greek and Latin roots have enabled the French at least until recently to avoid the need to import an abundance of words from abroad. The patois or pidgin versions of French may have established themselves in many corners of the world, but with little effect on the language of the mother country. The greatest threat to its purity is English, not so much that of its neighbor and old adversary, (which the French are happy to regard as a badly pronounced form of their own language) but that of its overseas form, American.

Older English loanwords usually have an Edwardian flavor to them and relate to the leisure pursuits of the English gentleman; snobbery in France set great store by English horses and horsemanship and welcomed terms like *jockey, turf* and *handicap*, making them their own. The French have an unerring way of altering the sense, form or pronunciation of English words to give them a Gallic flavor (only a Frenchman can say *club* like a Frenchman) and the word "snob" itself has become almost complimentary on French lips, used much as the English use *chic*.

Technological terms, lacking any sort of elegance, are harder to Gallicize. Correspondents to French newspapers debated for years whether or not to accept the admittedly gross word "bulldozer" into the language, but the jargon of interplanetary hardware and its spin-offs is universal and irresistible; as are the *supermarché* goods, "*le tee-shirt*" or *le pull* "pullover" the Frenchman now wears with his Venetian *pantalons*.

The French complaint is not simply that they are borrowing so much from English (on any day, a French newspaper may have one English word in every 170), but that others are

Provençal: the Language of the South

Provençal is the traditional language of the southernmost third of France and a quarter of its population. It has few if any mono-lingual speakers left, but survives in the warm rustic dialects of Limousin and the Auvergne, Gascony, Béarn and Aquitaine, as well as those of the Mediterranean littoral. It is not a patois (an old French word meaning "rough local speech") but the remains of the *langue d'oc*, an independent language of great distinction, spoken by a people to whom their Gallo-Roman brethren of the north were quite alien, in speech as well as in manners.

The southern tongue, closer in sound and spirit to its Mediterranean neighbors, Italian and Spanish, than to the harsher voices of the north, was that of a sophisticated society, a feudal democracy that had its glittering courts, but also an unfettered peasantry. These two classes were to produce between them a unique class of man, the troubadour, who immortalized the Provençal tongue and carried southern ideas of chivalry and love throughout western Europe. Kings were not above claiming the title of troubadour – Richard Coeur de Lion was one – but the ranks of the *ménestrels* were open to anyone of sufficient lyrical talent.

At the time of the first known troubadour, Guillaume IX of Aquitaine (b. 1070), *fin amors* or "courtly love" is already an established tradition, for in his bawdier verses the poet-duke delights in making fun of it. The source of the tradition and its language may be in Limousin, birthplace of the first great Provençal poet, Bernart of Ventadorn (1148–95, the son of a brushwood gatherer) but it soon became a refined literary convention; Limousins, Gascons, Catalans, even Italians, all composed in Provençal, and its influence spread rapidly to inspire among others, the German *Minnesänger*.

The most obvious difference between Old Provençal and Old French, one that still persists in speech, is the Provençal retention of the Latin feminine ending *-a* (*ville, villa*). The modern traveller jouneying south will hear, becoming more pronounced, the final *e* which in the north is completely mute. The masculine ending *-or* is another feature of Provençal closer to Spanish than to French; the modern word *amour* derives appropriately from the language of the troubadours and their audiences.

A more ironic legacy from Provençal to French was *croisade* (the French ending *-ade* is borrowed from Spanish and Provençal *ada*). It was by means of the Albigensian Crusade of the thirteenth century, ostensibly to put down religious heresy, that the north destroyed the power of the southern courts. Without the patronage of the nobility, the troubadour milieu in which the literary language had flourished was all but destroyed and Provençal began its decline.

For centuries afterwards, southern peasants continued to speak in dialects quite different from the imposed *langue d'oïl* of the north. Provençal words continued to pass into French, often ones that describe a purely southern phenomenon, like the *Mistral*. The name comes from the Latin *magistralis*

A typical Provençal town or bastide, perched on a hilltop, like an eagle's eyrie.

"masterful wind." *Cigale*, too, is a Provençal word, for the song of the cicada is heard only in the warm south; a more widespread species, the ortolan bunting, carries its Provençal name *ortolan* "gardener" across much of Europe, if only occasionally to Britain.

What is left of the *langue d'oc* continues to retreat, harried towards its end by the imposition of compulsory French-medium education and the decline of rural populations. Only in remoter Gascony, which still has the most distinctive of accents, Béarn and the Auvergne *massif*, is one aware that the language of the people of the Midi is quite different to that on their televisions.

not borrowing from them. Few *diplomates, chefs, maîtres d'hotel, costumiers* (even soldiers, wearing the Béarnaise *beret*) would share this sombre view, that borrowings from the French are *passé*.

French beyond France

The borders of France have been fiercely contested throughout her history yet they fail to fulfil any function such as, for example, the inclusion of all French-speaking regions of Europe. Just as German, Catalan and Basque-speaking areas overlap into France, the area where French is spoken extends beyond the political frontier, principally into Belgium and Switzerland, but also into the north-west corner of Italy.

The Walloon dialect of southern Belgium shares the historical roots of the dialect of neighboring Picardy but political inde-pendence from France has allowed it to follow a different evolutionary course. The southern half of Belgium's population speaks Walloon, the linguistic boundary following a line that has existed for more than 1,000 years except for Brussels which, although lying in Flemish Brabant, is bilingual.

In Switzerland, French is a minority language spoken by just a million inhabitants, mostly living in the western cantons of Geneva, Neuchâtel and Vaud. The cantonal system of government in the Swiss Confederation has always ensured that French has nothing to fear from the numerically superior German Swiss who occupy the greater part of the country. The 100,000 French speakers in the Val d'Aosta region of

PROTOCOL AND POLITICS

The historical prestige of the French language is nowhere more evident than in the world of international affairs. Whatever his native language or status, the *diplomat* (one vested with a "diploma" authorizing him to represent his government abroad) acquires a French style and title once he appears at a foreign court and presents his credentials.

L'État c'est moi: the court of Louis XIV, "The Sun King." The lustre and language of his court were copied throughout Europe.

The *envoy* (literally "messenger") may be a minister plenipotentiary (*plein pouvoir* "with full powers") armed with a *carte blanche* (literally blank paper on which he may write his own conditions on the understanding that they will be accepted, that is absolute freedom of action); or simply a *chargé d'affaires* looking after his country's interests in the absence of a more senior minister. He may issue *communiqués* or write an *aide mémoire*, a "memorandum," with the aid of specialist *attachés* in commercial or military matters, some of whom may be engaged in secret surveillance (*sur veiller* "to keep watch on") by means of *espionnage*.

The impetus given to political change in Europe by the destruction of the French monarchy brought into being new ideas of government, expressed in French idioms. With its cry of "*Liberté, Egalité, Fraternité*," the French Revolution gave new life to Ancient Greek themes such as *democratie* and *patriotisme* while rattling down the *guillotine* on aristocrats' necks. *Patriotisme* soon found a name for those guilty of an excess of it, thanks to Colonel Chauvin, a Napoleonic soldier whose love for all things French became a source of embarrassment even to his own countrymen. *Chauvinist* has now been adopted as a term of abuse for anyone perceived as having an excessive pride in his (or her) sex.

There appeared for the first time the sinister figures of the *agent provocateur* (one whose business it is to urge others to commit crimes against the state) and the *saboteur* (from *sabot* or wooden clog, thrown into machinery to bring it to a halt). Worst of all, the Terror of the Revolution brought into being the *terroriste* and *terrorisme,* which passed into lexicons of countries that never knew revolution.

The previously inoffensive *bourgeoisie* (townsmen with their own businesses and the middle classes generally) became marked with an ineradicable stigma after centuries of useful service, and it was French that first gave the world *socialisme* and *communisme* as well as their attendant and all-pervading *bureaucratie*.

Italy find it difficult to keep alive their linguistic heritage in an area where, unlike its role in Switzerland, the language has no official status.

Beyond Europe, the continuing influence of France's former empire is found chiefly in Africa and America but also in small islands scattered over the world's three oceans. Many former French colonies belong to the loosely associated *Communauté française* which actively maintains cultural as well as economic links. As the official language of the infant republics of central and north-west Africa, French is the essential lingua franca over a vast area of the continent even though in many countries French speakers are but a tiny educated minority.

Because of the traditional prestige of French and the insistence on correctness in the way it has been taught around the world, the ambition of many is still to speak the language of the mother country, rather than the local patois or Creole. *Créole,* a word borrowed from Spanish, applies particularly to the languages of the West Indies, where it is spoken by the descendants of both slaves and European settlers. In France's far-off overseas departments – Martinique and Guadeloupe in the Caribbean, Réunion in the Indian Ocean – the French education system keeps local speech habits from diverging too far from the parent language.

There are forms of French that have evolved free of all parental supervision, the patois of Mauritius or the creole of Haiti, its vocabulary enlivened by English, Spanish and words brought from Dahomey in the days of slavery. Although French is the official language,

FRENCH BEYOND FRANCE

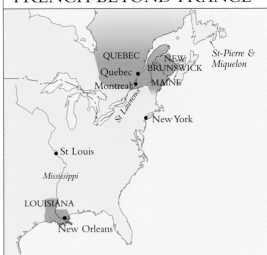

Predating its rival English in Canada by a century and a half, French is the everyday language of a quarter of Canada's population of 29.6 million. While it shares official language status with English in the country as a whole, French is the dominant language of Quebec province. Quebec, whose capture in 1759 marked the end of French sovereignty in Canada, is a French city, its inhabitants spending their lives in a French milieu. Beyond Quebec, French speakers are present in substantial numbers in New Brunswick.

The old colonial French of Louisiana (acquired by the USA from France in 1803 – the Louisiana Purchase), is no more than a patois along with some Creole French. "Cajun," a form of French also spoken in Louisiana, arrived when its speakers were driven out of seaboard Canada in the 1750s.

The *Vieux Carré*, the French Quarter of New Orleans, flies the flag of its old owners in many of its street names. It marks the end of one of the many roads taken by the ancient language of Rome over a period of 2,500 years.

Creole is the mother tongue of Haiti's five million inhabitants; outside Europe, only Canada has a greater number of people whose language is French or a form of it.

French in Canada

The survival of French in Canada is a tribute to the tenacity of the colony settled there when the English seized their territories in the Seven Years' War. Twenty-four per cent of Canada's present population is French-speaking and most live in Quebec Province. The first French colonies were in Nova Scotia and New Brunswick, but many of the settlers of Acadie, as the region was known, were driven out by the British in the early eighteenth century. They sailed south to join the French colony in Louisiana, where their descendants are known as Cajuns (Acadians). Living in isolation in the swamplands of Louisiana, Cajuns kept alive their distinct identity and their language, inevitably colored as time passed by English – one name they have for their language is "Yats," a shrinking of the English, "Where y'at?" A quarter of a million, perhaps more, speak "Yats" (or "Bougalie") or have some knowledge of it, but so small a number in a sea of English must eventually vanish. In the meantime, Cajuns have drawn attention to themselves with a folk music as distinctive as their language.

If it had not been for the expulsion of the Acadians, Canada's maritime provinces would have remained as French as the two tiny islands of St Pierre et Miquelon (pop. 6,000) off the Newfoundland coast, which remain as a French toehold. As it is, French is now a minority language in the Atlantic provinces.

As a result of political isolation from the homeland, Canadian French has retained characteristics of the language of the eighteenth century. At the time, the language of the colonists was commended for its purity, but a modern Frenchman is put off by its somewhat monotonous intonation and lack of articulation. Examples of archaic vocabulary include *fiable* meaning "reliable" and *nuisance*, which owes its survival to the presence of the same word in English. When a word has two different meanings in the two languages, English has tended to take over, as in the use of *opportunité* or *occasion*, but given the chance, the French Canadian prefers to coin new words rather than borrow from the English.

National pride now encourages French Canadian writers to use their language with no feelings of inferiority. In the past, however, they would turn to France for models of literary style, so the written language never diverged greatly in usage across the Atlantic. At all events, identification with France has always been preferable to identification with England.

General de Gaulle's *"Vive Quebec libre!"* (uttered publicly on a visit there) finds its echo in the somewhat draconian legislation of the Quebec provincial government to expunge the influence of English. Nevertheless, the number of French speakers in Canada is in overall decline, through no-one's fault, except nature's.

ITALIAN: A DIVERSITY OF DIALECTS

Italian, the Latin language that stayed at home, has remained closer to the ways of its parent than most of its relatives. In its formal, literary sense it is not an "old" language but is largely the creation of one man, Dante Alighieri (1265–1321); in its everyday, spoken form it is a language of many dialects, those separated by the greatest distance often being all but incomprehensible to each other. Sard, the dialect of Sardinia, preserves features of Latin that were old when the Roman Empire was young and is effectively a language, albeit now waning, in its own right; the Sardinian peasant shares his heaven with the most ancient of Romans, calling it *kelu*, pronouncing it with the hard, Classical Latin *c* of *caelum*, which other Romance languages have softened.

The language of the peninsula has travelled less extensively than French, Spanish or Portuguese and has gained no permanent foothold as an official tongue beyond Italy. The powerful maritime traditions of cities such as Genoa and Venice were of an essentially Mediterranean nature; although a Genoese, Columbus, discovered the New World and a Florentine, Amerigo Vespucci, had his name (somewhat fortuitously) given to it, both sailed under Spanish colors and it was to Spain and others that the benefits of their endeavors went. Millions of Italian speakers now live in the New World as a result of the mass immigration of the nineteenth and twentieth centuries. By far the most live in the United States, the rest mostly in Argentina (one and a half million) and Brazil (half a million) where their language is now used only at family and local community level, in any case heavily

influenced by English, Spanish or Portuguese.

If the extreme conservatism of the Sardinian form is the result of its geographical isolation, the profusion of dialects on the mainland came about through political isolation. Italy was never subject to one unifying power until the nineteenth century. After the Western Empire of Rome had fallen, Italy attracted one wave after another of Germanic raiders but none helped to create a new national identity in the way that the Franks did for France.

The first were the East Germanic Ostrogoths, at the end of a road that had brought them from the Baltic, by way of the Crimea, to Italy. Theodoric, the Ostrogothic leader who ruled Italy from 493 to 526 (spurning Rome and using Ravenna, to the north-east, as his capital) was an Arian Christian and though anathematized by the Roman Church, governed the peninsula with a rough civility for thirty years. The Ostrogoths' stay was too short to have any real effect on the resident form of Vulgar Latin, but they seem to have left behind one useful invention, the pocket. The modern German and Italian words for it are remarkably similar, *Tasche* and *tasca*.

Roman rule was re-established briefly by the Byzantine emperor Justinian (483–565) but at the end of the sixth century most of Italy had fallen once again into the hands of Germanic invaders, the Langobards. Although contact between them and their Italian subjects was limited during their two centuries of rule, many of their words survive today, especially in the dialects of the north, where the region of Lombardy still bears their name. The words that have passed into Italian often exhibit forms

THE LATIN FAMILY

The political unity that eluded Italy from Roman times until the nineteenth century ensured the survival of regional dialects *(right)* bearing the marks of contact with French, German, Spanish and Arabic.

similar to modern German: *scherzare* (German *scherzen*) "to joke," *strofinare (streifen)* "to run." An extraordinary number of parts of the body have Langobardic names: *guancia* "cheek," *schiena* "back," *milza* "spleen" and *stinco* "shin." This odd fact does not constitute proof of great physical intimacy between the Langobards and their subjects; they were all words used originally in the butchering of animals. Even the German *Zahn* appears in Italian as *zanna*, the tusk of a wild boar and now, by extension, that of an elephant. Some of these German loanwords may have come with the Franks who vanquished the Langobards in 774, but it is impossible to distinguish them; Langobardic and Franconian were closely related "West Germanic" tongues.

Town and country tongues

The one uniting force in Italy's Dark Ages was the Roman Church, but its influence was limited to the power of the forerunners of *Don Camillo,* the parish priests. Each town and parish developed local peculiarities in its treatment of Vulgar Latin, beginning the diversity of local dialects that has come down to the present.

The greatest threat to Christian Europe at this time came from the spread of Islam. Halted by Charlemagne's grandfather, Charles Martel, when they invaded France from Spain in 732, the Muslims nonetheless held sway over the whole of the Mediterranean. Sicily fell to them at the beginning of the ninth century and they occupied it for 200 years. Although Sicilian dialects preserve legacies of the Arabic occupation, words like *zammataru* (the manager

of a cheese factory) have not, for obvious reasons, gained currency in the national language; it is hardly a commonplace occupation.

The Arabic words that did effect a successful entry into Italian came later, when the young and thrusting maritime republics of Genoa and Venice drove the Arab *barcas* from their trade routes at the time of the Crusades. *Dogana* "customs," *magazzino* and *tariffa* made their way into Europe through Italian trade with the Levant as did *zecca* the (money) "mint." The small coins produced by the mint, *zecchini*, later reached France and England in the form of "sequins," while the color azure, *azzuro*, was derived from the Arab name for the semi-precious stone called *lapis lazuli* in medieval Latin.

In Venice the word *arsenale*, originally a workshop, assumed its military meaning, since borrowed by all the Romance languages and by English. New commodities with new names came with the Arab traders, *cotone* "cotton," *zucchero* "sugar," *limone* "lemon," *arancia* "orange" and *carciofo* "artichoke" among them. In slightly different forms these words also appeared in Spanish, the two versions competing for adoption into French and thence into the languages of northern Europe.

Rather surprising newcomers to the affairs of the Mediterranean in the eleventh century were the Normans, who took control of Sicily and southern Italy. The kingdom of Naples and Sicily which they established proved a relatively durable feature in subsequent Italian history, but it was never to be ruled by Italians. The Normans were ousted after 100 years by the

The Apennine spine of Italy brought isolation and often near-inaccessibility to many towns and villages. Together with the old political divisions, this encouraged the survival of strong local dialects. Those most widely separated, such as Piedmontese and Calabrian, differ almost to the point of incomprehension. And, as in other countries, cities are marked by strong local accents.

Sard, the fast-disappearing language of Sardinia (above) is the most conservative of neo-Latin languages, but carries Catalan and Castilian borrowings. Nowadays it is a purely oral medium.

CREATOR OF MODERN ITALIAN

Dante Alighieri (1265–1321) seated at his desk. Dante almost single-handedly created the basis for the modern Italian language. His greatest work, *The Divine Comedy*, is one of the masterpieces of European literature, a comprehensive survey of the theology, philosophy and literature of his time, its poetic language soaring over the multitude of dialects that characterized the peninsula.

The following generation provided two more giants of Italian literature, Boccaccio and Petrarch. Petrarch's poetry and Boccacio's bawdy *Decameron* – its themes recognizable over the generations as common to most European societies – have provided inspiration for many writers, from England's first great poet, Geoffrey Chaucer, to modern film makers.

Medieval Venice dominated European trade with the east. It was the "port of entry" for many Arabisms into European languages, and its local dialect was the basis of "lingua franca," the polyglot tongue used by Mediterranean seafarers. The term has now come to define any popular language used between people speaking different tongues, or of different interests.

Hohenstaufen rulers of Germany who came to control an empire extending from the Baltic Sea to the Malta Channel.

In thirteenth-century Sicily, at the cultured polyglot court of the Hohenstaufen Frederick II, the first experiments were made in the use of the unsung vernacular of Italy as a vehicle for literature. The "Sicilian" poets used French and Provençal as their models, and the language that emerged was an almost unrecognizably ennobled version of the local dialect.

Dante Alighieri

To their northern neighbors in the eleventh and twelfth centuries, all the inhabitants of Italy were simply "Lombards." The concept of "Italian" was still unknown. Latin was the written language, the local dialects of town and countryside merely individual spoken versions of a common inheritance. To each other, Italians were *Veneziani, Genovesi, Fiorentini, Pisani* and the like, subjects of the powerful city-states and the colorful, violent dynasties that were to rule throughout the Renaissance.

In response to the Sicilian example, Tuscan poets started to compose in the vernacular but all early attempts were to pale into insignificance with the appearance of Dante Alighieri (1265–1321). No one man has ever had such a far-reaching influence on the development of a language as Dante had on Italian. Dante was a native of Florence, the "city of flowers" of the ancient Romans and throughout the Renaissance the fountainhead of Italian culture.

The supreme poet of the *Divina Commedia* was a gifted philologist. His *De Vulgari Eloquentia*, after a picturesque account of the history of language, explores the "fourteen" dialects of Italy in a vain search for the source of the literary language of the day. Once he had forsaken theory for practice he relied on Florentine and Tuscan forms but borrowed also from the Classical Latin of his "master" Virgil, from medieval Latin and the other Italian dialects. The result is infallibly appropriate to the ideas he expresses.

Many centuries were to pass before Italy could call itself one nation, but a start had been made on "one language." Dante's Italian presents little difficulty to the modern reader thanks to the reverence accorded to it, to him and his fellow Tuscans, Petrarch and Boccaccio, in following centuries. Many of the transitions from Vulgar Latin to Italian did not arrive at a settled form until long after the *Trecento* ("three hundred" is the Italians' convenient term for the fourteenth century) and variations that existed then can still be heard in modern Italian dialects. Although the ending -*iamo* (*parliamo*) was soon adopted as the "correct" standard the older *parlamo* can still be heard in many regions of Italy, including Tuscany itself.

The coming of age of the Italian vernacular coincided with the start of a period of great linguistic innovation. The new language had to keep pace with the practical genius of the Italians during the late Middle Ages and the Renaissance; not only in the arts but also in political, economic, military and nautical matters, Italy was Europe's main source of new ideas and inventions.

The growth of banking gave new meaning to the words *credito* "credit" and *interesse*

"interest" and introduced the concept of *bancarotta*. The word *banca* itself came from *banco* "money-lender's table." The modern sense of the word "post" also evolved in Italy as *posta*, the place where horses were changed, and came to mean a system of sending letters.

Warfare was another field in which Italian terminology spread throughout Europe. The invention of gunpowder produced new weapons like the *cannone*, literally "a large tube" from the Latin *canna*, the threat of which called for new forms of fortification. Constantly besieged by unfriendly neighbors, the city states developed the *bastione* "a large construction," the *ridotto* (now *ridotta*) "redoubt" from the Latin *reductus* "a refuge," and the *parapetto* a defensive wall as high as a man's chest or *petto*. All these defensive measures were designed to resist an "attack," a word which derives from the phrase *attacare battaglia* "to join

battle," coined by the Italians at this time.

The domination of commerce and shipping by the Venetians and Genoese resulted in more than the export of a technical vocabulary (*bussola*, French *boussole* "compass," literally the small box in which the compass was "boxed," is one word which, unlike Italian shipping generally, broke out of the Mediterranean). In Corsica, under French rule since the eighteenth century, a dialect based on Tuscan is still spoken, while the possessions of Venice at one time stretched along the Dalmatian coast as far as Albania. Mediterranean sailors of different nationalities overcame their communications problems with the lingua franca, a simplified form of Venetian.

In the commercial sphere, Venice was the first city to produce a *gazeta*, now *gazzetta*, so-called after the small coin which was its price.

The Italians profited from other countries'

inventions to surpass the rest of Europe in almost every practical field. The most revolutionary invention of the age was printing, not an Italian innovation but taken up by them enthusiastically and with skill, using the appropriate Germanic word *stampare* to describe it. Another imported industry was the production of fine porcelain called *maiolica*, an Italian corruption of *Majorca*. A method of firing fine pottery had been introduced from the Balearic Islands in the fourteenth century. The town of Faenza, where the technique was perfected, entered the French language and the conversation of collectors everywhere as *faience*.

Through the resourceful adaptation of Vulgar Latin and their own dialects, Italians were able to coin new words to meet the needs of new situations. Hundreds found their way not only into other Romance languages but into Germanic and Slavonic as well. Artists, architects and musicians the world over still use Italian words in the senses they were first given at the time of the Renaissance. Although the flow of Italianisms into other European languages began to diminish in the seventeenth century, they have held fast in the arts, particularly music *(see pages 86–7)* in which performers take all their written instructions in Italian, and painting in terms like *impasto* (color laid on thickly), *fresco* (painting on to wet plaster) and *chiaroscuro* (light and shade), commonly used among artists everywhere.

A formal language

Until very recent times "Italian" was spoken only by a tiny, literate minority of courtiers, scholars and writers. In the sixteenth century the controversy as to how this "Italian" should develop, the perennial *questione della lingua* which afflicts all languages, threatened to produce a linguistic schism. The most powerful voice in the debate, Cardinal Pietro Bembo (1470–1547), maintained that Classical Tuscan models should be followed, Petrarch in poetry and Boccaccio in prose; not Dante, because his language was too catholic. The Accademia della Crusca was founded in Florence in 1582 to settle the argument. The first of its dictionaries, published in 1612, took note of many of Bembo's recommendations and did much to rationalize spelling.

Scholarly debate on a national language had little effect upon the vitality of the dialects. The flourishing of Neapolitan in the eighteenth century owed much to the lyrics of the magnificent popular songs of the southern capital. Centuries of Spanish rule had imposed the formal courtesies of Spain on her subjects and it was from Naples that the now-universal *signore* and *signora* spread to the rest of Italy. Neapolitans, prominent among Italian immigrants to the United States, used a borrowed Spanish word, *guapi* "the handsome ones," to describe themselves. From this self-flattering description, the derisory "wop" appears to have come. The informal greeting *ciao*, on the other hand, is Venetian, a contraction of the Latin *sclavus*. Not all Italians are aware that they are saying "I am your slave" many times a day.

From the north the principal foreign influence on Italian ideas, customs and language came from France, and by far the most loanwords to enter Italian over the last three centuries have been French. Many Italian phrases are *calques* or literal translations of French ones, as in *mano d'opera* for *main d'oeuvre, colpo di stato* for *coup d'état* and *luna di miele* for *lune de miel* (but originally English "honeymoon"). Words created by the French from Latin and Greek sources have passed freely, although not without objection from purists, into Italian, recent examples including *turista, revista, ristorante* and *automobile*.

The height of French influence on Italian affairs came in the wake of Napoleon's invasion in 1796. The example of the French Revolution inspired the republican movement to seek a unified Italy, partially achieved in 1861, but as a monarchy under the House of Savoy. Before Rome was added to the kingdom in 1870, Florence enjoyed a brief reign as capital, a fitting tribute to her great contribution to the culture and language that, it was hoped, would help unite Italy. Unity was

Florence, briefly the capital of ltaly (1865–70) as the modern nation emerged, still has a claim to pre-eminence, as the birthplace of Dante, as Italy's literary heart, and as a repository of Renaissance culture.

achieved politically, but language has proved to be another matter.

The official attitude toward dialects has been unsure of itself. The Fascists attempted to abolish them altogether but it was a vain ambition: pure Italian was too refined a mode of speech to be imposed by compulsory education, and dialect too deeply rooted. Nowadays, dialect and the standard language tend to meet half-way in the speech of most Italians. Sardinians are often complimented on the correctness of their Italian but in reality they have had to learn a foreign language, a situation that has its parallel in the "correct" English of the bilingual Gaelic-speaking Scottish Highlander.

Like all modern tongues, Italian has had to adapt rapidly to the technological change of the twentieth century, and to the intrusion of English, which, mostly in its American form, is making itself felt to an increasing degree. If English words continue to be introduced at the present rate it will put a great strain on Italian spelling which, although eminently regular and well-suited to its own language, cannot always cope with eccentricities of Anglo-Saxon origin.

Few Italian words have gained worldwide currency in the twentieth century, and at least two are not a matter for national pride; although *pasta* in all its forms is enjoyable enough (and *Chianti* is now something more than part of Tuscany), *fascista* and *mafia* are better done without. Both words have now taken on international careers; one as a description of extreme right-wing politics, the other synonymous with organized crime.

ITALIAN MUSICAL TERMS

Italian is the language of music, using which a Korean soloist may play a German concerto with an American orchestra conducted by a Czech. Italy rose to its pre-eminence in modern music in the seventeenth and eighteenth centuries, when its masters were in demand throughout Europe. Musicians everywhere now take their instructions in Italian. Some commonplace terms are listed.

A cappella Unaccompanied choral music, "In the style of the chapel"
Accelerando Becoming faster
Adagio Slow
Adagietto Slightly faster than slow
Affetuoso With emotion
Affrettando Increasing in speed and feeling
Agitato Agitated
Allargando Becoming slower, "widening"
Allegro Lively, fast
Allegretto Slightly slower than *allegro*
Alto A high male voice or its female equivalent
Amoroso Lovingly
Ancora Again
Andante Moving steadily
Andantino Slightly faster than *andante*
Animato Animated
Appassionata Passionately
Appoggiatura An ornamental note
Aria A song, usually operatic
Arioso Song-like
Arpeggio A broken chord, sounded one note at a time
Assai Very
Attacca Continue playing without pause between movements
Basso A low male voice
Basso profundo A very low male voice

Bravura Technically difficult to perform; often merely flashy

Buffo Comic

Cadenza Extended (originally extempore) vocal or instrumental passage

Cantabile Flowing and lyrical

Cantata Work for chorus and orchestra

Canto Song or melody

Capriccio Short, spirited composition, "caprice"

Coda Concluding section of movement or piece

Coloratura Virtuoso, often very high operatic singing

Comodo Leisurely, "easy"

Con brio/fuco With spirit/fire

Concerto A work for solo instrument and orchestra, "a concert"

Concerto grosso Major Baroque orchestral work, "great concerto"

Continuo Bass line to a Baroque composition, "continual"

Crescendo Becoming louder, "growing"

Decrescendo & Diminuendo Becoming quieter

Divertimento Entertaining work for small ensemble

Dolce Sweetly

Dolente Sorrowfully

Dopo After

Doppio movimento Double the speed

Espressivo Expressively

Falsetto A high male vocal register

Finale Last movement

Forte Loud

Fortissimo Very loud

Giocoso Cheerfully

Grave Slow

Grazioso Gracefully

Intermezzo Short composition or musical interlude

Largo Slow, "broad"

Larghetto Slightly faster than *largo*

Legato Smoothly, unaccentuated

Leggero Lightly

Lento Slow

Libretto Words of an opera

Maestoso Majestic

Maestro Master (title for distinguished musicians)

Maggiore Major

Mezzo-forte/piano Moderately loud/soft

Mezzo soprano Slightly lower than soprano

Minuetto Minuet

Missa A mass

Moderato A moderate speed

Molto Very, much

Moto perpetuo A composition based around a continually repeating musical phrase

Niente Almost inaudibly soft

Nobilmente Nobly

Obbligato Independent passage accompanying main theme

Oratorio Major work for chorus, orchestra and soloists

Ostinato A constantly repeated phrase, often in the bass, "obstinate"

Partita A suite

Pianissimo Very soft

Piano Soft

Più More

Pizzicato Strings to be plucked, not bowed, "pinched"

Poco A little

Prestissimo Very fast

Presto Fast

Rallentando Becoming slower

Ritardando Becoming slow

Ritenuto Held back (in speed)

Rondo A composition with a regularly recurring theme

Rubato Take liberties with ("rob") the speed

Scherzo Rapid, often good humoured piece or movement, "joke"

Scherzando Light-heartedly

Sempre Always

Sforzando Sudden increase in volume, "forcing"

Smorzando Dying away

Solo A passage played or sung either alone or with accompaniment

Sonata A composition for solo instrument and piano accompaniment, "sounded"

Sonatina A little sonata

Soprano A high female voice

Sostenuto Sustained

Staccato Detached, short notes

Subito Immediately

Tempo Speed at which a piece is played, "time"

Toccata A rapid, technically demanding solo keyboard composition

Tremolo Nervous effect created by string players rapidly repeating same note

Troppo Too much

Tutti The full ensemble, "all"

Veloce Quickly

Vivace & Vivo Lively

Voce Voice

....Volti subito! Turn the page quickly!

SPANISH: CONQUISTADORES' LANGUAGE

At the height of Arab civilization in the tenth century, the survival of a Romance language in Spain must have seemed a forlorn prospect. Although the common speech of most people in Islam's most westerly caliphate was descended from Vulgar Latin, the written form had been totally eclipsed by Arabic and Hebrew. Within a few hundred years, the situation had been reversed. Colonial Arabic had been driven out during the Reconquest (not without leaving a permanent mark on the Iberian languages) and Spanish and Portuguese had become major colonizing languages in their own right.

Today, six times as many people speak Spanish beyond Spain as speak it in its native territory; one country alone, Mexico, has far more speakers of Spanish than Spain, a situation which parallels that of English, its greatest colonial rival. Portuguese is far more important as regards numbers of speakers in Brazil than it is in Portugal, and both Spanish and Portuguese have great potential for growth in their colonial settlements.

Spain was Rome's first major overseas province. Native resistance to the legions gave Spain a reputation among the colonizers as a *horrida et bellicosa provincia* but once the Celtiberian and Lusitanian tribes had been subdued in the second century BC their languages died out rapidly to be replaced by a local form of Vulgar Latin. Only in the Pyrenean north did an aboriginal tongue survive, that of Basque, which is alive and kicking today.

At the break-up of the Roman Empire, Spain, like the rest of western Europe, fell prey to waves of Germanic invaders. The Vandals, remembered in the Arabic Al-Andalus, now Andalusia, pressed on into northern Africa, the Swabians settled north-western Spain, now Galicia, while the third and most powerful Germanic tribe, the Visigoths, became masters of the rest of the Iberian peninsula until it was invaded by the armies of Islam in 711.

Gothic influence on the language of the Hispano-Romans was slight but it did inspire a lasting taste for Germanic Christian names like Alfonso and Fernando. Of everyday words, only a few oddities like *ganso*, almost identical to the modern German *Gans* "goose" (English "gander") have come down to modern Spanish. A larger number of Germanic words entered the language from Frankish or Old French when the Carolingians established the Spanish march as a bulwark against the Islamic invader. The title *marqués* "marquis," ruler of the march, dates from this period as does another loanword the Spanish have cause to remember, *franco*, originally a "free man." Military vocabulary was similarly influenced, adopting words such as *tarja* "shield, target" and *guante* "glove, gauntlet."

The Arabic contribution to Spanish is not markedly dominated by political, administrative and military terminology, but conquerors always leave their mark in these fields. The Arabic leader, the *Emir*, gave Europe a new word for a naval commander, the Spanish *almirante*, French *amiral* and the English "admiral."

Caliph was similarly taken over as *algalife*, and *alférez*, originally a horseman, has come to denote a junior officer in the Spanish army.

THE *RECONQUISTA*

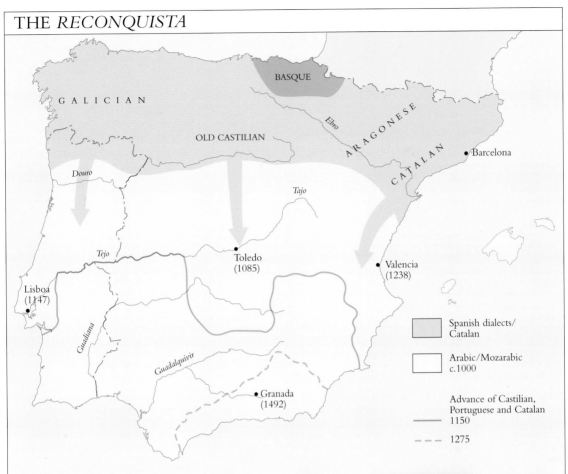

GALICIAN

BASQUE

OLD CASTILIAN

Ebro

ARAGONESE

CATALAN

• Barcelona

Douro

Tajo

Tejo

Toledo
(1085)

• Valencia
(1238)

Lisboa
(1147)

Guadiana

Guadalquivir

• Granada
(1492)

| | Spanish dialects/ Catalan |
| | Arabic/Mozarabic c.1000 |

Advance of Castilian,
Portuguese and Catalan
——— 1150
- - - - 1275

Above The Arabic invasion of western Europe began
in 711 when Islamic forces crossed the Strait of
Gibraltar (its name derives from *Djebel al Tariq;* Tariq
was the Moorish conqueror of the Rock). They swept
through Spain and raided deep into France until
defeated by Charles Martel at Poitiers (732). The
progressive *Reconquista* "Reconquest" of Islamic Spain
began in the eleventh century, spearheaded by the
forces of Castile, whose dialect in time came to be the
official language of all Spain. The Mediterranean shore
was reconquered by the forces of Aragon and Catalonia
and the Atlantic seaboard by the young nation
(founded 1139) of Portugal. The last Islamic kingdom
in Spain to fall was Granada in 1492.

Right The architecture of La Mezquita "The Mosque"
in Córdoba is one of many visual remains of Islam's
presence in Spain. Many more reminders of "Islam in
Europe" fall upon the ear, for many hundreds of words
in Spanish were borrowed from the Moors.

The most striking feature of these and other Arabic loanwords is that nearly all are nouns and appear together, in their hundreds, in the front of the dictionary, thanks to the absorption into Spanish of the Arabic article *al-*. This peculiarity seems to suggest that neither the Berbers, who made up the bulk of the Moorish settlers in Spain, nor the Mozárabes, the "almost Arabs" (Christians of native stock, living in the Arab south), had much understanding of Arabic grammar.

The most significant contribution made by the Arabs to the Spanish way of life, and consequently to the language, was the introduction of new methods of agriculture and new crops. The *naranja* "orange" and *limón* "lemon" came to thrive in a new soil, while Arabic names also became attached to everyday products like *aceite* "olive oil" and *zanahorias* "carrots." Water, the most important factor in the lives of desert dwellers, is equally vital to agriculture and the Arabic *wadi* survives in the names of many Spanish rivers beside the *Guadal*quivir, literally "large river," and *Guadal*araja "river of stones." Arab irrigation skills even made possible the cultivation of rice. Their word for it, which has passed into Spanish as *arroz*, had in fact been borrowed by them from the Greeks at a much earlier date. They brought with them also that most precious commodity *azúcar* "sugar," while to feed stock they planted *alfalfa*, and for clothing *algodón* "cotton."

Surrounded by orange groves and rice fields, the architecture of southern Spain possesses many unmistakably eastern features, especially the small white houses built of *adobe*, bricks dried in the sun, rather than baked, and *azulejos*, still the word for roof tiles, even if they are no longer always *azul* "blue." The usual word for a village, *aldea*, is also Arabic. At the other end of the architectural scale, a palace or fortress is an *alcázar*, but this is an Arabic corruption of the Latin *castra*, a military camp. Palaces and houses alike have their shady *alcobas* "alcoves" (originally "tent") where the nobility at least would pass the time playing at *ajedrez* "chess" or listening to the *laúd* "lute."

The arts and sciences that the Arabs had adopted from the Greeks flourished in Moorish Spain, most of all alchemy *(alqui-mia)*, a word that now conjures up visions of charlatanism and hocus-pocus but which, in its original sense, was a serious matter. From Arabic through Spanish it has given to the laboratories of the world *alambique* "alembic, distilling apparatus," *elixir, alcohol, álcali* and *quilate* "carat." In astronomy, many individual stars still possess their Arabic names, including Aldebaran and Rigel.

In mathematics, the greatest Arab bequest was the use of zero in their numerical system. The word *zero* came through Italian rather than Spanish, but the Spanish version of the same Arabic word, *sifr*, was *cifra* which in French became *chiffre*, meaning any numeral, passing to English as "cipher," changing its meaning yet again. And to the despair of school children everywhere, the Arabic *al-jabr* "the reunion of broken parts" became "algebra."

Most of the Arabic scientific terms that have gained currency throughout Europe and the world were not transmitted specifically through Spanish. Traffic between the two languages mostly concerned the everyday life and needs of the Mozárabes. Trade and the migration of Mozárabes took many Arabic terms into the dialects of the Christian north, long before the *Reconquista* allowed Spanish as a whole to absorb the full linguistic legacy of the desert people.

The reconquest

The Reconquest was not the work of one sustained military campaign but began at the time Arab conquests had reached their northernmost limits, continuing sporadically until the removal of the last Moorish foothold from Granada in 1492. The Christian kingdoms of Galicia, Leon and Navarre all had their moments of glory and ignominy in the first three centuries of the Reconquest but in the eleventh century, with the recapture from the Moors of the ancient capital of Toledo in 1085, Castile and Aragon emerged as the two powers that were to complete the task.

This political development was of vital importance to the subsequent history of the language, its ultimate consequence being that Castilian, once the humble dialect of a small region in the Cantabrian mountains became, as the language of administration, law and literature, the official language of all Spain. Aragon, by incorporating Catalonia under its crown, put paid to any chance of Aragonese obtaining similar prestige but helped Catalan *(see pages 96–8)* enjoy both a golden political and literary age.

The taking of Toledo had many far-reaching effects. It was restored to its role as capital by the Castilians (Madrid did not become the chief city of Spain until 1561) and there was established a school of translators which disseminated throughout western Europe the accumulated knowledge of both Arabs and Jews, the latter enjoying a period of great influence as a cultural bridge between Muslim and Christian. For the local population, the increasing use of Castilian as the language of official business erased the Mozarabic dialects to such an extent that central Spain, now called New Castile, became Castilian-speaking.

Castilian had evolved from Vulgar Latin along lines similar to those in Italy and in many ways Castilian and Italian are close to each other, far closer than either is to their French sister. Unlike French, Castilian has few diphthongs, the two most characteristic being the almost universal Romance *ie* for *e*, as in those two most Spanish institutions, the *fiesta* and the *siesta* (from Latin *sexta*, the sixth hour of the day) and the strictly local development of Latin *o* to *ue*, as in *bueno* "good" or *pueblo* "people."

Of older, more fundamental changes, many were not yet reflected when in the twelfth century there appeared the first great work in Spanish literature, the poem of The Cid (Cid is the Arabic *sidi* "Lord"). The Latin *f-* was still written as such although it is certain that in Old Castile, it was already pronounced *h-*. The peculiarity spread southward with the Reconquest to give the modern Spanish forms *hablar* "to speak" (from Latin *fabulare*), *hermoso* "beautiful" (*formosus*), *hijo* "son" (filius).

In total command of central Spain, Castilian remained virtually landlocked by Galician-Portuguese in the west, Basque in the north,

Catalan in the east and Arabic to the south until the reign of the "Catholic Monarchs" Ferdinand and Isabella in the latter half of the fifteenth century. In 1492 Granada, the last bastion of Islam in Spain, capitulated. In the great crowds witnessing the surrender was a Genoese seaman, known to the Spanish as Cristoforo Colón, with the key that was to unlock a new world to Spain and the Spanish language.

Some idea of the Castilian spoken by the *conquistadores* can be inferred by roundabout route from the language of the Spanish or Sephardic Jews who were expelled from the country in the same year as Columbus's landfall in the Bahamas. In Morocco and the Balkans, where the exiles made their homes, their Judeo-Spanish language survived, preserving until recent times archaic forms of medieval Castilian and Mozarabic. Many "Sephardim" now live in the United States and Israel, descendants of those whose contribution to European culture was inestimable.

Spain advanced spectacularly in the sixteenth century, providing employment and prospects of preferment to hidalgos like Cortés and Pizzaro. Often impoverished bravos with a claim to gentility (the word *hidalgo* "son of something" neatly describes their pretensions), they carved out an empire of breathtaking size, one of permanence so far as their language was concerned; Spanish is quite as successful a language of colonization as Latin was before it and English since.

It was a golden age also for Spanish literature, reaching its peak at the end of the century in the plays of Lope de Vega and the prose of Cervantes. As in other Romance languages as they emerged from the medieval to the modern age, the most important source for neologisms, newly coined words, was Latin, in the case of Spanish by way of Italian. Ties between Spain and Italy were strong, even if Spaniards like the Borgias were not always the most worthy of Italian citizens.

Political involvement in European affairs assumed new dimensions when Charles I of Spain (1500–58) became Charles V, Holy Roman Emperor. Spanish soldiers became a familiar sight on the battlefields of Europe, but although they were respected as fine fighting men, they were often mocked for their swagger and ostentation. *Matamoros* "Slayer of Moors" became the stock Commedia dell'Arte figure of the braggart captain. As they travelled Europe they introduced it to new amusements like *dominos* and *hombre*, played *serenadas* to the local beauties on *guitarras*, the Spanish form of the old Greek *kithara* which had passed into Latin to give its name to a variety of stringed instruments, including the Austrian *zither*.

Most of the words that passed from Spanish to other languages of Europe came from their seafaring achievements. Latecomers to the sea, the Castilians at first borrowed their nautical terminology from the Italians, *piloto* "pilot," *brújula* "compass" and *fragata* "frigate," for example. In succeeding centuries, original Spanish sea terms made themselves known: *armada* "fleet," *flotilla* "small fleet," *embargo* "seizure, sequestration" and the somewhat less truculent *estivador* "stevedore, docker" who loaded and unloaded *cargo*, an earlier Spanish loanword meaning "load."

OLD SAILORS FIND THEIR BEARINGS

The bustling, cosmopolitan ports and web of seaways criss-crossing the Mediterranean from earliest times were sailed by mariners speaking a dozen languages or more. The need for mutual understanding gave rise in later times to the *lingua franca*, the "Frankish tongue" (suggesting a strong French influence) by which the Spanish *hombre de mar* discussed maritime business with the Greek *nautes* among the masts of barca, xebec, caravel and galley in the neutral entrepot of Venice.

Phoenician and Greek sailors traversed Homer's "wet lanes" without the aid of a compass or any other navigational device. Few journeys took the old mariners out of sight of land for any length of time, with the shore-line usually "in the offing" – in distant sight.

It was the perfect place to refine the early arts of navigation, bounded to the north, south and east by the continents of Europe, Asia and Africa, and with the Canaries, the "Fortunate Isles" of Ptolemy (second century AD), to the west.

Without the compass's magnetic needle (introduced, perhaps from China, in the Middle Ages) to indicate "north," position finding depended on the acquired skills of observation – of prevailing winds and tides, of the depth of water under the keel, and above all, of the position of the sun, whose rising and setting supplied the first longitudinal markers.

The Greek "east" was *Eos* "dawn," the Latin *Oriens* "rising." Romance and other languages continue to use their derivations of *Oriens* (and *Occidens* "west," "setting") to describe east and west in general terms. German *Morgenland* "morning land, east" and *Abendland* "evening land, west" echo the old usages of the Mediterranean.

North and south were also established by the sun – its position at noon and the fall of a shadow. "South" remains "midday" in the Latin-derived French *midi*, Spanish *mediodia* and Italian *mezzogiorno*.

The seven stars of the Great Bear constellation (Latin *septentriones*), circling the Pole Star as night progressed, provided a general description for the north, *septentrion*.

Modern cardinal directions, the succinct and monosyllabic Germanic "north," "south," "east" and "west," have come into universal use. While the northerners introduced "north" and "south" to the compass, their "east" and "west" (the sun's rising and setting) are as old as Indo-European time. The first is related to the Greek *Eos* and the Sanskrit *Usas* "dawn," and the second to Latin *Vesper* and the Sanskrit *avastat* "evening."

CONQUISTADORES' AMERICA

Portuguese

Spanish

English, French and
Dutch Creole

The Latin languages of Spain and
Portugal are, next to English, the most
successful of European colonizing languages.
From the Rio Grande to Cape Horn, Spanish is the
official language of all countries on the continental
mainland with the exception of Brazil (Portuguese) and
the Guyanas, a total in excess of 300 million people.
The number is expected to increase rapidly by AD
2,000, ensuring that Spanish and Portuguese will retain
and improve their importance among the world's
languages. The old Amerindian languages, however,
have not been completely destroyed; they are still used
by about twenty million.

Central America

Spanish gained its first
substantial foothold on
the American continent
when Hernán Cortés, a
hidalgo from Estremadura
in Spain, and his band of
adventurers landed in
1519 and overthrew the
Aztec empire of
Montezuma. In their
endless search for new
and golden empires to
conquer, the
Conquistadores carried
their language north into
what are now the
southern states of the US
and south to Chile and
Argentina. Although,
since that time, Castilian
Spanish – *Castellano* – has
been Mexico's official
tongue, Nahuatl, the
language of the Aztec
empire, Mayan and other
Amerindian languages are
spoken by several million.

Forms of the Mayan
language are also spoken
in the countryside of
Guatemala.

South America

Amerindian languages
have survived more
successfully in South
America, mostly in
Ecuador, Peru, Bolivia
and Paraguay. Pre-
eminent among the old
languages is Quechua, the
tongue of the Inca
empire overthrown by
Pizzaro. The future of
Quechua was secured
when the Spanish Catholic
missions adopted it to
propagate Christianity. A
third of Peru's population
speak Quechua, and it is
also used in neighboring
Ecuador and Bolivia,
bringing the total to
about ten million people
in all. Another language

of the Andean highlands
is Aymara, with adherents
in Peru and Bolivia. One
other Amerindian
language, Guaraní, has
retained a strong position;
it is the language of most
of the population of
Paraguay, although
Spanish is the medium
of education.

Argentina, Chile and
Uruguay are the most
"European" of South
American countries and
Spanish is the official
language of all three.
There are about 300,000
pure-blooded Indians left,
almost all of them in
Chile.

Brazil

Portuguese has been established in Brazil as long as Spanish has in the rest of Latin America, and (excepting Mexico and the Central American states) has more speakers (over 150 million) than Spanish. Less than half of one per cent of the population, living in the remoter regions, speak an Amerindian language.

Caribbean

Among the principal Caribbean islands, Spanish is the national language of Cuba and the Dominican Republic, which shares the old Spanish island of Hispaniola with the Creole-French-speaking republic of Haiti.

The cargoes of gold and silver brought back to Spain by the Indiamen were not all that was unshipped in Cadiz and Seville. A country whose own agriculture had become run down, clipped bare by huge flocks of sheep which were, to the Spanish, the only dignified form of farming, welcomed new forms of food: *patatas, tomates, maïz, cacao, ananás, tapioca, cacahuetes* ("peanuts," French *cacahouettes*). They proved in the long run to be more beneficial than the gold and plate, which caused rampant inflation before the sources dried up.

The explorers and settlers nearly always took an approximation of the native Indian names for the exotic crops, as they did for the fauna of South America, beasts like the *tapir, jaguar* and *llama*. Only occasionally were they inspired to name things themselves. *Vainilla* "vanilla" from *vaina*, a scabbard and so called because of the sheath-like shape of the pod, was such a word; another was *armadillo*, the "little armored thing."

Although South, Central and much of North America is dominated by Spanish names, a few older, aboriginal ones survive, as

in the *pampa* of Argentina and the *sabana* "savanna," a Caribbean word like *huracán* "hurricane." Shakespeare had King Lear invoke "hurricanoes," making the word more Spanish than it really was, and from similar travellers' tales he also took the idea of cannibals. The word had at first been a perfectly innocent Spanish corruption of the Caribs' own name for themselves.

Since the seventeenth century, Spain's fortunes in Europe have not prospered. Wars of succession and fratricidal conflicts have exacted their toll on a nation that opened up much of the world to other Europeans. The continental empire of Flanders, Milan and Naples was lost in 1713, and Spain never again rivalled France, England or Austria as a great power, or as a provider of new terms for European vocabularies.

Spanish in Latin America

The vitality of the language may have been sapped by historical circumstance in Spain itself, but in the New World it had a lasting triumph from Mexico to Argentina. The Spanish spoken in South and Central America is close to that of the mother country although there are great differences between the more and the less educated. It is quite clearly Castilian despite an overlay of local vocabulary and idiom; a pampas gaucho, possibly of Welsh stock, is unlikely to use the same figures of speech as a highlander from Bolivia or a Mexican peon, either of whom might in any case be happier talking an Indian language. One feature common to the pronunciation of all Spanish America is the so-called *seseo*, the tendency to make *s, z,* and soft *c* into the same sound *s,* but the phenomenon is common enough in Spain, especially in the south.

Many Spanish words, no fewer than those of English which have made the transatlantic journey, have taken on fresh and sometimes surprising meanings in their new homes. *Galera,* a word with a variety of definitions in Spain, ranging from a van or wagon to a house of correction for women, loses both wheels and stigma in Mexico and the Caribbean, where it is simply a shed or hut.

Both in Spain and in South America, once the colonies gained their independence, an important element in political life has been the power of the military to depose and install governments, usually including themselves. The frequency with which the *generalissimo* (title accorded at one time even to the Chinese President Chiang Kai-shek) or other *supremo* makes a *pronunciamento,* and establishes yet another *junta,* has led to the adoption of the terms by political commentators everywhere. In the art of modern warfare, the Spanish technique of *guerrilla* "little war" is recognized everywhere. The word has a modern ring, but it describes the tactics employed by the Celtiberians against the Romans 2,000 years ago, and by Spanish patriots fighting the French during the Napoleonic Wars.

The area of the world where Spanish is most influenced by another language, and at the same time has the most influence itself, is the United States. American English has long been indebted to Spanish through the legacy of the south-western states which were once part of Spain's empire. That spectacular feature of

the landscape, the canyon, is the Spanish *cañon,* the "large tube" of Latin descent and while the Spanish *cañon* also applies to an artillery piece, in Colombia it is a tree-trunk and in Peru a highway.

Many Spanish loanwords refer to horses and cattle, the essential means of livelihood of the settlers. Now, thanks to the cinema, the *rancho, corral, rodeo, mustang* and *stampede* have travelled a long way from the Old West. "Mustang" comes from an old Spanish form *mestengo* and was originally applied to wild cattle; and if the "stamp" part of stampede seems more Germanic than Romance, it is because *estampida* was a Frankish loan to Spanish. It once referred, among other things, to a medieval dance; *estampa* "stamp" or "engraving" comes from the same source. Nowadays even *gringos* (a corruption of *griego* "Greek" but used to describe the unintelligibility of English-speakers) take leave of each other saying *hasta la vista* "until the next meeting" or *hasta mañana* "until tomorrow." In doing so they are using the Arabic preposition *hasta,* borrowed by the Spanish 1,000 years ago.

The Catalan bridge

The Catalan language is almost an exact reflection of Catalonia's geographical position as a bridge across the eastern Pyrenees between southern France and Castilian Spain; it is closely related to Spanish but at the same time shares many affinities with the Provençal dialects of its northern neighbor. It is descended from neither, but is a member of the Romance family in its own right, having developed its own characteristics while they were forming theirs, from the common Latin stock that they had jointly inherited.

Catalan has no official position in Spain or France, where it is heard in Roussillon, but it retains much of the vitality it possessed in the Middle Ages, when it was the official language of the Kingdom of Aragon. Barcelona was the heartland from which it spread, during the years of the *Reconquista*, down the coast to Valencia and to the Balearic Islands. Today, something like a fifth of Spain's population of thirty-nine million speak Catalan, although all are now bilingual, and the language shares the somewhat microscopic honor of official recognition, with French, in the tiny Pyrenean republic of Andorra.

At the height of Islamic power in Spain, the county of Barcelona was a feudal institution of the Franks, part of the Spanish march set up as a barrier against the Moors. From the time of William the Hairy (died 897) the counts were effectively masters in their own home, swearing allegiance as it suited them either to the Caliphate or to the northern overlords. There followed a period when the Catalonian language developed rapidly, and the name of Catalunya first appears in 1114.

Medieval Catalan and Provençal were strikingly similar in many ways, leading many scholars, including the illustrious Dante, to believe that Catalan was simply a form of Provençal. The misconception gained ground because the Provençal cult of the troubadours had many adherents in Catalonia, and Provençal, or *Llemosi* (from Limousin, the likely cradle of the cult), was effectively the first literary language of Catalonia.

Modern Catalan retains much of the abrupt, robust quality which first became evident in the Middle Ages; the Castilian brother and sister, *hermano, hermana* are *germa, germana* in Catalan, while the common Spanish diphthong *ie*, as in *cielo* "sky, heaven," is plain *e* in Catalonian *cel*. Where French and Spanish have settled on words of similar meaning derived from different Latin sources, Catalan often retains both. A Catalan farmhouse is *mas* (like French *maison* from Latin *mansionem*) but an ordinary house is the Spanish *casa*. There are few words that are purely Catalan. One is *gos* "dog," said to be an abbreviated form of *canem gothicum*. If the native Iberian form of *perro* seems a reasonable enough thing to have around the house, *canem gothicum* hints at a truly terrifying hound baying in the ruins of a deserted castle at midnight.

Another peculiarity of the language is found in the names of the days of the week. Monday is neither French *lundi* nor Spanish *lunes*, but *dilluns*. In Vulgar Latin *diem lunis* was a common alternative for *lunae diem*, so the ancient form survives now only in Catalan, and some parts of Provence. The *ll-* form is a development unique to Catalan. In the earliest examples of the written language it was already used to represent the distinctive pronunciation of initial Latin *l-*, (as in English "mil*l*ion") for words like *llit* "bed" and *llet* "milk."

The power of Catalonia and its language was at its greatest between the twelfth and fifteenth centuries when, under the kings of Aragon, its rule was extended to Sicily, Corsica, Sardinia and, for a time, Greece. Only in Sardinia has the language survived, where a

PORTUGUESE: POTENTIAL FOR GROWTH

modified form of Catalan is still heard around the town of Alghero.

The marriage of the Catholic monarchs, Isabella of Castile and Ferdinand II of Aragon, in 1469 began the decline of Catalan prestige, although Naples was added to the realms of Aragon. Castile and Castilian became dominant, to such an extent that in 1640, in the middle of a war between Castile and France, the Catalans sided with the French. Forty years later they rose once again against Madrid in the Wars of the Spanish Succession, and as a result their universities were abolished, books could no longer be printed in Catalan, and Castilian was imposed as the language of education and religion.

Faced with the prospect of becoming merely a dialect of Castilian, Catalan found a rebirth, the *Renaixença*, in the upsurge of nineteenth-century nationalism. Scholars, mostly amateur, reconstructed the old language from the speech of the uneducated, but compromised in the use of learned Latinisms supplied by Castilian, as they had come to describe essential features of modern life. By this means the vitality of the language was assured: such respect for everyday usage was the reason for the success of the Catalan *Renaixença*.

With about nine million speakers in its homeland, Portuguese is one of the "smaller" European languages. Its potential for growth, however, surpasses that of almost all others for it is the national language of Brazil. Brazil is a huge and still underpopulated land larger in size than the United States but, with 105 million inhabitants, it has only half the population.

Portuguese shares identical origins with Spanish, another language with great growth potential in South America. It descends from Old Galician, one of the Iberian Romance dialects of northern Spain to which the formal Spanish of Castile also owes its source.

The fortunes of Portuguese and Galician *Gallego*, show how important it is for a region to achieve political independence if its speech is to survive as language rather than as dialect. At the time of Arab rule in the Iberian peninsula, the shared parent, Old Galician, was spoken only in the north-west corner of the peninsula, its southernmost limit coinciding roughly with the River Douro. As the most westerly form of Iberian Romance, it had much in common with Castilian, Aragonese and other forms of Spanish, but had evolved peculiarities which marked it off from them.

The Reconquest of the old province of Lusitania, an area more or less coinciding with modern Portugal, was begun from Galicia in the eleventh century and completed by the end of the twelfth. During the campaign, Alfonso VI of Castile made a gift of Galicia to the Burgundian brothers Raymund and Henry for their support against the Moors, the boundary between the brothers' territory being the River

Minho which has remained the northern frontier of Portugal.

To the north of the river, the county of Galicia remained loyal to Castile and thereafter to Spain. Its dialect suffered inevitably from the formal use of Castilian and was ultimately reduced to the level of a patois. To the south, ties with Castile were severed and Portugal emerged as an independent nation, apart from one brief interruption in the sixteenth and seventeenth centuries, with a language it could call its own.

The close kinship of Spanish and Portuguese is apparent even to those with the mildest knowledge of them. It is in pronunciation that the important differences are found for the same Romance vocabulary forms the basis of both languages. Most of the spoken differences are reflected in the spelling, like the Portuguese nasal ending *-ão* where the Spanish has *-ón* or *-ión*, or the disappearance of intervocalic consonants *-n-* and *-l-*, giving the Portuguese *mão* instead of the Spanish *mano* "hand," *pessoa* for *persona* "person," *dor* for *dolor* "pain." Other differences make spoken Portuguese difficult for the Spanish speaker to follow (various pronunciations of the letter *s* and the "swallowing" of countless unstressed syllables) but the more open pronunciation of Spanish is easier for the Portuguese to understand.

Alone among Romance languages, Portuguese has kept the names for the days of the week that were introduced optimistically by the early Christian Church. Monday is *segunda feira*, Tuesday *terça feira* and so on until *sexta feira*, Friday. While pagan deities continued to be commemorated throughout the rest of Christendom, Portugal adhered to these devout but rather uninteresting substitutes. In its development of Latin, Portuguese has been generally more conservative than Castilian. *Fabulare* has emerged as *falar* rather than *hablar* "to speak" and the Spanish *hacienda* "estate" is the Portuguese *fazenda*.

Overall, the similarities between Portuguese and Spanish in their evolution from the Vulgar Latin are far more evident than the isolated differences, however curious the latter appear. The same is true of the numerous Arabisms in both languages. The emergence of Portugal as an independent nation came at a time when the momentum of the Reconquest was at its greatest. Lisbon was taken from the Moors in 1147 and the Mozarabic dialects of the center-south were absorbed by Old Galician. The Arabic words that entered the language are the same agricultural, commercial and artisan terms that are found in Spanish, but a few survive that have disappeared in Spain, like *alfaiate* "tailor." Another Arabic word peculiar to Portuguese is *alfandega* "customs post," taken from the name of a town that stood on the former border between Christianity and Islam.

The language of discovery

Driven from mainland Europe, Islam was as strong as ever in Africa and the Near East as though there stretched a medieval "iron curtain" between Europe and the Orient. The need to circumvent the barrier brought the dawn of the great age of exploration and discovery, and the birth of the great colonial empires. Some means, other than the traditional overland

The search for a sea route to the Indies lay behind the age of discovery, pioneered by the Portuguese and the Spanish. The driving force behind Portugal's efforts was Henry the Navigator (1394–1466) *(right)* who sent his caravels south along the coast of Africa, establishing the route first to the Cape of Good Hope (rounded by Bartolomeu Diaz, 1487), and then to India itself. Lisbon *(below)* saw the departure of da Gama's fleet in 1497 and its triumphant return. The way to the East, and to European empires, was open.

routes, had to be found to reach the wealth of the Indies and the oriental spices on which European palates had come to depend. The Portuguese emerged as the great pathfinders.

Their *naos* or galleons discovered Madeira and the Azores, settling their language in these previously uninhabited islands. Staging down the West African coast, they succeeded finally in rounding the Cape of Good Hope and in 1498 the great captain Vasco da Gama reached India. Almost by accident, Pedro Alvarez Cabral discovered Brazil in 1500 when his convoy was blown off course on its way to India. Within a few years Portuguese ships hove into the astonished view of the Japanese.

Back from the China seas, Portuguese merchants introduced Europe to words like *pagoda* and *mandarim(n)*, and to *chá*. Other European languages have since adopted a different name for the beverage imported by the Dutch as *tee*, but the Portuguese continue to prefer *chá*, as does the British Army, from its tradition of service in the East.

From Ceylon (now Sri Lanka), their most valued possession in the east, the Portuguese carried the word *anaconda*, Tamil for a species of local snake, to the jungles of Brazil where they attached it to a local serpent. From Malayan waters they brought back a *lanchara* "launch" to western harbors. They also left many of their own words behind, especially in India, where they were picked up by the

English whose Indian bungalows usually had Portuguese *varandas* where the *aia* ("tutor" but really a nursemaid) looked after the children. The word *caste* in its Hindi sense was also a Portuguese legacy, meaning "pure" (of race) and derived from the same Latin source as the English word "chaste."

The Portuguese empire in the east was commercial rather than colonial and did not long survive the inroads made upon it by northern Europeans, the Dutch and English. Neither, however, could remove one strong trace of the Portuguese years, the presence among Eurasians of common Portuguese patronyms like Pereira and Da Silva.

Until the race for African colonies began in the nineteenth century, Portugal's many coastal stations there were hardly used except as supply depots for the slave trade. Such communication as there was between the Portuguese and the Africans (English *negro*, French *negre* and German *Neger* derive from the Spanish and Portuguese *negro* "black," although the Portuguese more commonly use the term *preto*) was rarely conducted at a profound level; it was *palaver*, from *palavra* "word or speech." Even before the years leading to independence, the use of Portuguese in the colonies of Mozambique and Angola was limited to the educated minority, although Creole forms exist. The one country where Portuguese took root as fruitfully as Spanish and English in their former empires was Brazil, where it is now the national language of a heterogeneous population of 156 million.

Speakers of other Romance languages find it easier to recognize familiar words in Brazilian Portuguese than in the accents of the mother tongue. Through constant contact with South American Spanish, "Brasileiro" has modified many of the more distinctive sounds of European Portuguese, opening out vowels that all but disappear in the parent language. "Brazilianisms" have begun to usurp the position of Portuguese words in their own homeland.

In these and other differences, Brazilian Portuguese tends to close ranks with Spanish and other Romance languages. Portuguese for example calls a train a *comboio* "convoy" while Brazilian favors the international *trem*. In course of time, the size and potential of Brazil will doubtless cause its language to eclipse the prestige of its parent, and Portuguese, which assumed its individuality out of a proud spirit of independence from Spain, may lose many of the characteristics that distinguish it from its neighbor.

Beyond Brazil, the once-enormous range of Portuguese interests has left no real mark on world languages, but a number of Creole or pidgin forms are spoken in places as far apart as the Cape Verde Islands in the Atlantic, and Macao on the China coast. The Creole of the Cape Verde Islands is close to that of Portuguese Guinea, now Guinea-Bissau, on the nearby mainland.

In the east, the once-important Malayo-Portuguese Creole has vanished, as has Macanese, the variety of Macao, but traces of a form spoken in the Moluccas persist in the Philippines, to which it was carried. They are the last echoes of the voices of da Gama, Magellan and the men who sailed with them.

ROMANSCH: THE ALPINE TONGUE

The high Swiss valleys of the Grisons in eastern Switzerland hear most western languages in the course of the year. No part of Europe is more dramatically beautiful, either in summer or winter and, being Swiss, the inhabitants cope happily with German, French, Italian or the English of the tourists who come to ski, climb or simply to rest. But the natives of the Grisons possess a language of their own called Romansch, one of a group of Latin dialects known collectively as Rhaeto-Romance and spoken from the headwaters of the Rhine to the Italian-Yugoslav frontier.

The Roman province of Rhaetia was established in 15 BC as part of the Rhine/Danube frontier to discourage the southward migration of the Germanic tribes. It reinforced the natural barrier of the Alps, extending from present-day Switzerland, through the Tyrol, to Bavaria. The importance of this mountainous region was primarily military, but when the legionary garrisons abandoned it to the Alemanni and later to Bavarians, the civilian population stayed behind in sufficient numbers for Romance speech to persist in many of the more isolated valleys.

The remoteness of these communities meant that there survived in the vernacular many Latin words, which elsewhere gave way to northern substitutes. While the Germanic *blank* provided France, Italy and Spain with new words for "white," Rhaetia kept the Latin *albus*, which gave the modern form *alf*; in Romania, similarly cut off from the mainstream of the evolution of the Romance languages, it survives as *alb*.

The term "Rhaeto-Romance" refers principally to the Romansch of the canton of the Grisons in eastern Switzerland, but it is usually extended to include the "Ladin" spoken in the Dolomites and the language of Friuli to the north of Venice. Ladin and Friulan, however, are under serious threat of extinction from Italian. A mere 10,000 speakers of Ladin survive precariously in a few valleys near the Austrian border, while Friulan has been in regular contact with Italian for so long that it can hardly be considered as anything other than an extreme form of the Venetian dialect.

Languages have always been dangerous weapons in the hands of politicians, and, when it has suited their purpose, Italians have been only too content to see Romansch simply as a variant of their own language, a fact used by Mussolini to justify territorial claim to the Grisons. The claim was successfully refuted by the expedient of having Romansch recognized as a national language of Switzerland. The result was an extraordinary compromise, whereby Romansch now enjoys the status of "national" language, but it is not an official language, except in the Grisons.

Throughout their history the people of the Grisons have used any means available to preserve their bastion of independence and linguistic individuality. They joined the Swiss confederacy only to avoid being absorbed by some great power during the Napoleonic Wars. Before that they had governed themselves through three centuries of anarchic, not to say blood-stained, democracy. The name "Grisons" (German *Graubünden*) dates from the mid-fifteenth century, when *les trois ligues grises*, "The Grey Leagues" formed by the local land-

The remote, beautiful and, for long, fiercely independent valleys of eastern Switzerland have used their historic isolation to preserve a distinctive form of the Latin language introduced by the Romans.

owning peasantry, united to do away with the remnants of feudal and episcopal jurisdiction over their lands and drive off the Austrian invader.

The Grisons "republic" never established harmonious coexistence between its various warring factions, particularly after the Reformation, when the majority of the population became Protestant, while about a third remained Catholic. The two principal dialects of Romansch subsequently became associated with the rival versions of Christianity. Surselvan, so called because it is

spoken "above the forest" of Flims, high in the Rhine valley, is the Catholic idiom, and Engadinish, centerd in the upper valley of the Inn, that of the Protestants. Religion was also the chief instrument in the creation of written Romansch, but here too, there exist two standards. The older, more conservative version of the written language is found in the Engadine, where printing was introduced as early as the mid-sixteenth century. Today almost all Romansch-speakers are bilingual.

ROMANIAN: ROMANCE IN ISOLATION

Surrounded by languages with which it has only the most distant kinship (Slavonic), or none at all (Hungarian), Romanian is a remarkable survival of the Latin language many hundreds of miles from its nearest Romance relative. It is spoken within its own borders by upwards of twenty million people and by many more beyond them; two and a half million in Russia and another million or so scattered throughout Greece, the former Yugoslavia, Albania and Bulgaria.

The standard language, often called Daco-Romanian (the Roman of Dacia), has a number of related but not easily comprehended dialects, sufficiently distinctive almost to qualify as languages in their own right, but all are on the wane. Aromanian (Romanian of the south) is spoken by scattered minorities throughout the Balkans. Istro- and Megleno-Romanian are now all but moribund.

The survival of a Romance language north of the lower Danube is a mystery for which there is no easy explanation. Despite being cut off from the rest of the Romance-speaking world for over 1,000 years and overrun by Goths, Gepidae, Avars, Bulgarians, Slavs and Magyars, the Roman province of Dacia preserved a language as Latin in its structure and roots as French or Italian.

The unresolved debate as to how Romanian survived hinges on the fact that the Roman legions, first dispatched there by the Emperor Trajan, occupied the territory for a mere 165 years. Furthermore, Dacia can hardly have been the most attractive of Rome's colonies, and few of its original colonists would have had Latin as their mother tongue. For these reasons many

refuse to believe that the language has been handed down directly by the descendants of those first settlers, preferring the theory that the region was repopulated by Romance-speaking people later.

A more appealing version of the history of the language holds that, in the mountains of Transylvania, communities left behind when the province was abandoned by Rome continued to use the language of their old masters, clinging to it tenaciously while chaotic movements of populations came and went around them. Those who support this theory point to the diversity of dialects in Transylvania, which argues that the language has been established there for an extremely long time.

The exact location of the Romanians during the Dark Ages may never be known. What is certain is their complete isolation from the development of Romance in the west, a factor which has made Romanian more conservative than its cousins. Because it has developed along such unfamiliar lines, the authentic Latin grammar is often hard to recognize, as are many common Latin words that have changed their pronunciation.

Until the last century, when loans from French and the international lexicon of Latinisms began to restore the balance, over half the vocabulary of Romanian was Slavonic. For centuries the only written language in the area was Church Slavonic, so that when Romanian was first put to paper, it was in the Cyrillic alphabet. The early Romanian religious texts were naturally full of Slavonic loans, like *sfînt* "saint," but, as the language established itself, words of Romance origin came out of hiding to take their place in the liturgy. Most of the Romanians of the Dark Ages probably lived as semi-nomadic shepherds and the terminology of agriculture and the names of many crops are Slavonic. Words adopted during this period of important social change include *morcov* "carrot," *bob* "bean," *hrana*, a general word for food, and *plug* "plough."

When the Slavs encountered the Romanians they gave them the name *Vlach*, whence the Kingdom of Wallachia. "Vlach" appears elsewhere in the words the Germans applied to Romance-speakers and the Anglo-Saxons gave to the Celts in the west of Britain. The Slavs themselves were not the most warlike of the peoples disputing the lands around the Black Sea. When they fought, it was usually in the service of the Bulgarians, who gradually adopted the language of the more numerous Slavs. Nevertheless, many military terms in Romanian were borrowed from Slavonic, including the word for war itself, *razboi*.

Other languages that added to the rather impoverished vocabulary of Romanian were Magyar and, in more recent times, Turkish. The Magyars were evidently more successful merchants and craftsmen than the Vlachs, many of their loans to Romanian belonging to the realm of commerce. Hungarian is still spoken in a small area of central Romania, the only alien language represented by any significant number of speakers apart from a colony of German speakers, the only one to survive the mass exodus of Germans from eastern Europe after the Second World War. Romanian itself is not confined to the borders of the modern state, being spoken in its Moldovan form in the small republic of Moldova, previously part of the former USSR.

It was not until the nineteenth century that Romanians were able to catalogue and analyse their language to see exactly what it was. The union of Moldavia and Wallachia in 1859 greatly accelerated the process and the new capital at Bucharest became the focal point for the development of the modern language. The Romanian Academy has had to work much harder than its counterparts elsewhere, busily creating written standards from a disparate oral heritage, and at the same time having to select and accommodate countless new words and expressions relating to the technological advances of recent times. French, as the most prestigious of the Romance languages, was the obvious model, providing essential words like *garaj* "garage" and *timbru* "postage-stamp."

CHAPTER SEVEN

Voices of the north

The distant and unlettered ancestor of English, German, Dutch and the Scandinavian languages was a latecomer to history. By the time it entered the affairs of Europe during the last centuries before Christ, the place of Greek in history was already secure and the Latin of Rome had begun its reduction of the Celtic language to the status of a minor offshore tongue.

Little is known of Proto-Germanic, as it is called, apart from speculative reconstructions. It was the language of rough illiterates to whom any sort of written record was unknown. It was left to contemporary Greeks and Romans to give an account of the barbarians whose life seemed unutterably crude to the urbanized Mediterraneans.

The dialects of these remote northern people shared a distinctive nature quite unlike those of Celtic and Latin, an individuality now thought to have been acquired over many generations from an unknown tongue enveloped and absorbed at some time in prehistory. The Germanic vocabulary, on the other hand, contained an abundance of words that were clear evidence of its relationship to other European tongues and its membership of the Indo-European family.

If a language can be said to have a birthplace, then that of Germanic was probably in southern Scandinavia. It is a conjectural cradle, for by the time others became aware of them, the Germanic tribes had already occupied the great northern plain of Europe from the North Sea to the River Vistula. Those in Scandinavia had moved north to make contact with the nomadic Lapps, while on their southern borders they were confronting the Celts along the Rhine and the Roman garrisons along the Upper Danube.

Their language had already lost the relative homogeneity it once had. At first no more than regional and mutually comprehensible varieties of the same tongue, three branches soon became clear and more pronounced as each group of speakers made its singular impact on the history of the continent as a whole: the East Germanic, conveniently called Gothic, of the tribes who had settled the easternmost Germanic lands around the Vistula; the North Germanic or Old Norse of the Scandinavian peoples; and the West Germanic of those who were living between the Elbe and the North Sea. With no simple epithet like "Gothic" or "Norse" to describe them, the West Germanic dialects were to become the most widespread of all, through their main descendants German, Dutch and English.

When not on the move, the Germanic way of life contained much that would have been familiar to their more settled descendants 1,000 years later. They lived in scattered homesteads of wood-framed buildings infilled with wattle and daub, engaged in mixed farming, growing

(North)	(West)
Icelandic	German
Danish	Dutch, Frisian
Norwegian	English
Faeroese	Afrikaans
Swedish	Yiddish

Men of Groningen, Holland. The elements *-ing* or *-ingen*
("people,""people of") occur commonly in Germany,
Holland and England as part of placenames, showing a
common linguistic ancestry.

barley, oats and wheat, and breeding cattle. They brewed beer and mead and hunted wild pig, elk and aurochs (a species of wild cattle that became extinct in the sixteenth century) in the great forests that covered northern Europe. Others who had made their homes along the North Sea and Baltic shorelines fished the abundant shoals of cod and herring and were destined to become great seafarers and traders.

Whatever their main pursuits, the tribes possessed a social structure that contained the seeds of later democratic forms of government. Matters of importance were debated by an elected assembly or "thing" (modern Danish *Folketing*, Norwegian *Storting*, Icelandic *Althing*, Manx *Tynwald*) but allegiance was owed to a chosen leader or *kun-ing-gaz* (Old English

cyning, then *cyng* "king") who ruled a community of freemen, half-freemen and serfs.

Laws were applied ruthlessly and punishment included the drowning of criminals in bogs. The preserved remains of these *Moorleichen* "swamp corpses" have provided posterity with grisly fashion notes; the men wore woollen and fur cloaks over long trousers, and lace-up shoes, the women long woollen gowns and cloaks, and girdles around their waists.

As a pagan people, the Germanic tribes were haunted by an array of spirits, daemonic wights, kobolds (from whom the mineral cobalt derives its name), dwarfs and giants living in the woods, the pools and the earth itself. Reliable freemen, *Adelbauern*, were nominated to cope with these spectral threats and to foretell the future by casting stones.

From the mists of their past, the northern tribes had brought with them a pantheon of gods to be feared and respected, the greatest of whom, *Tiwaz,* was the Sanskrit *Dyaus-pita*, Greek *Zeus* and Latin *Iupiter* "Jupiter," father of heaven. In course of time, *Tiwaz* gave way to *Thor*, the god of thunder and *Wotan*, the one-eyed wanderer who feasted the valiant dead, brought to Valhalla by the battle maidens. The gods have gone, but days of the week still celebrate them: *Tiwaz* Tuesday, *Wotan* Wednesday, *Thor* Thursday and *Freya* Friday.

The Gothic migration

The Roman historians Tacitus and Pliny the Elder, to whom we owe the surviving portraits of the early Germanic tribes, lived at the height of Rome's power. Fewer than 500 years later a Germanic king, Theodoric (454–526 AD), ruled Italy. Theodoric was a Goth, one of the East Germanic people who swept like a savage wind across Europe, destroying the Western Roman Empire.

According to their own tradition, the Goths were of Scandinavian origin, and placenames still existing there, including the island of Gotland, mark the source from which they sprang. They migrated from Sweden to what is now East Germany and Poland by way of the Baltic islands (some of which, like Gotland, Bornholm and Rügen, bear the names of the two old East Germanic tribes). By the third century AD they had deserted their Baltic lands and carried their language eastward beyond the Carpathians to the Black Sea. Here they formed into two major groups, the Ostrogoths who settled lands to the north of the Crimea and the Visigoths, who made their home around the lower Danube.

The earliest literary remains in any Germanic language is a translation of the Bible by the Visigothic bishop Ulfilas, who lived in the fourth century. Written in an alphabet part Runic, part Roman, part Greek, Ulfilas's work survives chiefly in the *Codex Argenteus*, now in the care of Uppsala University, Sweden. It provides almost all that is known about the nature of the East Germanic dialects and their evident affinity to the Old Norse of Scandinavia.

Although traces of their language, latterly known as *Krimgotisch* (Crimean Gothic), persisted in southern Russia until the eighteenth century, the Germanic tenure of the eastern lands was brief. Within a couple of centuries of their arrival, they had been driven back westward by the tide of Hunnish invaders from Asia. Taking a lead from the Asiatics, the Gothic tribes began their own series of conquests. The Ostrogoths became masters of Italy while the Visigoths drove through France and occupied the Iberian peninsula. Their predatory relatives, the Vandals, carried their infamous work into North Africa from the Gibraltar Strait to Carthage.

So far as the survival of the Gothic dialects was concerned, all this might never have happened. At no time as numerous as those whose lands they conquered, the Goths were first reduced in France, then in Italy. The arrival of the Islamic Moors in 711 put an end to them in Spain, and their culture, customs and language vanished from Europe. All that is left

THE GERMANIC FAMILY

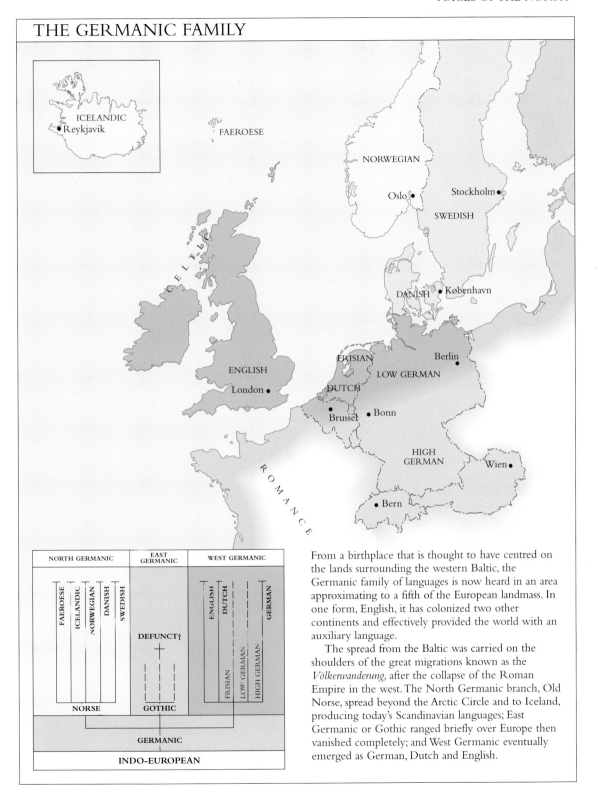

ICELANDIC
• Reykjavik

FAEROESE

NORWEGIAN

Oslo •

Stockholm •

SWEDISH

C
E
L
T
I
C

DANISH • København

FRISIAN

ENGLISH

Berlin •

LOW GERMAN

DUTCH

London •

Brussel •

• Bonn

R
O
M
A
N
C
E

HIGH
GERMAN

Wien •

• Bern

NORTH GERMANIC	EAST GERMANIC	WEST GERMANIC
FAEROESE · ICELANDIC · NORWEGIAN · DANISH · SWEDISH	DEFUNCT†	ENGLISH · DUTCH · GERMAN · FRISIAN · LOW GERMAN · HIGH GERMAN
NORSE	GOTHIC	
GERMANIC		
INDO-EUROPEAN		

From a birthplace that is thought to have centred on the lands surrounding the western Baltic, the Germanic family of languages is now heard in an area approximating to a fifth of the European landmass. In one form, English, it has colonized two other continents and effectively provided the world with an auxiliary language.

The spread from the Baltic was carried on the shoulders of the great migrations known as the *Völkerwanderung,* after the collapse of the Roman Empire in the west. The North Germanic branch, Old Norse, spread beyond the Arctic Circle and to Iceland, producing today's Scandinavian languages; East Germanic or Gothic ranged briefly over Europe then vanished completely; and West Germanic eventually emerged as German, Dutch and English.

are a few loanwords in Spanish and the name of the province of Andalusia (Vandalusia) and in France, the old kingdom of Burgundy. The first Burgundians were an East Germanic people whose name survives not only in France but also in the Baltic island of Bornholm *(Borgundarholm)* from which they had originally come.

The Burgundians played no part in the wilder Gothic migrations but had settled in France after a savage defeat at the hands of the Huns. They were soon Gallicized and their language, apart from a few words in the French dialect of Bourgogne, had vanished by the sixth century. The Goths, Vandals and Burgundians had passed through European history like wild geese, and the simile is not inapt; one of the words they left behind in Spanish was *ganso* "goose" (German *Gans*).

Old Norse

Old Norse, the language of the Vikings, is the parent from which all modern Scandinavian languages descend. Danes, Norwegians, Icelanders and Swedes can look back with mischievous glee to the days when their ancestral tongue brought terror to foreigners unfortunate to hear the berserkers for the first time, but they are forgiven. In Britain, the impact of their language proved to be far more lasting than their legendary villainies, while the largest European nation, Russia, owes not only the foundation of some of its great cities to them, but also its name.

Old Norse is first recorded in Runic inscriptions. The Runic alphabet is the earliest form of Germanic writing and is thought to

A page from the *Codex Argenteus,* a fourth-century translation of the Bible and the earliest literary remains in any Germanic language. A *codex* is not a book but a bound volume of manuscripts.

have originated in northern Italy, making its way by some unknown route to the Baltic. The Norsemen, for whom it had occult as well as practical uses, believed it to be the work of Wotan, "The Great Wordmaster" himself.

Runic (or *Futhark* from its first six letters) appeared for the first time in the third century AD in southern Sweden, but the period of its greatest flowering was the Viking Age. Countless stones in Scandinavia attest to the valor and far-flung adventures of those whose memories they celebrate. "He went boldly, wealth he gained, out in Grikkland, for his

SCANDINAVIAN: VIKING INHERITANCE

heir." Grikkland was Greece, the name by which the Norsemen knew the eastern empire.

They had made their way there from the Baltic through Russia, which they called "Greater Sweden." Its inhabitants called them "Rus," from which the name of the country derives. Carrying their boats from one great river to another they traversed the whole of Russia and founded Novgorod and Kiev.

Viking influence in the east lasted until the twelfth century, by which time their realms there had become entirely Slavicized. But the runes had other exploits to celebrate. The western oceans and its islands were as irresistible to the men of Norway and Denmark as Russia was to the Vikings of Sweden. The effect of the Norse dialects and vocabulary on the languages of Britain is described elsewhere *(see page 134)* and they occupied completely the oceanic Faeroes (*Faeroer* "sheep islands") and Iceland.

The last great adventure for the Norse language took it to Greenland where settlers, moving on from Iceland, established a colony that lasted for 400 years, until the climate, combined with the antagonism of the Eskimo or Inuit, wiped them out.

Most Scandinavians are quite sure that their language was the first European tongue to be heard on the North American mainland, the "Vinland" of the Icelandic sagas. Much evidence, both real and manufactured, has been marshalled to support the claim, including archaeological finds, but the best evidence is still that of the sagas and in the questing nature of the Norsemen.

The outward surge of the Scandinavian adventurers from the ninth century onward had the effect on the old common language, or *dönsk mál* (Danish tongue), of diversifying it into two main groups, the West Norse of Norway and Iceland and the East Norse of Denmark and Sweden. Both forms came to add color to English, for, while Danish appropriated much of midland and eastern England, the Norwegian raiders settled the north-west of the Western Isles of Scotland, the Orkney and Shetland Islands where their dialect, once known as *norrònt mál*, survived into modern times as Norn.

No European language of the time could remain untouched by Latin. The Romans knew of Scandinavia, a term first recorded by Pliny the Elder, and for centuries had been in contact with the Germanic barbarians along their northern frontiers. Useful words made their way north, carried by Frisian traders and others: *sekkr* "sack," *kerra* "cart" and *kal* "cabbage," among them, from the Latin *saccus*, *carra* and *caulis*. Returning heroes from the campaigns in Britain, and later those Norsemen who had made their homes there, gathered from the Old English new words that were ultimately from Latin sources; *straeti* "street," *gimr* "gem," *mylna* "mill," *mynt* "coin," from the Latin *strata*, *gemma*, *molina* and *moneta*, made their way into Scandinavian vocabulary by way of Old English. There were touches of southern luxury, too, in *pipari* "pepper" and *vin* "wine," which arrived in the Norse language soon enough for Leif Erikson to give to his discoveries in north-east America the name *Vinland* in the tenth century.

A bay for longships: the Faeroes or "sheep islands." The name "Viking" probably descends from the Old Norse *vik* "bay, inlet," the kind of place the raiders anchored their boats, and set up camp.

Common Scandinavian was never in danger of losing to Latin its own distinct identity. The greater part of its vocabulary shared, as it does today, the antique Germanic traditions of its neighbors to the south and west. It might acquire odds and ends from the sophisticated south, but its roots were in northern soil. The land itself was an important influence on the language (at one time there were four different ways to say "forest" in common Scandinavian) while words for the basic business of life — eating, drinking, hunting and farming — were linguistic anchors in preventing the drift away to other cultures.

Placenames still reflect the early homes of the Scandinavians. The ancient words *heimr,* "home," *-vin* "meadow," *-land* "land" and *-setr* "place" identify thousands of towns and villages, although often modified by the centuries; the old community of *Bjorg-vin* "mountain meadow" exists only as a distant memory in the modern city of Bergen.

The great area occupied by the Scandinavians, and their tradition of venturing far beyond their own territories, made fragmentation inevitable. The process was accelerated by the emergence of national states, roughly corresponding to the modern boundaries of Denmark, Norway and Sweden. When the Christian Church, by way of German and English missionaries, established its hold over the young nations in the tenth century, Scandinavians became part of the mainstream of European history, rather than marauding intruders who came and went like a summer storm.

The Christian Church encountered little resistance to its mission in Scandinavia, its kings preferring the promise of Paradise to the halls of Valhalla, where they were required to be available for *Ragnarok,* the last battle at the end of the world. And, more practically, the Church

THE HANSEATIC LEAGUE

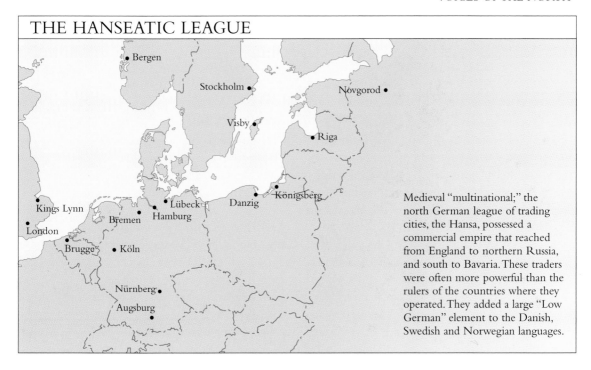

Medieval "multinational;" the north German league of trading cities, the Hansa, possessed a commercial empire that reached from England to northern Russia, and south to Bavaria. These traders were often more powerful than the rulers of the countries where they operated. They added a large "Low German" element to the Danish, Swedish and Norwegian languages.

of Rome could offer them what Odin could certainly not – Papal recognition, the international seal of approval.

With the Church came new Latinisms. Like the earlier examples, many of the new words entered the old Norse languages by way of English and Low German. *Messa* "mass," from Latin *missa,* and *arkibiskopr* "archbishop" came by way of Old English, *domkirkia* "cathedral" and *klokka* "bell" from Low German. The filtering of words from one language to another, via a third, often resulted in changes of meaning as well as of form. The Latin word *hospitalis* "hospitable," for example, became *spittal* (hospital for lepers) in Low German and finally, in Old Danish, *spitalsk* "leprous." It was a far cry in meaning from that of its Latin source.

The Hanseatic influence

While Latin enriched the Norse languages, Low German came almost to engulf them. Middle Low German was not, like Latin, the well-bred language of scholars but the everyday speech of aggressive German traders, the Hanseatic League. The League was an association of (mostly) German cities, the most important of which, Lübeck, Hamburg and Bremen, sought and achieved a monopoly in the Baltic herring fishery. With feast days in the Roman and Eastern Orthodox Churches lasting almost from one year's end to the other, fish was a vital part of the continent's diet; control of the great herring grounds of the Baltic gave to the Hansa towns a stranglehold on north European trade.

At one time or another between the thirteenth and fifteenth centuries, almost all the great trading cities of northern Europe found it advantageous to belong to the League, from London and King's Lynn in England, to Novgorod in Russia. Among the most important beyond Germany was Visby, on the Swedish island of Gotland. Its inhabitants, known as *Osterlings* "Easterlings," may have given to English the word "sterling" according to a nineteenth-century authority.

The Low German of these "merchants-militant" (they were prepared at all times to fight for their monopoly; *hansa*, in Gothic, meant armed band) took firm hold around the Baltic shores. Money, as always, talked, and in Denmark, Norway and Sweden the language it used was Low German. It became the fashionable language of the upper classes and the official language of the Danish court.

It was easily assimilated into Scandinavian because the languages were closely related in structure and pronunciation and, as a result, thousands of Low German words entered the northern vocabulary. The Danish *borger* "citizen," now had a *borgmester* "mayor" and could do his shopping at the *skomager* "shoemaker," *skraedder* "tailor" or *slagter* "butcher," one who "slaughters."

Not all Scandinavians took kindly to the German introductions. In 1489, in the Telemark province of Norway, a bizarre incident of manslaughter was reported to the authorities. Two travellers at a wayside inn were drinking together when one toasted the other in Low German. "I don't like that gabble" said the other. "Let us speak our fathers' and mothers' tongue." Voices were raised, knives were drawn and the speech of Scandinavia acquired its first martyr.

Away from the towns, where the clerks murmured in Latin and the merchants argued and bid against each other in Low German, the farmers and hunters continued to use one or other of the several Norse dialects. The eastern variant of Denmark and Sweden, aided by political and social change, came to prevail throughout Scandinavia as the West Norse of

Norway went into decline, helped on its way by a Swedish royal house (after 1319) and the Black Death (1349), which all but wiped out its most literate class, the monks and priests.

Decline of old Norwegian

Only in Iceland did the western dialect survive and flourish. Danish became the principal literary language of Norway. By 1537, all pretence was swept away when it was decreed that Norway "would not, hereafter be or be called a kingdom of its own." Officially at least, Norway and its language ceased to exist. Sweden and Swedish escaped a similar fate when Denmark's long-cherished desire to unify all of Scandinavia under a Danish king was thwarted by an alliance of Sweden and the Hanseatic League in 1523. As a result the language of Sweden, now markedly different from that of Denmark, flourished in both speech and writing. The Reformation helped widen the gap; Latin was driven from the Church, and the Bible, in Danish and Swedish translations, became accessible to anyone who could read his native language. Only Norway, which for many years was denied even its own printing press, lacked a Bible in its own language. In religion, as in all other things, Norwegians had to make do with written Danish.

By the mid-sixteenth century, the languages of Sweden and Denmark had begun to develop along independent national lines. One Swedish archbishop could even urge the use of "Good old Swedish words" in churches and schools. Politically, the Scandinavian kingdoms were far from stable but their languages had begun to

The midwinter festival of "Up-Helly-Aa" in the Shetland Islands keeps alive a Viking tradition. Norn, a form of the Norse language, survived there until the eighteenth century. "Vole," the name of a common English rodent, comes from Norn, as does "bonxie," another name for the great skua.

take on their distinctive natures. From this unsettled age, linguists date the beginnings of the modern Scandinavian tongues.

Apart from visitors to Scandinavia, few people from beyond it will have heard one or other of its languages spoken, and will be most unlikely to differentiate between them. Danes, Norwegians and Swedes are as a rule linguists *par excellence* and are at home with the languages of other countries – at least in western Europe – they visit. On their own territory, more often than not, they will greet the German or the English speaker in his own language, and often with a clarity to equal that of the visitor.

Despite this adaptability, their own languages show no signs of withering away although they are spoken in total by no more than seventeen million people, spread over thousands of miles.

The reason lies partly in the fact that the history of the Scandinavian countries has been of their own making; languages tend to come under threat when the destinies of their speakers are taken over by others, as happened to the once-widespread Celtic tongues. Where an intrusive language has become particularly insistent, the Scandinavians have quickly invested its words with Nordic characteristics, an ability the English language has demonstrated for 1,000 years.

Later foreign influences

German has always proved the most influential neighbor. The Low German of the Hansa merchants began to wane in the sixteenth century as the herring shoals on which their prosperity was based moved their breeding grounds from the Baltic to the North Sea. In its place came High German, which soon made inroads into Scandinavian life and language. It became a language both of learning and of social importance, and many of its words have remained naturalized citizens of the Scandinavian tongues.

In the seventeenth and eighteenth centuries, French emerged as a cultural rival to High German. Adapting French words was not always easy, but the Swedes accepted the awkward nasal sounds of words such as *balcon* and *restaurant*, adjusting the spelling to *balcong* and *restaurang*. The French suffix *-euse* has lately found an unlikely partner in the German word *Schminke* "make-up;" together they create a very Danish make-up girl, *sminköse*.

English did not begin to make much of an

impact until the Industrial Revolution, but it has since become the principal foreign influence on Scandinavian languages. Some words have been swallowed whole and unchanged: the Danes, like others including some French, make no effort to adapt words like "teenager" and "weekend," but the Swedes particularly give Nordic spellings to words like *najlon* "nylon," *bejbi* "baby" and *bagg* "bag."

The Scandinavians have not allowed foreign words to enter unopposed; Swedes have referred to the *Engelska sjukan*, the "English sickness" that corrupts their native speech, in which they are at one with nineteenth-century Germans, twentieth-century Russians and, at all times, the French.

The ground swell of nationalism throughout Europe in the nineteenth century hinged as much upon language as on anything else, and in Norway it found a sympathetic echo. Their old West Norse had been moribund for centuries; Danish was the official written language used by the educated urban population. Two solutions were proposed, either to make Danish more "Norwegian" in its spelling, or to invent – better still, recreate – the old Norwegian. In the event, both solutions were adopted, and Norway today has two official languages: *Bokmål* or Dano-Norwegian and *Nynorsk*, or New Norwegian. *Bokmål*, the first language of about eighty per cent of the population, has moved progressively away from Danish over the past 100 years.

A new language from the old

Nynorsk, the minority language, was developed in the nineteenth century by Iva Aasen, a linguist of genius. By bringing together a number of existing rural dialects, Iva Aasen created a single language that was reminiscent of the long-lost Norse. His labors were rewarded in 1885 when New Norwegian or *landsmal* "country language," as it was first called, became an official second language. It is intensely conservative, especially as regards German borrowings. Thus the Dano-Norwegian *frihet* "freedom" became *fridom* in New Norwegian.

With its two languages, Norway is unique among Scandinavian countries. But the resolute linguistic nationalism of Norwegians is a characteristic Nordic attitude. Nowhere is it more evident than in Icelandic and Faeroese, the two smallest linguistic groups. Icelandic, spoken by about 260,000 people, is deeply conservative. English borrowings are frequent in speech but are barred from the written language, however distinguished their antecedents. Thus "psychology" translated into Icelandic becomes "soul science" (happy enough, if slightly Caribbean in mood) and "cigarette," a word with which most people are satisfied, is rendered *vindlingur* from the word for "wind" or "twist."

Of all the Germanic languages, Icelandic has remained closest to its ancestral form, thanks to this policy of purism. The Danish of Iceland's former rulers remains the Icelanders' first foreign language although English, as elsewhere, has gained ground. Faeroese, which has a distinct Icelandic look, has reasserted itself in recent times, and is the chief language in the "sheep islands," sharing official status with Danish. It is spoken by 44,000 people.

GERMAN: HIGH AND LOW

German is the mother tongue of more than ninety million people and is the most widely spoken language in Europe, apart from Russian. Nine out of ten German speakers live in Germany proper and Austria, the rest in neighboring countries where historical political changes and the re-drawing of frontiers have severed large groups from the main body. Switzerland, part of the German-speaking area since the collapse of the Roman Empire, has the most, but here German shares national status with three other languages. It is widely spoken in the French provinces of Alsace and Lorraine, but has no official approval there; it is the historic High German dialect of Luxembourg, where now it shares official rank with French; it is the language of the "Liège cantons" in eastern Belgium and retains a hold in Italy, in the South Tyrol.

Elsewhere beyond its borders, in central and eastern Europe, German has lost more ground than any other major European language – all of it to Slavonic since the end of the Second World War. When the Third Reich collapsed in 1945, thirteen million Germans fled or were ejected from lands their ancestors had occupied since the Middle Ages in Poland, East Prussia and Czechoslovakia. A colony that had existed in Russia since the reign of Catherine the Great was dispersed, although it was large enough to have formed a German-speaking Soviet republic on the Volga between the two world wars.

Only one German-speaking colony in eastern Europe survived the exodus, in Romania. The forebears of this outpost had arrived from Germany in the Middle Ages to settle in Transylvania and on either side of the Romania-Yugoslavia border. Known as Transylvanian Saxons and Danube Swabians, they were neither Saxon nor Swabian; their dialects show that the "Saxons" had come from the Rhineland and the "Swabians" from the Odenwald. Some 300,000 people still speak German in Romania, the last of the once-widespread Germanic enclaves in eastern Europe. German's role as the most influential of foreign languages among the Slavs was replaced by Russian during the Soviet hegemony, but has once again gained ground.

Elsewhere in Europe, German remains a popular second language, on an even footing with French, but it has been replaced by English where once it would have been an automatic choice. This is particularly true in Scandinavia where, because of the linguistic kinship and the almost imperially strong commercial ties of the Hanseatic League, it is still widely understood.

The Germans were latecomers in the race for a colonial empire beyond Europe and what they did gain did not last long. Small groups of emigrants in South and Central America and in Australia continue to talk their language among themselves, but the only community of any significance is the Pennsylvania Dutch colony in the United States. Numbering about 300,000, they are descended from Rhenish and Swiss emigrants to the New World in the seventeenth and eighteenth centuries. They are almost all now bilingual, often the first step towards extinction of a minority language, but their English remains colored in everyday speech by the German of their ancestors.

The two languages

The earliest known text in German dates from the eighth century and survives in the cathedral at Merseburg, near Leipzig. It is a simple charm or incantation for the release of a prisoner, contains a reference to the mythological warrior maidens, the Valkyries, and is written in what is now called Old High German. It gives evidence of the oldest form of the modern German language.

The term "High" German has nothing to do with excellence but reflects the landscape in which the young language lived. In its earliest form German was a number of dialects spoken by the tribes who spread south from their northern home during the Dark Ages. At some time before the first written form appeared in the eighth century, German had already become two languages: the "Low" German of the plainsmen in the north; the "High" German of those who had made their homes in the uplands and mountains of central-southern Germany.

Low German was spoken from the North Sea to the Middle Elbe by Saxons, Frisians (whose dialect was already taking on its own distinctive nature), and by Franks around the lower Rhine and in Flanders. Their dialect, Low Franconian, was the precursor of modern Dutch, and its speakers were in time to conquer Gaul and give their name, if not their language, to the modern French nation. And not a few words to the Gallo-Romans.

From the same Low German lands, Angles and Saxons set off across the North Sea to make their homes in Britain and to lay the foundation of the most expansive of Germanic

Remains of an ancient forest along the River Elbe, in northern Germany. The expansion of the Germanic people into southern and western Europe, the *Völkerwanderung*, began in this area.

languages, English. Thus Dutch, Frisian, English and the old Low German dialect of northern Germany are among the most closely related of languages, although the latter did not survive in a national sense. By the sixteenth century it was described contemptuously by one of its erstwhile speakers as "Barbaric Saxon."

The eastern boundaries of Low German corresponded roughly with the former frontier between West and East Germany, where the Saxons were in contact with the Slavonic Wends or Polabians (Slavonic *po* "on," *Laba* "Elbe"), with whom they intermingled. The Wendish Slavonic tongue persisted in this part of Germany, the Luneberg Wendland, into the eighteenth century, and many placenames on the modern map of northern Germany end with the Slavonic suffixes *-ow* and *-itz*.

In the center and south of Germany, tribal movements and settlement were taking place and were giving final shape to what are now the principal German-speaking regions. The tribes that were engaged in the expansion were the Alemanni, whose name survives in

THE GERMANIC FAMILY

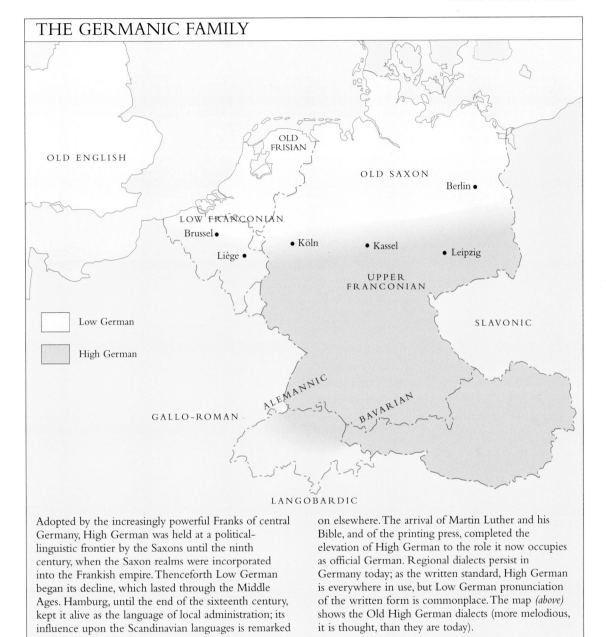

OLD ENGLISH

OLD FRISIAN

OLD SAXON

Berlin •

LOW FRANCONIAN
Brussel •

• Köln

• Kassel

• Leipzig

Liège •

UPPER
FRANCONIAN

SLAVONIC

Low German

High German

ALEMANNIC

GALLO-ROMAN

BAVARIAN

LANGOBARDIC

Adopted by the increasingly powerful Franks of central Germany, High German was held at a political-linguistic frontier by the Saxons until the ninth century, when the Saxon realms were incorporated into the Frankish empire. Thenceforth Low German began its decline, which lasted through the Middle Ages. Hamburg, until the end of the sixteenth century, kept it alive as the language of local administration; its influence upon the Scandinavian languages is remarked on elsewhere. The arrival of Martin Luther and his Bible, and of the printing press, completed the elevation of High German to the role it now occupies as official German. Regional dialects persist in Germany today; as the written standard, High German is everywhere in use, but Low German pronunciation of the written form is commonplace. The map *(above)* shows the Old High German dialects (more melodious, it is thought, than they are today).

Allemagne, the French name for Germany, Bavarians and Langobards.

The Alemanni were the first to carry the German language across the middle Rhine into Alsace, into Swabia (south-western Germany) and most of Switzerland. At the same time the Bavarians from central Germany occupied the upper Danube, pushed eastward into what is now Austria, and established a foothold beyond the Brenner Pass. All these gains were at the expense of the Celtic tribes, which had lost the protection of the Roman legions and were easy

Walther von Vogelweide (c. 1170–1230), great medieval German lyrical poet. His was the Age of Chivalry when epic and romantic poetry flourished under the influence of the southern troubadours, and many French terms entered German.

prey to the warlike and ambitious people from the north. Another migrant tribe, the Langobards, travelled even further, into northern Italy, where their name survives in "Lombardy" although their Germanic tongue had gone from there by the eleventh century. The expansion of the German language in western Europe was now complete, but its occupation of the southern lands initiated and imposed a lasting change on the language as a whole.

The Celts of the upper Danube and Alpine ranges whose own language, as in Gaul, had been replaced by Latin, now had to adopt the language of the new invaders. They brought to it an accent that was to prove irresistible to the men from the north; Aleman and Bavarian began to speak their own language in a quite ungermanic "brogue," in which – notably – the important consonants *p, t* and *k* became modified; *p* became *f, ff* or *pf, t* became *s* or *z*, and *k, ch*. Thus the south German came to call his village a *Dorf* instead of the *Dorp* of the north (English "thorp"); *Appel* "apple" became *Apfel* and *Pund* "pound," *Pfund.* The term "to eat," which in Low German (and Old English) was *etan*, changed first into *ezzan*, later *essen.*

These changes and others swept, not always consistently, through the vocabulary of the Alemannic and Bavarian dialects and then northward, into the Franconian of the Franks (originally "Low Germans") which had come to dominate central Germany. The spread was stopped at a linguistic frontier, now called the Benrath line (from a town at its western end) and the effective boundary between the Franks and their northern neighbors, the Saxons.

All this took place in fewer than 200 years, a speed no less remarkable than the willingness of the Germans to adopt the changes, now known as the High German Sound Shift. It was as if the English, having imposed their language upon the Celtic Britons of the west (as in time they did), chose thereafter to speak English throughout England with a Welsh accent.

With the dawn of a wider literacy in the eleventh century High German began its emergence as a language of international importance, taking on the pattern of the modern language. There are many differences of detail, particularly in the vocabulary, from which many old words disappeared (as they have done from English), to be replaced by many new ones.

The process of acquisition was long-standing. Although they had successfully resisted the advance of the armies of Rome at the height of its powers, the achievements of Latin culture had not been lost on the Germans. The first German *Wein* "wine" came from the Rhineland *vinum*, and the windmill (Latin *molina*, German *Muhle*) appeared as a useful technological innovation. Houses acquired a stone wall (Latin *murus*, German *Mauer*) and within, the chamber (Latin *camera*, German *Kammer*) and the kitchen (Latin *coquina*, German *Kuche*). The paved *Strasse* "street" appeared for the first time, an extension of the *strata* that led from Rome. The Latin of Christianity, adopted by the Frankish kings, further enriched the language, as it did wherever the Roman Church exercised its influence.

No western society in the Middle Ages could hope to escape the all-pervading influence of the French, their customs, culture and language. The knightly classes of western Europe were in constant touch with each other as brothers in arms on a crusade, guests at each other's weddings and jousting contests. In all these matters the French set the style and much of the vocabulary, and to the Age of Chivalry German owes the introduction of French terms like *Abenteuer* "adventure," *Turnier* "tournament," *Harnisch* "armor, harness," *Lanze* "lance" and that most potent of twentieth-century military terms, *Panzer*, also meaning "armor."

Troubadours from the south were also allowed to pass without let or hindrance, carrying their poetic mixtures of unrequited love and death for noble causes to the German courts. Their images and idioms were widely adopted by German poets like Wolfram von Eschenbach and Gottfried von Strassburg and those who followed them. From this period date the common German adjectives *fein* "delicate, cultured," *falsch* "false" and *stolz* "haughty, arrogant."

The influence of French upon German was not to end with the passing of the Age of Chivalry. From the end of the sixteenth century and for the next 200 years, French was the language of all polite society; even Frederick the Great (1712–86) despised his own language and its literature, as did the minor princelings and dukes whose patchwork of petty realms preceded the making of modern Germany. Common French words filtered down into the everyday speech of ordinary German people – *Papa, Mama, Onkel, Tante* – and came to be adopted in the seventeenth century.

Along the eastern marches of Germany, there was no such cultural interchange. From the tenth century, Germans had been moving eastward into the lands of the Slavonic tribes beyond the Elbe, clearing the forests and draining the marshland. New cities sprang up along the Baltic coast from Lübeck to Königsberg, and with them, the all-powerful Hanseatic League of militant merchants. By the fourteenth century, German influence had come to dominate the Baltic shores from Denmark to the Gulf of Riga.

For the Slavs whose lands came under German control, it was an unhappy time; their name had long been synonymous with the lowest menial – slave – and few of their words were thought to be of any use to their new masters. Trade with the east was reflected in a few words like *Zobel* "sable" (Russian *soboli*) and *Kürschner* "furrier" and the Wendish *korcma* became the German village tavern, *Kretscham*. The Slavonic *smetana* "cream" survives in the German *Schmetterling* "butterfly," and was picked up in passing by the Romany, whose "cream" is *smentena*.

REFORMATION: LUTHER AND THE PRINTING PRESS

Martin Luther *(right)*, whose lifelong struggle against the Established Church permanently changed the face of Christianity, was one of the greatest forces in modern European history. Born at Eisleben, Thuringia, in 1483, Luther entered the Church as an Augustinian monk. Appalled at the worldliness and extravagance of the Church, he attacked it in his famous *Ninety-five Theses*, nailed to the door of Wittenberg Castle Church in 1517. The Reformation had begun. Unlike the voices of earlier "dissidents," who could go to the stake, their views unheard, Luther's was heard everywhere, thanks to the power of the recently introduced printing press. It made him the world's first "best-seller;" his translation of the Bible into German ran to more than 100,000 copies. Luther's interest in the spoken language of his fellow countrymen ran deep and his Bible contains many dialect words and sayings. Such was its popularity that Luther-Deutsch became the foundation of the modern literary language.

The *Fraktur* alphabet *(below)* is the German "national" hand and was in use in northern Europe generally until the sixteenth century, where it is called "Gothic" or "Black Letter." It developed gradually during the Middle Ages, taking on a more angular appearance that made the work of the first type-cutters simpler, once printing was introduced.

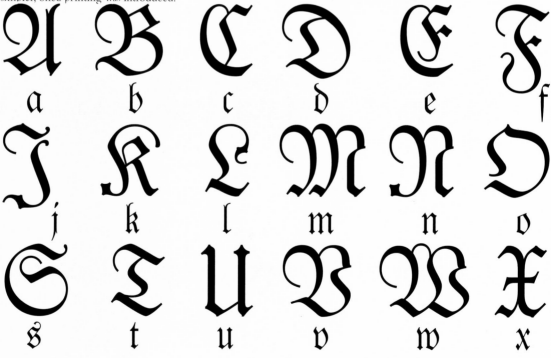

Johannes Gutenberg of Mainz is credited with the invention of printing from moveable type. The Press carried the Bible and the message of the Reformation to an increasingly literate world.

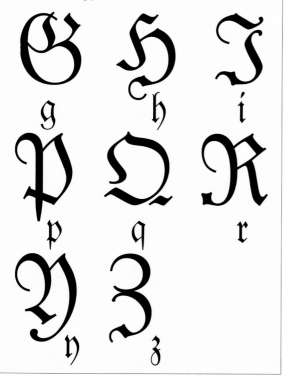

Modern German

Modern German begins with Martin Luther (1483–1546) and the Reformation. Throughout Germany, High German became the literary and spoken standard and Low German, which had exercised a strong influence in the Baltic lands and in Scandinavia, began its decline to the level of a patois. Luther was a Thuringian and his language belonged to the "east-central" variety of High German. The reformer himself believed that the form he used could easily be understood by *Ober- und Niederländer*, speakers of both High and Low German.

Luther's message was carried on the newly fledged wings of the printing press. The invention of printing from moveable type is usually attributed to a fellow German, Johannes Gutenberg (1398–1468), a Mainz goldsmith who, with his partner Johann Fust, cast enough type to set a whole Bible in 1445. It was in Latin; the first book to be printed in German appeared in 1461.

Printing made Luther the world's first bestseller. In the five years before his translation of the New Testament in 1522, a third of all publications in German bore his name. After his complete Bible appeared in 1534 the press at Wittenberg alone produced 100,000 copies, and huge numbers were printed elsewhere. The spread of literacy that the introduction of printing afforded meant that Luther's Bible became part of the furniture of most German homes, ensuring that Luther's form of the language would eventually become the national standard.

The acceptance of Lutheran German made less headway in the Catholic south – Bavaria and Austria – which had its own version of the

A group of Amish elders, members of the Pennsylvania-Dutch (Deutsch) community that arrived in North America early in the eighteenth century. German settlers from the Rhenish Palatinate and Switzerland first reached there in 1683 and have kept alive the German language, the only place beyond Europe where it has resisted assimilation.

Bible, but even here, in course of time, Luther's forms and vocabulary asserted themselves. In Switzerland, where German was spoken in a number of diverse dialects, Luther's High German became the standard form. Conversation between Swiss, however, retained its own distinctive nature and is called *Schwyzertütsch*. By its use the Swiss define themselves as Swiss, not Germans on the wrong side of a frontier.

Within Germany itself, regional variations of the standard language are as numerous as the patchwork of autonomous regions that had made up the country for more than 500 years; at the end of the catastrophic Thirty Years' War (1648), Germany was divided into 234 distinct territorial units – bishoprics, counties, duchies, electorates, landgraviates, principalities and dozens of free cities – each of which was a law unto itself. There was no administrative and cultural heart of the kind that Paris provided to

the French and London to the English hundreds of years earlier.

Broad dialectal differences, far greater than those of English in England, continued well into the nineteenth century, when the post-Napoleonic years brought to Germany the unity that made it Europe's most powerful nation. The standard language, in its literary form used only by the cultural elite and a flourishing *bourgeoisie* in the growing cities, spread through compulsory schooling, with inevitable effect upon the dialects.

Regional variation remains nevertheless noticeable and the gap between ordinary conversational styles in Berlin and Bavaria is certainly as great as that between say, London and New York. Between Berlin and Vienna, it is even greater, with many differences in vocabulary and idiom; a Viennese housewife's shopping list might contain many items unfamiliar to the Berlin grocer, whose *Kartoffel* "potato" is the Viennese *Erdapfel*, and *Blumenkohl* "cauliflower" *Karfiol*. Similarly at the fruiterer's, where the Berliner's *Apfelsine* "orange," *Pflaume* "plum" and *Aprikose* "apricot" are the Viennese *Orange, Zwetschge* and *Marille;* and at the butcher's where, among other victuals, the Berliner's *Hackfleisch* "mincemeat" is the Viennese *Faschiertes.*

In scores of other terms, the northerner and southerner make their distinctive choices, the southern usage often reflecting a strong "Romance," particularly French, influence, as in *Plafond* "ceiling" instead of the northern *Zimmerdecke*, and *Kouvert* "envelope" rather than *Umschlag*. In the street, the Viennese will walk along a French *Trottoir* "pavement" and the Berliner will avoid the traffic by sticking to his *Burgersteig*. Here there is an echo of the London–New York gap, for the Englishman uses the Latin-derived "pavement" where an American prefers the Anglo-Saxon "sidewalk."

There is perhaps an element of southern fastidiousness and northern earthiness in the choices of word for "chair." The Berliner's *Stuhl* has its biological connotation, as "stool" does in English, so the Viennese is happier to call it *Sessel*. Conversely, the Viennese travelling to the north is well advised to drop his simple adjective *geil* ("rich," as in "rich food"); to a Berliner, it can mean anything from lewd and lascivious to the more unmentionable parts of an animal's anatomy.

Beyond Germany, modern German terms have lodged in the languages of others to convey concepts for which the local forms have no suitable expression: the somewhat fraught *Angst* "fear, anxiety;" *Schadenfreude* "a delight in others' misfortunes;" and *Weltschmerz* "world weariness." English and other dictionaries now include *Weltanschauung* "world outlook, philosophy of life' to add a little cosmopolitan erudition to commentators" columns in the *Zeitgeist* "the spirit of the age."

In the more esoteric world of the circus ring, lions everywhere obeyed instructions traditionally in German – the tamer's *schön* "fine, well done!" and *ruhig!* "quiet, calm down!." Nowadays, the big cats answer to instructions in other languages to the regret of purists and the active opposition of animal rights enthusiasts.

Yiddish

The language of adversity, fortitude and wry fun, Yiddish was born in the German Rhineland about the end of the tenth century. Its parent speakers were a Jewish colony that had emigrated from France and adopted the language of their new hosts.

Throughout the Diaspora, Jewish communities had created their own forms of the languages of those among whom they lived. In Europe, the main groups were the Sephardim of Spain (so called from the Hebrew word, *Sepharad*, for Spain) and the Ashkenazim of northern Europe. Of the two, the Sephardim enjoyed a happier history during the Middle Ages, ironically (in the light of recent history), while Spain was occupied by the Islamic Moors. It was a golden age for European Jewry, brought to an end when the Catholic monarchs Isabella and Ferdinand drove the last Moors from the peninsula in 1492. The Jews were sent packing at the same time, making their homes in Italy, North Africa, the Balkans and the Levant. Their language, a form of Romance known as Judeo-Spanish, survived and is still understood by perhaps a quarter of a million people.

Yiddish derives its name from a dialectal form of the German *Jude* "Jew." In its present form it is far removed from its earlier one, which evolved when the migrant Jews abandoned the Old French of their previous home and took to German. A few words survive in modern Yiddish that were first acquired from French – *bentshn* "bless" and *leyenen* "read" have their roots in the Latin *benedicere* and *legere* – but in essence Yiddish is German, albeit a German strongly colored by Hebrew (it is written in Hebrew characters, from right to left), Slavonic, some Romance and (increasingly) English.

The first two centuries of the Jewish presence in Germany coincided with a general movement of German influence eastwards, into Slavonic lands, and many Jews joined the migrations, mainly into Poland. The movement reached its climax in the years following the Black Death, for which the Jews were accused of somehow being responsible. When they were not massacred, they were confined to their own quarters; the *ghetto*, first used to describe the Jewish quarter in sixteenth-century Venice, became a fact of Jewish existence in Europe long before it was given its name. There were reasons enough to seek some stability in the wide and underpopulated regions of the east, and it was in the Slavonic lands, Poland particularly, that Yiddish thrived.

Before the First World War, more than half the population of many large towns, Warsaw included, were Yiddish-speaking. Some small towns were 100 per cent Jewish. Although there had been considerable emigration at the turn of the century, mostly to the United States, two-thirds of the world's twelve million Yiddish speakers remained in eastern Europe to face the awful consequences of the Second World War and the holocaust (Hebrew *Shoah*), as it has come to be known. Overwhelmingly, the Jews slaughtered were Yiddish-speaking.

The surviving language is a reflection of a history often all too synonymous with a Hebrew-Yiddish word that has passed into colloquial German – *Dalles* "misfortune" or "queer street'. The basic German component is combined freely with the vocabulary and usages of Slavonic, together with the Hebrew of the religion that at all times in all places sustained its speakers. All three combine sometimes in one term; the Hebrew *mazl* "luck" preceded by the German *schlimm* "bad" and followed by the Slavonic suffix *-nik* produces the Yiddish *schlimezalnik* – an unlucky person.

Wherever Yiddish-speaking communities have settled beyond their central and eastern European homelands, many of their words have entered and enriched surrounding languages, notably the English of New York and certainly the vernacular of show business. *Kosher* is as good a way of describing the genuine article as any English term, and readers of English newspapers are becoming used to *chutzpah* "cheek" or impudence on a grand scale. But Londoners have long used Yiddish "nosh" for food (German *Naschen*, snack between meals).

DUTCH: A PROUD INDEPENDENT

The land in which the ancestors of the Dutch made their homes was quite unlike anywhere else in Europe. The Roman historian Pliny described it in less than flattering terms. "Here, in the space of a single day and night, the ocean, far and wide, twice advances and recedes, occasioning such a struggle between the elements that one might doubt whether the entire region should be accounted to the land or the sea. The inhabitants build their huts upon artificial mounds above the reach of the highest floods, and when the tide is in they look like mariners in their barks, when it is out they look like shipwrecked sailors."

From such unpromising beginnings, the Dutch have made much. Since the Middle Ages, the Low Countries have been an outstandingly prosperous part of Europe, its inhabitants having won (with occasional setbacks) a battle with the sea to produce a fertile and productive land. And, holding no terrors for them, the sea also provided for the Dutch one of the most powerful of maritime empires.

In their triumph over such challenging conditions, the Dutch found their linguistic independence and the right to assert that their language is *not*, as many Germans have liked to think, simply a mis-spelled and mispronounced form of German. It shares a common ancestry, as English does, with the Low German dialects of the north, but the historic High German "shift" that turned German into a new language found no response from Dutch, which remained independently "low."

The temptation to think of Dutch as a form of German can be forgiven when one looks at many of the everyday words of the two languages. The German says *Mann* "man" and *Frau* "woman," the Dutchman *man* and *vrouw;* the German breathes *Luft* "air," the Dutchman *lucht;* many commonplace words change hardly at all between one language and the other, such as German *Stern* "star" and Dutch *ster, Stein* "stone" *steen, Baum* "tree" *boom* and *Licht* "light" *licht.* A number of Dutch words, however, bear no resemblance to German words of equivalent meaning, and pronunciation of them is no easier for a German than for anyone else.

Little is known of Dutch in its oldest form. Some fragments (a few psalms) survive from the ninth century and it is evident that the language was a Low German or Franconian dialect close to Old Saxon. As texts become abundant from the thirteenth century onward it is clear that Low Franconian, and not Saxon, had prevailed to become, in time, the modern Dutch language.

By this time France, the increasingly powerful neighbor to the south, was already making its political and cultural presence felt. Throughout the Middle Ages and well into modern times, unlikely Dutch names like Perceval, Clarisse, Yseut and Vivien testify to the popularity of medieval French fiction imported into the Low Countries, and hundreds of Latin-based words arrived to contribute to the growing material prosperity and a flourishing literature. Long before it had become the greatest seafaring power in the world, the Dutch nation had taken on board a sizeable maritime vocabulary from the French.

Whether on a *fregat, brik* or *korvet* (French *frégate, brigantin* and *corvette*), the *kapitein* and ordinary rating *matroos* (ultimately the same as the French *mâtelot*) steered a *koers* by means of a *kompas*, both borrowed from the French.

It was not just at sea that the Dutch relied upon a French vocabulary. Many essential and unrelated words that are the substance of everyday speech were imported from France: *feit* "fact," from the French *fait*, *schaak* "chess" from *eschac*, *punt* "point," *monteren* "to assemble" from *monter* and *kosten* "to cost" from *coster*. Some terms were translated literally and thus *petit-fils* "grandson" and *belle-fille* "daughter-in-law" became *kleinzoon* and *schoondochter* in Dutch.

The power of France over the Low Countries was generally more cultural than political. Netherlanders never ceased to think of themselves as an independent nation, even when their princes spoke habitually in French. William of Orange, the great Dutch leader in the struggle against Spanish rule, uttered his patriotic dying words in French, beseeching God to help his subjects – "*cet pauvre peuple*," as he called them. His prayer was eventually answered, but only after a long and bloody series of political events that directly influenced the nature of modern Dutch.

In 1585, a year after William's death, the great city of Antwerp fell to Spain, and with it collapsed the economic influence of Brabant, until then the dominant province. Power now passed to the northern provinces, especially to Holland, where the cities of Amsterdam, the Hague and Leyden flourished at the expense of Bruges and Antwerp in the south. The dialect of Holland also became the principal speech of the Netherlands, although thousands of influential immigrants from Brabant gave it a strong southern flavor.

The patchwork of Germanic dialects that had characterized Netherlandic speech became increasingly unified during the seventeenth century as the newly allied northern provinces grew to the status of a world power. A notable translation of the Bible authorized by the state, and the writings of Joost van den Vondel (1587–1679), the greatest of Dutch poets, helped establish the language "General Cultural Netherlandic." This language, based on the dialect of Holland, is the standard written form of Dutch today and is rapidly gaining precedence in speech over such regional dialects as still survive in rural areas. Only in northern Belgium does it remain principally a literary language. There, most of the five million "Dutch speakers" in fact speak Flemish or *Vlaams*, a Dutch dialect.

Dutchmen concerned about the purity of their language are today involved in a continual struggle. Centuries of trade with larger foreign countries have given many Dutchmen a pragmatic attitude towards communication: better to prosper in someone else's language than to be proud, monolingual and poor. On top of this, cultural domination is just as much a threat now as it was when William of Orange breathed his last French words 400 years ago. Today, however, the language that impinges most upon Netherlandic life is English with its essential role as the lingua franca of business and technology.

English has an economy of expression that makes it a useful language to many professions. In 1957 one Dutch shipping company listed

Eternal image of Holland: water and windmills. The
Dutch brought to landscapes and domestic scenes a
naturalism absent from the works of the classic south.
Where Italian gave English the "studio" terms of impasto
and chiaroscuro, the Dutch gave to it the open-air "easel"
and "landscape."

140 English-based words that were used for navigation alone. (But the English seafarer owes quite as great a debt to his Dutch counterpart, whether he is the *skipper* of a *sloop* or the *commodore* of a *yacht* squadron; these four words are of Dutch origin.)

Years of doing business with the world may have made the Dutch particularly susceptible to linguistic invasion, but they are also well-prepared to cope with the problem, to absorb what is beneficial and to reject what could be harmful. This unhysterical approach to language has allowed the Dutch to adapt a number of English words: *checken, relaxen, overlappen* and *cancellen* represent the easy transition from an English to a "Dutch" verb. Nouns have been adapted in a number of ways: there might be a slight modification in spelling, as in *teamwerk* "teamwork;" a Dutch ending as in *fitheid* "fitness;" a literal translation as in *schaduwkabinet* "shadow cabinet;" or a contraction as in *tiener* "teenager."

Frisian

The Frisian people once flourished along the North Sea, from the mouth of the Rhine to southern Denmark. Long ago they were absorbed into the states of Germany, Denmark and the Netherlands, but miraculously their language survives. A mere handful speak the rapidly vanishing form known as East Frisian in a tiny enclave in north-west Germany, and a few thousand coastal inhabitants of German Schleswig still speak one of the many dialects of North Frisian. In the Dutch province of Friesland, however, and on several offshore islands, up to 300,000 West Frisian speakers cling to their language, although all are necessarily bilingual.

In the towns of Friesland, such as Leeuwarden (Frisian *Ljouwert*), the capital, a compromise form called "town Frisian," half Frisian and half Dutch, is spoken, and street and town signs and public notices are frequently seen in both languages.

THE FRISIANS

Placid and well-ordered, short on fortresses but rich in flourishing farmland, the northern Netherlands province of Friesland is best-known today beyond its borders for the famous black and white Friesian cattle. Its present appearance cloaks a past in which it was one of the great commercial powers of northern Europe, with depots, like the (much later) Hanseatic League in Scandinavia.

The Romans (who left them alone) mention them in association with the mouth of the Rhine; at their greatest extent, they occupied the North Sea coastal area from the Rhine to the Ems. At Dorestad, near Utrecht, they maintained an important commercial entrepot until it was destroyed by the Vikings.

The affinities of Frisian and English are more apparent than real. The Frisians were among the Germanic invaders of Britain, where a few Midland placenames like Friston (Suffolk) and Frisby (Leicestershire) recall their settlements – as Swaffham (Norfolk) marks the early presence of Suevi, or Swabians.

Modern Frisian

Possible extent in Roman times

Frisian is of especial interest to linguists because it was for a long time believed to be the surviving link between continental Germanic languages and English; "Bread, butter and green cheese is good English and good Friese" runs an old rhyme. The basis for this theory is particularly evident in those Anglo-Frisian words that lost the nasal *n-* sound. Thus *gans* and *fünf* in German are *gós* and *fíf* in Old Frisian, appearing as "goose" and "five" in English. Despite many similarities, however (and evidence that Frisians were among the early Germanic arrivals in England), Frisian is no more like English than its other neighboring languages. It simply sounds like it at first hearing, particularly to a native of East Anglia, that part of England closest to Friesland. These two peoples met frequently, fishing the Dogger Bank, and shouted *"Avast"* ("stop") at each other when their nets entagled.

The literary West Frisian language nearly died of neglect in the eighteenth century, but the romantic era, with its renewed interest in tiny nations and forgotten tongues, gave it fresh life. In the last 150 years West Frisian speakers have fought determinedly for official and social recognition, extracting repeated concessions from the Dutch Government. A Frisian Academy was established in 1938. Five years later a Frisian translation of the Bible finally appeared. In 1955 Friesland primary schools were permitted to teach Frisian instead of Dutch as a first language. A year later Frisian was authorized for use in legal cases.

In order to safeguard the purity of West Frisian, nationalist academics insist where possible on vocabulary that is far removed from Dutch. Thus the word *hawwe*, one of four dialect versions of the verb "to have," was approved for use in written West Frisian because it was least like *hebben*, its Dutch equivalent. These academic stratagems shed little light upon the actual state of the language. Its survival, as with any language, will be decided in the streets rather than in the university.

Boers (Dutch "farmers") on the move, or "trekking," making an overland journey. Many Dutch words have made their way into English by way of Afrikaans:

"trek" itself, "spoor," "springbok," "gemsbok" (Dutch *gems,* "chamois"), "eland" (Dutch *eland,* elk), the self-explanatory "wildebeest," and "aardvark" (earth-pig).

Afrikaans: the laager language

Afrikaans, now the language of more than four million South Africans, began by chance in the seventeenth century. In 1652 a small group of Dutchmen established a settlement on the Cape of Good Hope as a victualling station for their East Indiamen. Among themselves, they spoke a number of Netherlandic dialects, with the language of South Holland Province prevailing. By the end of the century their speech had already changed considerably from that of Holland, and 100 years later it had become a separate language.

Linguists disagree as to exactly how Afrikaans developed, and why with such speed. It is sometimes described as a sophisticated Creole language, formed by the exposure of a Dutch minority to a displaced and polyglot population of slaves and traders. This theory points to the rapid simplification of Dutch as evidence of a pidgin lingua franca – the only way in which Dutchmen, Malayo Portuguese, French Huguenots, and Hottentots could effectively communicate. Other experts, especially among Afrikaners themselves, who naturally object to descriptions such as Cape Creole or "Kitchen Dutch" applied to their language, consider that Afrikaans is a perfectly natural development of Dutch, comparing the process of simplification to the changes that occurred in English some centuries earlier.

Afrikaans vocabulary has not been greatly affected by the jumble of nationalities that have gone to creating South Africa. A few words, including *baie* "very," have been introduced from Malayan, and those two very South African words *kraal* "cattle pen" from the Portuguese *corral,* and *mielies* "maize" from the Portuguese *milho,* have similar origins. But after more than three centuries of isolation most of the Afrikaans vocabulary remains based in Dutch.

Afrikaans began to achieve literary status in the late nineteenth century. Until then Standard Dutch had been the language of reading and writing. In the face of derision from the influential English population and disapproval from their conservative countrymen, especially in the Church, Afrikaner nationalists gave their language complete written respectability within a period of about fifty years. In 1914 Afrikaans began to be taught in schools; in 1925 it became an official Parliamentary language. The loss of political power by the white minority and the removal of the laws of *Apartheid* in the early 1990s brought a rainbow of official languages to the young "rainbow republic." Afrikaans and English retain a formal function in government and commerce, but have been joined as official languages by nine native African tongues. Principal among them are Xhosa, Swazi and Zulu, members of the huge Niger-Congo family of languages spoken throughout sub-Saharan Africa.

ENGLISH: THE UNIVERSAL LANGUAGE

The growth of English to its unchallenged leadership among the languages of the world is a phenomenon of recent history. The German philologist Jakob Grimm (1785–1863) was one of the first to recognize its potential: "In wealth, wisdom and strict economy, none of the other living languages can vie with it," he wrote. Grimm's observations were those of a man concerned with the nature of language, rather than the social or political reasons for its success.

At that time, English was spoken in Europe by little more than half the number whose mother language was French, twenty million against thirty-five million. According to some estimates, English was a poor fifth among European languages at the beginning of the nineteenth century.

The astonishing momentum with which the use of English gathered pace was not due to a wholesale recognition of the virtues attributed to it by Grimm, although they have helped. The reason lay far beyond Europe, in America where, five years before Grimm was born, John Adams had written: "English is destined to be in the next and succeeding centuries more generally the language of the world than Latin was in the last or French is in the present age. The reason for this is obvious, because the increasing population in America and their universal connection and correspondence with all nations will, aided by the influence of England in the world, whether great or small, force their language into general use."

The history of English soon embarked on the course that Adams had envisaged for it. It is estimated that today more than 400 million people speak English as their first language, with as many again using it as an official or second language. Even more are in the process of learning it; there are said to be more Chinese learning English than English-speakers in America. One ambitious forecast suggests that, some time in the future, most of the world will be tri-lingual; people will be masters of their own language, of English as spoken locally and of standard written English (far from impossible, given the advent of the Internet).

The arrival

The British king Vortigern was at his capital, the city now called Canterbury, when messengers reported to him that: "Unknown men, and what is more, men of huge stature, landed in enormous ships." The arrival of "Jutish" tribesmen on the Kent coast in 449 AD may have been the result of an appeal for military help from Vortigern, but its consequences for the world's community of languages were far more momentous than the outcome of any local fracas. The Germanic dialect of the "Jutes," together with those of their relations, the Angles and the Saxons, was soon to become known as *Englisc,* the language destined to become pre-eminent throughout the world, and the first to be heard beyond it, on the Moon.

The "Jutes" are something of an enigma. It is thought that they were a Frankish people from the middle Rhine, which would account for a complete absence of Norse among Kentish place-names, but many with Frankish elements: *-ingas* (now -ing, German *-ingen*), -ham and -ge (German *heim* and *gau*).

Primus in spatium: Americans arrive on the moon and the first language heard from outer space is English – "That's one small step for a man, one giant leap for mankind."

Whatever or wherever their homeland, the new realms of the Jutes did not extend beyond the south-east of England where, if they thought of themselves as anything, it was as "Kentings," taking the Celtic name of the old British kingdom and attaching their Germanic suffix *-ing* "people of" to it. For the rest of the country, Anglian came to dominate the north and east, Saxon the south and west, with the Angles providing the name by which the language became known. The first upon the English stage, the "Jutes" made their exit, to be recalled only in the name of the place from which history supposed they had come – Jutland.

At first glance, Old English does not appear to have much in common with the modern variety. Much of its vocabulary is foreign and its grammatical structure far removed from that of today. Like modern German, it was a highly "inflected" language, that is, the exact form of a noun, verb or adjective depended on the role it played in a sentence. *Stān* "stone" for instance, had six possible endings including *stānes* "of (the) stone" and *stanum* "to (the) stones." Gender was important but often illogical: words for "girl" or "maiden" *maegdēn* and "wife" *wif* were classed as neuter but "woman" *wifmann* was masculine.

But for all the differences between the *Englisc* of the conquering Germanic tribes and the English of today, a fundamental vocabulary runs through the language of the men who came in "enormous" ships to the language of the men who landed in spaceships on the moon, 1,500 years later. "That's one small step for man, one giant leap for mankind," said Neil Armstrong as he set foot on the moon's surface. Of these momentous words only "giant" is derived from a source other than Old English.

Eighty-five per cent of the Old English vocabulary has now vanished but the rest includes the most intimate and commonplace words in the English language: *mann* became "man," *mete* became "meat," *hus* "house," *etan* "eat," *drincan* "drink," *sprecan* "speak." With an Old English vocabulary, the modern English speaker still has a mother and a father, brother, sister and friends; he can walk or run, laugh or weep, sleep and dream. Most of these words have their recognizable echoes in the vocabularies of Scandinavia, Germany and Holland, and those of older languages, for they are part of the Indo-European stock.

The Germanic invaders took little from the language of the Celts they displaced and drove westward, but they had scarcely settled in their new home when Christianity, in the form of St Augustine and his fellow-missionaries, arrived in 597 AD. Most modern English words associated with the Church and worship – angel, candle, disciple, epistle, hymn, priest among them – were first adopted from the Latin by the Anglo-Saxons.

Although more than 400 Latin words were assimilated during the early centuries of Anglo-Saxon rule, the English converts occasionally dug in their heels and refused to accept the Latin term. In referring to the all-important Day of Judgement, they chose their own, expressive *Domes Daeg*, which still haunts the language in the nuclear age as "doomsday."

If *Englisc* had proved itself able, for the first time but certainly not for the last, to absorb and benefit from the impact of another culture, it was soon to be put to another more forceful test. It came as the Saxons themselves had come, across the North Sea, in the high-prowed ships of the Norsemen, distant cousins of the Anglo-Saxons, speaking a language not unlike their own. Twenty-five years of fierce campaigning gave to the Danes the greater part of northern and eastern Britain, which became known as the Danelaw. Their bid for sovereignty over the whole island was denied them by Alfred at the Battle of Ethandun (now Edington, Wiltshire) in 878, and the south-west remained Saxon.

The dividing line between the two realms followed the line of the old Roman road known as Watling Street, between London and Chester. The division remains apparent to this day in the country's placenames. Nearly 1,500 of Scandinavian origin still exist in England, more than 600 of them ending in *by*, the Danish word meaning "town." Grimsby, Rugby and Derby were three major settlements in the Danelaw. Other common Scandinavian words were *thorp* "village," *beck* "brook," *thwaite* "field" and *toft* "a piece of land," and they are as commonplace in the north and east as the

Anglo-Saxon *den* "pasture," *hurst* "wooded hill," *hythe* "landing place," and *ham* "village manor," are in southern England.

The Old Norse language of the Danish settlers so closely resembled the Old English of the Angles that the two societies were able to communicate on a basic level and to intermarry. Several thousand new words enriched the language. Many have disappeared, or survive only in dialects, such as that child of language intermarriage, "bairn," identical almost to the modern child in Scandinavian, *barn*. Among the words that have survived are earthy, everyday terms: egg, birth, dirt, skill, sky, call, die, get, give, scare and scowl (the hard *sk* and *g* sounds are typical of words borrowed by English from Norse at this time).

Beyond the new vocabulary, a more profound change was occurring where the Anglo-Saxons and Scandinavians lived side by side. In order to simplify the business of communication, those who lived in the north and east began to shed some of the more complicated Germanic endings to their nouns and verbs. The sort of "modernization" of a language that reformers conspicuously fail to achieve was begun unconsciously in tenth, and eleventh-century Britain by illiterate men and women who wished merely to talk to their neighbors.

The French connection

On Christmas Day, 1066, William of Normandy was crowned King of England. Although he was of Norse origin, he did not speak a word of English nor did he ever feel obliged to learn the language of his new

OLD ENGLISH

GAELIC

NORTHUMBRIAN

• York

Grimsby •

• Derby

• Rugby

OLD
BRITISH
(WELSH)

M E R C I A N

KENTISH

OLD BRITISH
(CORNISH)

W E S T   S A X O N

☐ Danelaw

── Watling Street

Within 150 years of the arrival of the Anglo-Saxons in the fifth century, *Englisc* was the language of England and its speakers were called Angles, wherever they had come from (the original Angles are recalled in Angeln, northern Germany). The first small kingdoms were seven in number: Northumbria, Mercia, East Anglia, Kent, Essex, Sussex and Wessex.

There were four main dialects: Northumbrian, Mercian, West Saxon and Kentish, of which West Saxon, the form spoken in Wessex, became something of a standard during the reign of Alfred the Great (849–899). By then a new element had arrived, the Norse-speaking Vikings. They raided and plundered sporadically in the south, including London, but achieved no permanent settlement there.

In the north and east they had greater success, setting up permanent communities, in many districts outnumbering the English. The Viking settlers were from Denmark and the lands they held became known as the Danelaw, divided from the Saxon south by the line of the old Roman Watling Street. The Old English "street" was no paved town thoroughfare, but a roman road, or *strata*, a word borrowed by Germanic people from the old Empire.

MIDDLE ENGLISH

NORTHERN

WELSH

WEST
MIDLAND

E A S T
M I D L A N D

• Cambridge

Oxford •

London •

KENTISH

S O U T H E R N

CORNISH

Englishman and Dane continued to fight each other throughout the tenth and into the eleventh century, but behind the campaigning the process of assimilation was proceeding. As many as fought each other were living and working side by side. A new nation was in the making, and its language was Old English modified by Danish and some Norwegian of those who had settled in what is now Cumbria.

The old Germanic language was about to undergo its greatest ever change, with the arrival in 1066 of the French-speaking Normans. English, in whatever accent it was spoken, was relegated to the role of servant; French ruled. When English regained its sovereignty after 200 years – a period during which it is described as Middle English – it is seen from contemporary writings to have acquired a strong French element in its vocabulary. Dialects persisted, however, in matters of local usage, of which the principal were Northern, East and West Midland, Southern and Kentish. It was the East Midland form, including that of London, that was to emerge as "Standard English." In 1415, a king and nobles of French stock led a small army of English yeomen into battle at Agincourt, and all called themselves Englishmen.

kingdom. The noblemen and clerics with whom he replaced the old English ruling classes spoke, as he did, the *langue d'oïl*, the tongue of northern France, which was henceforth the language of government and all its institutions. Those few Englishmen who succeeded in holding on to their lands and titles did so by holding their tongues, at least in their native language.

The change had little effect upon the daily lives of the common people, who clung to the old language except where they sought some small preferment as bailiffs or as clerks in the proliferating religious houses. For generations, these men provided the linguistic bridge between the cultures, but the gap inevitably closed, rendering translators and interpreters unnecessary; Norman baron married Saxon wife, a Saxon nurse tended his children who, in the manner of all children in all ages, began to speak like those with whom they had constant contact. By the time Edward I (1239–1307) came to the throne, some children of Norman descent were having to learn French from textbooks, and Edward himself chose to speak English as his main language.

An event more far-reaching in its effect than anything devised by man accelerated the rise of English through the social hierarchy. The Black Death completed its fearful journey through England in 1350, having carried off a third of the population in less than two years. Those who survived among the English-speaking artisans and laborers discovered they were now a rare and important breed. As their services became more highly valued, so the language they spoke acquired a greater status.

The façade of "French" officialdom finally collapsed in 1362 when Parliament admitted that French was "much unknown in the said realm" and that ordinary citizens in legal proceedings had "no understanding of that which is said for them or against them." Three hundred years after the Norman invasion, the language of the people had become the official language of the land.

The old Norman nobility, long since challenged to declare its allegiance to either the English or the French thrones, knew on which side of the Channel its bread was buttered. At Crècy, Poitiers and later Agincourt the noble scions of Norman stock fought the French alongside a yeoman, Anglo-Saxon infantry, and called themselves Englishmen and their language English.

Henry V's instructions to his men at Agincourt in 1415 would scarcely have been comprehensible to the Saxon house-carls who fought with Harold against the Norman invader. The process of unconscious simplification that had begun in the ninth century, when Dane and Englishman lived side by side, continued throughout the period of Norman rule. The illiterate masses – wainwrights and washerwomen, peasants and pickpockets – had little time for the complexities of grammar. Verbs and adjectives began to shed their confusing endings and irregular forms and the plurals of nouns began to be expressed simply with the letter *s*. Most significantly, nouns lost their gender as the unlettered English became increasingly unwilling to remember that while *woman* was masculine, *wife* was neuter.

CHAUCER'S ENGLISH

English came into its own in the work of its first great poet, Geoffrey Chaucer (*c.* 1345–1400) *(right)* whose masterpiece, *The Canterbury Tales*, is a vivid portrait of his countrymen and women. Chaucer was a tax officer, ambassador and sometime soldier, and was for a short time a prisoner in France. In his lifetime the old chasm between a French-speaking nobility and the lower classes, whose language was English, had been bridged, and English was the language of all. French was an acquired language and Chaucer makes the point clearly when he describes (with some affection) one of the Canterbury pilgrims, the Prioress *(below)*. "And Frensh she spak ful faire and fetisly, after the scole of Stratford atte Bowe, for Frensh of Paris was to hir unknowe…"

Few men of his time had Chaucer's breadth of learning or experience of other European countries and their achievements. He was widely read in Latin, French and Italian and admired the works not only of the ancient masters but of his great contemporaries, Dante, Boccaccio and Petrarch. He was dispatched, on at least two occasions, to Italy on the King's business. Boccaccio particularly was an inspiration, providing themes for some of the stories related in *The Canterbury Tales*. No portrait of a nation at a moment in time surpasses that of the English men and women, both high and low, streetwise or aware of their dignity, described by Chaucer in the Prologue to his marvellous account of the great pilgrimage.

RENAISSANCE ENGLISH

In 1485, when Henry VII proclaimed himself King of England among 1,000 corpses on Bosworth Field, English was well established as the spoken language of the land. One hundred years later, it was a major literary language as well, defended by patriots with a passion generally reserved for religion or politics. "I love Rome, but London better,"'wrote Richard Mulcaster, teacher of Edmund Spenser, the Elizabethan poet. "I honour the Latin, but I worship the English."

The Renaissance appeared to underline the importance of Latin as the language of culture. But throughout Europe there were men like Mulcaster who were coming increasingly to favor their native tongues; and these included more worldly men than academics, like the Elizabethan printer who, given a Latin tome to set up in type said: "Though, sir, your book be wise and full of learning, yet peradventure it will not be so saleable."

Thomas More *(above)*, exemplar and victim of his times (he was sent to the headsman's block by his friend, Henry VIII,

---

It was while in this highly plastic and adaptable state that the English language was invaded by the French. During the first two centuries of Norman rule, nearly 1,000 words of French provenance found their way into the English, mostly reflecting the master and servant, rulers and ruled relationships. The Old English *calf, pig, ox* and *sheep* became *veal, pork, beef and mutton* somewhere along the way from the Saxon *slaughter yard* to the Norman *table*. The Englishman had now to recognize an alien *government, royalty, authority* and *parliament*. Even if his *sovereign* was a *tyrant*, he would have to pay his *taxes* to the *exchequer* or *exchange* his *liberty* for a *dungeon*.

Once the Norman had decided he was no longer French but English, the clear-cut line between the aristocracy and the masses became blurred. New classes of men, merchants and guild craftsmen, proud of their independence, emerged, and with them "a distinct nation, no longer a mere overseas extension of Franco-Latin Europe." The English now had greater access to the language of their erstwhile masters and in this period in the history of the language, where it was known as Middle English, many thousands more French words were borrowed.

This new vocabulary belonged no more to one section of society than to another, and combined with the old language felicitously to produce an English that "all understanden." The new French introduction *gentle* could be combined with an English suffix and become *gently* or *gentleness*, or *gentleman* and *gentlewoman* when attached to English nouns. With the English prefix *un-*, a man could undress; with the French *dis-* he could disrobe as well. English could supply the suffixes to French words in forming *spiritless* and *peaceful;* French

for refusing to deny Papal authority in the king's realm), wrote his most famous work, *Utopia*, in Latin, but fifteen years after he died it appeared in English.

Elizabethan poets and playwrights found as much adventure in their language as their buccaneering contemporaries Hawkins, Drake and Raleigh encountered across the oceans of the world. Not all the new terms that entered English during their ebullient times were new mintings: twentieth-century commonplaces like "craggy," "dapper," "drizzling," "glance," "gloomy" and "grovel" were disinterred by men like Edmund Spenser (*c.* 1552–99).

The summit of Elizabethan endeavour was reached by William Shakespeare *(left)* whose vocabulary included words that had never before appeared in print, like the (now crudely mis-used) "obscene," "pedant," "indistinguishable" and "submerged," as well as dozens more that had only recently come into English usage. Shakespeare's English, like his birthplace, was "East Midland." From his lifetime, his English came to be regarded as the country's written standard.

suffixes could follow English roots as in *talkative* and *washable*.

The resources of two languages thus gave English a rich and sophisticated vocabulary. The Anglo-Saxon "book," so close to the Germanic *buch,* now shared its shelf with *volumes* from France; *work* was now also *labour* which could either *begin* or *end* in English or *commence* and *finish* in French. These matching English-French words or doublets, and there are thousands of them, do not always mean quite the same thing; they offer shades of meaning and qualities of sound that were to make English the treasure trove for later poets and dramatists it had already become for Geoffrey Chaucer (1345–1400). His *The Canterbury Tales* (written in the years around 1387) is still an accessible joy to those willing to learn a few archaic words and adjust to the Middle English spelling, as the stories are eternally fresh.

New words from old

Typical of this new race of Englishmen was Thomas More (1478–1535). His most famous work, *Utopia*, was written in Latin but he was no conservative when he came to use his native language. From Latin materials, More made new and lasting English words. From the Latin *exaggerare* he created *exaggerate* and similarly words like *absurdity, comprehensible* and *exact*.

He was not alone in his attitude to language. His was an inquisitive and adventurous age and words symbolic of this restlessness, *exploration* and *discovery*, entered the language from Latin and French; the north-easterly *brisa* that bellied the canvas of the Spanish Indiamen now filled northern sails as breeze. More than 10,000 new words made their way into "English" between 1500 and 1650. Most were derived from scholarship Latin but others were reintroductions from

Other English lexicographers are known only to the world of academics, but Samuel Johnson survives as an outstanding personality thanks to his Scottish biographer, James Boswell. A man of encyclopedic knowledge, high principles, witty conversation and eccentric personality, Johnson was a natural "TV personality" 200 years ahead of his time, (though he would have been unlikely to approve of that medium).

earlier English speech, unearthed by exuberant writers like poet Edmund Spenser (1552–99), who championed the use of archaic words and even invented a few of his own. *Bellibone*, meaning "pretty girl" (perhaps a contraction of *belle et bonne*), was not a successful innovation, more's the pity, but his onomatopoeic *chirrup* for the chirping of a bird, has survived.

The summit of achievement in the language was reached by William Shakespeare (1564–1616), who seized avidly upon new words while putting old ones to even more splendid use. In a performance of any of his plays, all but the best-educated of his audience would have encountered a number of unfamiliar words. *Accommodation, assassination* (far from its root in the Arabic for "hashish-eater"), *obscene* and *submerged* all appear for the first time in one or another of his plays.

It was an uninhibited and extravagant period, when men could use old, unknown and invented words and spell them as they wished. The printing press and moveable type which had encouraged a great flowering of literature now began to insist upon consistency and writers themselves began to look for some generally accepted rules. The age of schoolmasters had begun.

The obsession of the eighteenth century with rules and permanence in language was a reflection of the spirit of the time. The Age of Reason, as it has been called, respected logic and symmetry, qualities apparently epitomized by Greece and Rome. An educated man still read Homer, Sophocles, Terence and Plautus with pleasure, but he found much of the drama and poetry of sixteenth-century England full of embarrassingly unfamiliar words. The man who could appreciate the "foreign" Horace had difficulty understanding his English Chaucer.

The satirist Jonathan Swift (1667–1745) urged the setting up of an academy of learned men after the manner of the French and Italians, who had already done so, to regularize the grammar, throw out the "bad" words and restore the good. Fortunately, the idea was never taken up. The closest that England ever got to such an institution was in one man, Samuel Johnson (1709–75). The sole compiler of a massive dictionary, Johnson did more than any other man to "fix" the English vocabulary, although he recognized that it was not in the power of any man to "embalm his language and secure it from corruption and decay."

Johnson was a child of his classical times and fond of polysyllabic words of Greek and Latin origin, including in his dictionary a number of dreadful mouthfuls like *incompossibility* and *digladiation*. He was severe on what he called "colloquial barbarisms," new words that had established themselves in current usage without any perceptible authority. Luckily for the language, he and his contemporaries were powerless to check the flood of new words that continued to enter the language from abroad. Words that are now used more frequently than ever before, like *cartoon* and *dentist, publicity* and *routine, syndicate* and *canteen,* entered the language from French between 1650 and 1800; the artistic Dutch provided *easel, sketch* and *landscape,* their seafaring countrymen *boom, cruise, sloop* and *yacht* and the one word in English that must be shouted into a gale for best effect, *Avast!*

"Colloquial barbarisms" arrived from distant continents. The Indian *bungalow* joined the English *house* and the French *mansion* as part of the townscape. The Americas had provided new words almost from the time of their discovery; *tobacco* and *cannibal* (an alternative form of *carib*) were among the earliest arrivals from the Spanish Main, followed in subsequent centuries by a stream of new terms from the Amerindian north (*moccasin, skunk, toboggan, tomahawk, moose, caribou*), center (*hammock, hurricane, canoe, barbecue*) and south (*buccaneer, jaguar, tapioca*).

Since Johnson's *Dictionary* was published more than 200 years ago, English has undergone great superficial change but the grammatical rules and conventions laid down by his contemporaries and confirmed by subsequent generations of schoolmasters have remained virtually intact. Johnson would find that *The Times* newspaper, which first appeared a year after his death, was quite readable, if not wholly to his liking, although what he would make of some tabloid headlines defies the imagination.

There has been no stemming the historic tide of imported or borrowed words or of newly coined terms, and the language has been enriched rather than weakened by them. More often than not, traditional means and materials are used for the new mintings; the "automobile" is assembled from ancient components, Greek *autos* "self" and Latin *mobilis* "moveable," although the British still prefer to call it a "car," a word of ancient Celtic origin.

The English vocabulary continues to pick its fruit from exotic trees. An American author has demonstrated its omnivorous nature by compiling a children's story of 172 words in everyday English that contained thirty-two different languages. But non-English words are on the lips of English speakers everywhere, every day. Recounting his family's fortunes to a friend, a middle-aged Englishman was heard to say "My *father's tobacco kiosk* was *blown* to *smithereens* in the *blitz.*" It is perfectly good colloquial English, yet none of the italicized words has its origins in England. *Father* and *blown* have their roots in the ancient Indo-European mother tongue; *tobacco* arrived from the Spanish Main in the sixteenth century; *kiosk* was imported from Turkish in the seventeenth century; *smithereens,* literally "little pieces" from the Gaelic of Ireland in the nineteenth; and the German *Blitz* (shortened from *Blitzkreig* "lightning war") descended from the skies in 1940. Demobilized, "blitz" took on a civilian function as in "a blitz on paperwork."

English has already become the lingua franca of the Internet and the World Wide Web. It is salutary to reflect that this astonishing innovation has evolved through a system of mathematics with roots in ancient India and a language born 1,500 years ago. The concept of a *Weorold Wïd Web* might baffle Alfred the Great, but the individual words would mean exactly the same to him as to us.

English in America

And who, in time, knows whither we may vent
The treasure of our tongue, to what strange shores
This gain of our best glory shall be sent ...
What worlds in th'yet unformed Occident
May come refined with th'accents that are ours?

Elizabeth I was on the throne of England when Samuel Daniel (1562–1619) wrote the lines above. Within a year or so of his death, the settlement of English speakers in North America ("th'yet unformed Occident") had started and a process had begun by which his poetic hypothesis would be answered positively: from "a language of small reach," English has emerged unchallenged as the global language, in compass if not always in "accents that are ours."

In the decades following the young nation's Declaration of Independence in 1776, English was one of the lesser languages of Europe in number of speakers. The Victorian years of imperial expansion carried it to the four corners of the world, mainly as the language of the master to the servant, but its most potent settlement had yet to assert itself. It had taken place 200 years earlier when colonists from England "planted" the eastern seaboard of North America. By 1800 more than a quarter of all English-speakers were American and now the position is reversed; for every native English-speaker in Britain there are at least four speaking English in America. It is to this fact, together with the legacy of a now-vanished empire, that English at the end of the twentieth century owes its position as the language of

second choice for the greater part of the world.

American English was born imperceptibly, at the moment when the first settlers began to use commonplace words of the American Indians, or "native Americans" as political correctness now requires they should be called. The settlers soon learned what a *wigwam* was, what *moccasins* (now worn by more people than ever haunted the great plains) and *squaws* were, and were able to attach names to alien beasts like *raccoons, skunks* and *opossums,* for which there were no English counterparts. The first Europeans borrowed many words from the natives during their first century or so of occupation, but only a few of these "wigwam" words survive today in their original form. The local languages nevertheless live on in the landscape itself from the self-descriptive *Mississippi* "big river" to *Chicago* "garlic field."

The new Americans did not restrict their verbal borrowings to native American words. Although they were the most numerous, English speakers at times found themselves in contact with other western Europeans, particularly the French. The St Lawrence River had provided the French with a route to the Great Lakes and beyond and their footprints remain in the scores of placenames of obvious French ancestry from Detroit, by way of St Louis, to New Orleans. Once the English began to penetrate the heartland of the continent, they found a number of ready-made French names for unfamiliar natural features; *bayou, butte, crevasse, prairie* and *rapids* were among the early obstacles encountered by the French, and named by them.

There are more French words familiar to

THE 'AMERICAN' ACCENT

Two centuries of questing mobility, an urge to be moving on to better things (the "frontier spirit"), have given American English a freedom from the local and often disparate dialects characterizing the older, more static languages of Europe. The consistency of spoken American English was noticeable to a visitor within a few years of independence; nevertheless, there are differences of pronunciation which enable one American to recognize the place from which another has come. The regional dialects that have been identified in America almost all belong to those regions first colonized, from New England to the southern states, with transitional zones between. For the rest, the term "General American" is applied to cover the speech of about two-thirds of the country. Great cities are almost linguistic laws to themselves as a result of being the magnets for the mass immigrations of the nineteenth and early twentieth centuries.

In search of Utopia: the first colonists from England arrive in America, depicted in this highly romanticized painting *Landing of the Pilgrim Fathers* by G. H. Boughton (1869). Between 1620 and 1640, 200 ships, with 15,000 immigrants, arrived in New England. They spoke the Elizabethan English of Shakespeare, their accents in the main those of the English East Midlands, London and the West Country.

millions of Americans to whom buttes and bayous are simply words rather than observed landscape features. The cent and dime (from the French *dixieme* "tenth") are both French borrowings, although the dollar has travelled a greater distance. It is the Anglicized form of the German *thaler*, first cast from silver mined in Joachimsthal, in the Erzgebirge. Latterly, the French suffix *-ee* has been put to work. Paying no heed to its accent or essentially feminine nature (the masculine form should be é, as in *fiancé*), Americans have tacked it on to whatever word appears to need it. *Draftees, retirees, divorcees* and *trainees*, a mixed bag if ever there was one, can be either male or female and most have found acceptance in the English of the British Isles.

The Spanish borrowings are greater in number than those from the native American tongues or from French but also all belong to the landscape of the south-western states, for long a part of the Spanish-speaking world, or to the cowboy culture *(see page 96).* There are so many of these that the survival of the word "cowboy," instead of the Spanish *vaquero*, is a little surprising. His *poncho*, originally a military cloak in old Spain, is a straightforward acquisition, but the ten-gallon hat is a curious distortion. It derives from the Spanish *galón*, the "braid" with which the Spanish decorated their headgear. In English, the extra "l" turned the hat into an improbable liquid measure.

If the French and Spanish spoke a language of wide open spaces, a domestic warmness was brought to American English by Dutch settlers. Their *cookies, coleslaw* and *waffles* are as much a part of the American table as the *canyon* and *butte* are part of its western landscape, and far more widely used on a daily basis. The same is true of other Dutch-derived words; the Dutch *baas* is the boss, wherever he is found, and *dumb dope* and *poppycock* (particularly the latter) are as much part of English in England as they are in the more gentle forms of American invective.

The *wurst* had yet to come to the table with the Germans who arrived in America in increasing numbers during the eighteenth and nineteenth centuries. They brought with them *sauerkraut, noodles, pretzels* and the black bread of Westphalia, *pumpernickel. Bums* and *loafers* appeared, whatever their nationality, acquiring a German appellation. The *hamburger* and *frankfurter* carry their places of origin like a national flag. Scandinavians, Italians and Chinese have added to the culinary vocabulary of America with *smorgasbord*, infinite disguises for *pasta*, and *chow* generally, including *chop suey*.

Less *conspicuous* are the words that arrived in the holds of slave ships. Words like *jazz, gumbo* and *voodoo* are among the better-known, but it has lately become established that popular expressions such as *do your own thing, be with it,* and *bad mouth* "to abuse, generally behind the subject's back," are literal translations from African language for use by whites who are *hip,* from the African *hipikat* a "with it" person.

The list of words absorbed from other languages by American English and still in use is not great: fewer than fifty from French, about eighty from Spanish, thirty or so from Dutch and another fifty from German. Their influence, however, is far greater than their numbers would indicate; the simple French word *prairie* "meadow" or "grassland" has been incorporated into scores of compounds from *prairie dog* to *prairie schooner*, the last an all-American word that first occurred on the New England coast in the early eighteenth century.

The list of loanwords and their by-products in American English is all but endless, but the English language on to which they have been grafted was replete with borrowings from other languages long before it took root in America. It was already accustomed to the phenomenon and knew how to benefit from it.

The English have traditionally been highly critical of American speech, but visitors to the former colony in the decades following independence were already noticing a remarkable consistency of accent and freedom from regional dialects. "We hear nothing so bad in America as the Suffolk whine, the Yorkshire clipping or the Newcastle guttural," wrote an English traveller in the 1820s.

Noah Webster

American English found its own great lexicographer in Noah Webster (1758–1843). A patriot through and through, he wrote, "As an independent nation, our honor requires us to have a system of our own, in language as well as in government. Great Britain, whose children we are, should no longer be our standard; for the taste of our writers is already corrupted and her language on the decline. . . she is at too great a distance to be our model and to instruct us in the principles of our own tongue." Webster's first successful publication was entitled *The American Spelling Book* (1783), which was reprinted many times over; in 100 years, more than eighty million copies were sold. The characteristic American spellings of words like *color, favor, theater, center* did not at first appeal to him, but by the time his great *American Dictionary of the English Language* (1828) appeared he had been won round; in his dictionary old words like *musick* and *physick* have dropped their *k*, *-re* endings have become *-er*, *cheque* and *risque* have lost their Gallic flavo(u)r to become *check* and *risk*. Many today might argue with him about whether "English" English has become more corrupted than American, but it has accepted some of his innovations.

There were and still are major differences in accent, but the Bostonian will find it easier to communicate with his counterpart in Atlanta, Georgia, than a Londoner will with a Glaswegian with only a third of the distance intervening. This homogeneity in speech is known to the television generation of philologists as Network Standard, but it has its origins in the seventeenth century.

The first shiploads of settlers from England spoke a variety of regional dialects but in the New World they were obliged to live and talk as neighbors. Pennsylvania was particularly cosmopolitan, with Quakers from all parts of England sharing the land with Scots, Welsh and Germans. When the push westward began, dialects which were already under pressure became the more confused as one wave of settlers broke upon another and mingled with it. Regional expressions inevitably developed but in such a mobile society they rarely had the opportunity to take root. Today a few isolated areas maintain distinct regional dialects but elsewhere something like Network Standard prevails.

Even where different expressions exist for the same thing (the Elizabethan *turnpike* in New England, the *thruway* in New York, the *freeway* in California) the regional distinction is often forgotten and the terms used interchangeably.

The English travellers who remarked on the uniformity of American speech frequently noticed that Americans were using words,

CONTINUED ON PAGE 147

FIRST AND LATER AMERICANS

The arrival in America of Europeans blanketed the entire continent with their languages. Those of the native Americans, north and south, were of a number and complexity that may never be resolved – huge distances over which to spread, vast plains and mountains, rivers forests and jungles fragmented ancient speech families into thousands of different languages. Many have survived but far more became extinct.

The French

Jacques Cartier, a *maître-pilote* of St Malo, was the founding father of French fortunes in North America. After a first trip to the mouth of the St Lawrence (1534), his second voyage (1535–36) led to the foundation of French Canada. Later, intrepid Frenchmen carried French influence through the Middle West to the Mississippi delta (1682), where the

Blackfoot

Cree

Iroquois (Mohawk, Cherokee)

Cheyenne

Dakota Sioux

Navajo, Apache

Creek, Seminole

Pre-Columban Americans

The Amerindians arrived from Asia between 10,000 and 20,000 years ago, crossing a land bridge where the Bering Strait now separates the two continents. They were Mongoloid, probably hunters (the bison followed the same route from Asia to America). In small family groups they spread south. At the dawn of the modern era the population of the whole continent was about four-and-a-half million – a seventh of the population of Europe at that time. When the Spanish arrived it was three times larger, concentrated in the Aztec and Inca empires of Mexico and Peru. The number of languages once spoken in South America may have run into thousands, many of them becoming extinct, with their speakers, before records began. No more than 600 have any record, and many of these have now vanished.

North American tribes

North America possessed no equivalent to the Aztec and Inca empires; only a million people, about seven per cent of the whole, lived in the north. Those in the more populous east – natives with whom the first North European settlers came into contact – had adopted a semi-agricultural way of life, while the scattered tribes of the west pursued the old nomadic life. Tribes such as the Comanche had no more than a few thousand members, but their hunting territories were larger than the British Isles. There were families of tribal languages, often greatly dispersed. The Athabascan family includes some languages spoken in north-western Canada as well as the Navajo and Apache of New Mexico and Arizona; the Algonkian family includes the languages of the Wyoming Cheyenne and the Seminole of the south-eastern states.

The Spanish

First to explore America north of the Rio Grande, the Spanish found it less than enchanting. Adventurers like de Soto and Coronado ranged through what are now the southern states, seeking gold but finding none. Spanish settlement, from the Mississippi to the Pacific, began in earnest in the eighteenth century, establishing the "hacienda culture" encountered by French and Anglo-Saxon pioneers as they moved west. By 1850, the Hispanic territories in the north had fallen to the United States, but Spanish kept its grip on the map. Throughout the south and west, placenames recall Spanish Franciscan missions which provided the first European contacts for many of the natives. The "Village of the Queen of the Angels" (Los Angeles) and the "Mission of the Sorrows of St Francis" (San Francisco) are now of global fame.

Sieur de la Salle claimed the whole of the Mississippi valley for France, naming it Louisiana. France ceded its interests in Canada to the British (1763), and in 1803 sold the huge Louisiana territory to the young United States (the "Louisiana Purchase"). Like the Spanish, the French left their footprints in placenames, some topographical (Detroit "strait," Vermont "green mountain"), others recalling French homelands.

The British

The first English colony was set up on the Atlantic seaboard at Jamestown, Virginia (1607); the New England settlements followed (1620) and by the end of the seventeenth century all the coastal provinces from Maine to Georgia were British. A brief Dutch presence, during which they bought Manhattan Island and named it New Amsterdam (1624), came to an end when it was seized by the British (1664) and renamed New York. When the first census (1790) was taken by the United States, the population was four million, all but ten per cent of British stock. The British presence in Canada compared with that of the French until the War of Independence, when Loyalists from the new republic moved north. By 1800, English speakers were as numerous as the French, and, in time, the British came to dominance.

The great migrations

The nineteenth and early twentieth centuries transformed America's ethnic appearance. One-and-a-half million Germans arrived to give their own color (and beer) to cities like Cincinnati and Milwaukee, and as many Irish came to the eastern cities. (The mass Irish immigration followed an almost apocalyptic famine in Ireland caused by the failure of the potato crop and shameful British maladministration.) More than a million Scandinavians brought their way of life to the upper Mississippi. The flood reached its peak in the first decades of the twentieth century, with most new arrivals coming from southern Europe (particularly Italy), the old Austro-Hungarian lands of the Hapsburgs, and the Baltic and Slavonic countries of eastern Europe. The adoption of English was the first priority of the newcomers, each providing fresh color to the language of the first colonists.

meanings and pronunciations that had gone out of date in England many years earlier. The American season of the fall was traditional English usage in Shakespeare's time, but replaced by the Latin-derived "autumn." Playing cards still form a *deck* in America, having become a "pack" in English. "Mad" to an Englishman means insane but to an American it indicates *anger* as well, a meaning familiar to the Elizabethans. Chaucer would have understood the manner in which an American says "I guess," but the English scarcely ever use the expression.

Even more striking is the past participle of the verb "to get." *Gotten* which has not been used in England for the past 300 years, is still part of standard American speech. The conservative tendencies are even more apparent in accent; the short *a* (as in "hat"), used by Americans in *dance* and *bath*, is closer to Elizabethan speech than the broader sound now favored in standard English, like the *r* emphasized by Americans after a vowel, as in *third* or *are*.

For the most part, the conservative tendencies of American speech are concealed by the ebullient and often ingenious modern uses, what H. L. Mencken called "the national fancy for the terse, the vivid and above all, the bold and imaginative."

Modern American English is the prodigal son of Standard English. It says unforgivable things and is quickly forgiven. The Englishman may wince at each new Americanism but within a few years he is using it at the dinner table. He is participating in a process that is as old as language itself. The speech of the first

settlers was no archaic, unchanged mode but a lively and youthful language, which had only lately survived and absorbed the impact of Norman French upon the peasant Anglo-Saxon tongue. It was equipped to encourage an inventive attitude among those who used it.

The jumble of languages spoken by immigrants was a fertile source of inspiration, if not confusion. The ability of the common man to make himself heard placed his slang, invectives and malapropisms on an equal footing with the "correct" language of the cultivated. Creating new words from old is one of the most basic ways of changing the language. The English do the same thing, but the Americans do it faster. Nouns quickly become adjectives and verbs; why *take a vacation* when you can simply *vacation* or run something over with a steam-roller when you can *steamroller* it? The heavyweight machinery is not, however, needed, to "steamroller" other people's arguments in favor of one's own.

The readiness of English, like its Germanic relatives, to form compounds created by joining together words or parts of words, has been a favorite of American English. One American dictionary listed more than 100 compounds beginning with the word *yellow* from *yellow jacket* "a wasp" to *yellow-bellied sapsucker* "a woodpecker." This simple system of word building is condensed to include blend or portmanteau words: *motel* puts together *mo*tor and ho*tel*, and *telecast* a *tele*vision broad*cast*.

American English is not a moderate language. The fireside tales of frontier folklore demanded their own vocabulary. Words like *ripsnitious, absquatulate* and *flusticated* have not

survived although others like *ripsnorting*, attributed to Davy Crockett, have made a home in the English of England. *Super* attached to the front of any word gives it a status it frequently does not deserve, and public performers marginally better known than their contemporaries are called *superstars*, until superseded by *megastars*.

The tendency to use big words has been encouraged by an urge for gentility in some quarters of American society. Dirt, along with death, age and depression has been swept under the carpet of euphemism. Thus a *coffin* becomes a gruesomely elegant "casket" and the undertaker responsible for its provision a mortician; old people shed the stigma of senility to become *senior citizens*.

Alongside this vocabulary of elegant self-deception is a robust and vivid common talk, what H. L. Mencken called American Vulgate, arguing that ordinary American expressions — *rubberneck, rough house, has-been* and *lame duck*

City of hope: New York's population was built on a vast flight from despair – Gaels tortured by famine and repression, Jews escaping pogrom and persecution, Italian fugitives from poverty. All sought a better life and mostly found it. Together with immigrants speaking a score of other tongues, they made New York and other great American cities the vital centers that they have become.

among others – reveal an imagery and imagination that has been lacking from the language of England since the Elizabethan age. He went so far as to suggest Americanizing the orotund Georgian prose of the Declaration of Independence; "When in the course of human events, etc., etc." became "When things get so balled up that the people of a country have to cut loose from another country and go it on its own hook…" Mencken's version might well be preferable to current State Department officialese, which would have an "emergent nation in a self-determination situation as of now" if not "at this moment in time."

It is often forgotten how many American words, completely accepted today, were once considered barbaric by the English. The verb *donate*, the adjective *reliable* and the noun *standpoint* were all bitterly opposed when they first made the transatlantic journey. And the now indispensable *scientist* was labelled "an ignoble Americanism" by the London *Daily News* as late as 1890.

American English shows no sign of flagging, to the delight of publishers whose dictionaries, once serving for decades without change, are now promoted almost as annuals, boasting "thousands of new words." New terms and idioms, and many old ones with new or changed meanings, are spread more rapidly than ever thanks to television, but many last for no longer than a scriptwriter's contract.

English in Australia

The first English speakers to arrive in any numbers in Australia did so involuntarily as convicts or their guards put ashore at the penal colony of Botany Bay in 1788. Including their guards and 188 women, they numbered fewer than 800 people. Most of these reluctant expatriates were not hardened or violent criminals in the modern sense but victims of the savage penal code of the time. Most would have been transported for offences that would have drawn no more than a minor sentence or probation today.

More transportation, much of it from troubled Ireland, swelled their numbers until it was stopped in the 1840s but, by 1850 the English-speaking population had reached half a million. In the following decade it doubled as adventurers flooded in to seek their fortunes when gold was discovered. Growth afterwards steadied. Emigrants, mostly of British stock, arrived in a steady stream, a process that has continued to the present. Australia's population today is eighteen million, with the Anglo-Saxon contribution recently modified by numbers from other, mostly southern, European countries, particularly Italy and Greece. Others have arrived from eastern Asia, adding an exotic flavor to Australia's cities.

From the beginning, the new arrivals needed new words to describe their new home and for many of them they turned to the aboriginal inhabitants of the country, a minute population of perhaps 300,000 scattered across the huge landmass, a number now vastly diminished. The extraordinary marsupial *kangaroo* jumped across the world into many lexicons other than English, although there is some doubt now as to whether it was an aboriginal word; many aboriginals appeared not to understand it.

Budgerigar was certainly borrowed from the native population, from their *budgeri* "good" and *gar* "cockatoo," as was *dingo*, the wild dog with the reported attribute of being able to run backwards. The *boomerang*, a simple but potent wooden weapon, has spread like kangaroo into dictionaries other than English where latterly it has become a verb as well, used for anything, such as an insult, that "boomerangs" or an unfounded allegation that bounces back to the discomfiture of its original user.

Much of what was new to the new Australians could be satisfactorily named by combining English words. The eucalyptus, largest of Australian trees, was first described by Captain Cook as a "gum tree" and the name has stuck. While many compounds were self-evident, like "lyrebird," "woolshed" and "sheeprun," others took on a particular Australian meaning in the nineteenth century. The "swag" or loot in English thieving vernacular lost its criminal taint in "swagman," an itinerant workman who carried his possessions in a bundle or "swag" and his food in a "tuckerbox." Many colloquial expressions developed in this way, including the self-descriptive "no-hoper" and the "brickfielder," a hot, dusty wind. New Zealanders, whose speech shares much with Australia, will immodestly refer to themselves as "God's-owners."

When an Australian speaks of "the bush" he is not referring to a small tree or shrub, but what the English would regard as forest or uncleared land; he describes a flock of sheep as "a mob" and his country farm a "station" in "the outback," terms which suggest a wider landscape than anything in Britain. Some English words disappeared altogether in the open spaces, where a stream became a "creek," a pond a "waterhole" and the valley was replaced by a "gully."

The slang of Australia is distinctive, far-reaching and, unhindered by the social barriers of the old country, used widely in everyday conversation. Racy abuse like "ratbag" crop up, although accompanied by disapproval, in parliamentary debates.

The roots of the modern Australian colloquialism arrived with the transported convicts, who brought with them a ready-made dialect of their own from the crowded streets and gaols of Britain. Their argot was known as *flash*, a commonplace term among eighteenth-century villains in England to describe themselves and their language. In *flash*, an "old hand" was an early arrival, while a newcomer was a "new chum." The argot was at first so incomprehensible to speakers of Standard English in Australia that an interpreter was sometimes needed to assist the judge in legal proceedings.

Flash began to die out as the former convicts were freed and were joined by new emigrants, to whom it was a foreign language. It had, however, provided a fertile soil in which a new and vigorous speech could proliferate, even if it did so in a pronunciation closely akin to that of southern England and to the cockney of London.

Perhaps the most remarkable recent gift of Australia to the English language is the "walkabout." Originally used to describe the habit of the native aboriginals when they vanished for weeks on end from their settlement, it is now invariably used to describe the custom, favored by politicians, royalty and other public figures, of mingling with members of the public.

The English of Scotland

The English language has been spoken in Scotland, at least in its south-eastern part, almost as long as it has in England. Anglian invaders from Northumberland captured the Celtic fortress of Din Eidyn in 638 AD, combining Celtic and Germanic elements in its new name, Edinburgh. Over subsequent centuries and turbulent relationships between the two countries, Northumbrian or northern English spread throughout the northern kingdom, erasing the Celtic Old British of the south and east and, much later, eroding the Celtic Gaelic of the Highlands and Islands.

To the present day, however, the English of Scotland retains its powerful dialect; not all Scotsmen are completely comprehensible at first hearing to a *Sassenach*, a Gaelic word meaning "Saxon" and used indiscriminately by all Scotsmen to describe the southerner. An Englishman will more easily understand an English speaker born and bred on the other side of the world, and often a foreigner who has learned English as a second language, than he will many Scotsmen.

In its own kingdom, "Scottish" flourished throughout the Middle Ages and possessed a potent literature of its own, long after the regional dialects of England had begun to wane before the influence of standard English in the south. Decline set in with the Reformation and the introduction of an English Bible and finally the Act of Union of 1707, when the two countries became one. Even so, the division between the spoken and written forms persisted and are nowhere more evident than in the poetry of Robert Burns (1759–96). In one poem, *The Cotter's Saturday Night*, the local vernacular of lines like "His wee bit ingle, blinking bonnillie . . ." appear alongside others, "Princes and lords are but the breath of kings," which could have been written by one of his Georgian contemporaries in London.

Scottish borrowings, apart from those which travelled into the language from England, have been frequent throughout the history of the country, particularly from French. Burns' "Silver tassie" is the French *tasse* "cup" and a "doit," something small or worthless, is a borrowing from a Dutch small coin; "golf," also, derives from a Dutch word although the game in its modern form is a Scottish invention as are many of its universal terms like "tee" and "stymie" which began on Scottish "links" (an early Scandinavian acquisition) describing coarse coastal grassland. "Hogmanay," the Scottish New Year's Eve, has its origin in the French Picard *aguillaneuf*, a children's begging song sung on the night.

English in turn has benefited richly from the Scottish vocabulary. "Wraith" and "gruesome," "feckless" and "stalwart," "rampage" and "uncanny," "cosy" and "blackmail" are all words of Scottish origin which have made the journey into English, often through the novels of Walter Scott and other authors aware of the rich and colorful nature of the old "Inglis" dialect of the border reivers.

CHAPTER EIGHT

The Slavonic languages

The various Slavonic languages that now dominate eastern Europe, and much of Asia, did not erupt violently onto the linguistic map. Unlike the Latins and the Germanic tribes, the Slavs did not introduce their tongues to new lands by imperial conquest or spectacular migration; they simply multiplied and spread.

Their exact whereabouts, when they first attracted attention in the first century AD, is still open to some debate, but a light is shed on their prehistory by those known to have been their neighbors, the Balts and the Iranians. A certain amount of religious vocabulary, which has survived in such forms as the modern Russian *Bog* "God" and *mir* "peace" or "world," was borrowed from the Iranians, who, as the Scythians, once ranged through southern Russia. The quietly flowing River Don takes its name from the Ossetic Iranian *don*, which means simply "river" and is an element also in *Dniester, Dnieper* and *Danube*.

More significant, however, are the parallels in basic vocabulary between Slavonic and the Baltic languages, Lithuanian and Latvian. These are most striking in the names of animals, trees and parts of the body. The Slavs certainly enjoyed a long coexistence with the Baltic peoples, although the two groups of languages were not necessarily the immediate offspring of

a common parent. Lithuanian and Latvian are extremely conservative, retaining features of the original Indo-European language that have disappeared from the Slavonic languages.

Given this linguistic evidence of their prehistoric contact with the Baltic tribes and the Iranians, there is little reason to suppose that the Slavs had ever wandered far outside the area from which they eventually emerged to populate eastern Europe. This lay between the River Vistula and the middle reaches of the River Dnieper. The insalubrious climate of the Pripet marshes must have kept their numbers in check, for once they began to move, they increased at an astonishing rate. At first, Slavic expansion was restricted by the eastward migrations of the Goths, then by the onslaught of the Huns in the opposite direction, but, in the fifth century, the downfall of the kingdom of Attila and the mass transfer of Germanic tribes into the territories of the crumbling Roman Empire left vast underpopulated areas with no effective political organization. Into these areas the Slavs spread, not as warriors in search of an empire (there are no early Slavonic words for king, prince or emperor), but as peaceful farmers, whose principal social unit and world was the village, *mir* serving for both "world" and "village," and, probably significantly, also for "peace." It is easy to see how medieval Latin equated the words *Slav* and *sclavus* "slave."

Contact with western civilization was made chiefly through the Germanic peoples that had not left their homelands; *lyudi* in modern Russian is the German *Leute* "people, folk," while another word for people *Volk* gave *polk*, which now means a regiment of soldiers.

THE SLAVONIC FAMILY		
Russian	Wendish	Serbo-Croat
Ukrainian	Sorbian	Slovenian
Belarusian	Czech	Bulgarian
Polish	Slovak	Macedonian

Slav and Tartar, Chechen and Kazakh give Moscow as cosmopolitan a complexion as New York. The hub and capital of a still-huge empire, Moscow was founded 850 years ago as the principal city of Muscovy and, in the fifteenth century, of "All the Russias."

German methods of agriculture were superior to those of the Slavs; the Germanic *plug* with a metal ploughshare replaced the old wooden plough of the immigrants. The Slavs even borrowed a word for bread *chleb*, which is the modern German *Laib* and English "loaf," while through German from Latin they were introduced to *vino*. *Vinograd* is not a holiday resort for alcoholics; *grad* was originally the same word as the English "yard." Although it once meant vineyard, *vinograd* is now Russian for "vine." Another more surprising loan that seems to date from this early period is *tserkov* a "church," cognate with German *Kirche*. The Slavic settlers quickly advanced to many points

beyond the Elbe (*Leipzig*, for example, was *Lipsk*, from *lipa* "lime-tree"), but in the reign of Charlemagne the Germans decided that these intruders were no longer welcome and the tide of migration turned. As the Germans pushed westwards, a few enclaves of Slavonic speakers were left behind, the Polabians, who lived on the banks of the Elbe until the eighteenth century, and the Lusatians, known also as Sorbs and Wends (the usual German name for Slavs), who survive to this day around the towns of Cuttbus and Bautzen in East Germany. The group of languages, known today as Western Slavonic, comprises Lusatian, Kashubian (spoken in northern Poland to the west of the

St Cyril (capped) and fellow saints. He and his brother Methodius, "The apostles of the Slavs," were Macedonian Greeks who adopted the common Slavonic language. Old Church Slavonic became the literary medium for the spiritual realms of the Orthodox Church, adopting the role for Slavonic languages that Latin played for the Romance languages of the west.

Vistula), Polish, Czech and Slovak. The colonization of Bohemia, Moravia and Slovakia met with very little resistance, but there too the Slavs were subsequently to feel the pressure of the German quest for *Lebensraum*.

The eastern Slavs, ancestors of today's Russians, Belarusians and Ukrainians, settled the land as far as Moscow in the east and Novgorod in the north. They did not venture far beyond these points, because the grassy and arid steppes were the undisputed domain of the Turkic-Tatar horsemen, and, in the forests of the north, Finnic tribes led a life of fishing and hunting that was equally alien to a settled agricultural people. The third major movement of the Slavs was southwards into the Balkans; Slovenes, Croatians and Serbs colonizing what eventually became Yugoslavia (*jug* is Serbo-Croat for "south"), and another group to the east descending the Black Sea coast as far as Macedonia. It was here that contact with the Byzantine Empire shaped the future religion and culture of much of eastern Europe. This process began in Bulgaria, the first Slav state to be organized politically along the lines of feudal Christian Europe. The Bulgars themselves were a Turkic people from the Volga, but the land where they carved out their second empire was so thickly populated with Slavs that their own language did not survive. The great achievement of tenth-century Bulgaria was the translation of religious texts from Greek into a form of Slavonic, sometimes called Old Bulgarian, but more accurately described as Old Church Slavonic. The man who made this possible was St Cyril.

St Cyril and his brother St Methodius were Greeks from Thessalonika, who had learned the language of the local Macedonian Slavs. In 862 their linguistic abilities qualified them for a mission to far-off Moravia, for which purpose Cyril is said to have devised a system for recording the sounds of Slavonic, using the Greek alphabet wherever possible and, where this did not suffice, his own whim and genius. What Cyril created was not the Cyrillic alphabet at all, but the earlier Glagolitic (from *glagolu*, Old Slavonic for "word"). This was based on the Greek miniscule script, whereas Cyrillic was derived from the clearer uncial. In the end the mission to Moravia was not a success. After Cyril's death, Methodius aroused the hostility of the German bishops and was imprisoned for two years, but the example of the two "Apostles to the Slavs" was the origin of the written languages of Serbia, Macedonia, Bulgaria and, above all, Russia. Since the Slavs had spoken a common language but a few centuries before, Old Church Slavonic could be understood over the whole vast area they had recently occupied. At first it had a distinctly Macedonian/Bulgarian flavor but, as time went by, it took on characteristics of the languages of the various countries where it was used, in much the same way as the writing and pronunciation of medieval Latin varied from country to country in the Romance-speaking world.

The role of Old Church Slavonic in the diffusion of eastern Orthodoxy mirrored exactly that of Latin in maintaining the unity of the Church of Rome. Latin by now was already a dead language, but, not to be outdone, Old Church Slavonic died more or less the moment it was born. It artificially filled the need for a religious and literary tradition that the Slavs did not possess. In this capacity, it furnished the living languages with a model for future development in their syntax, grammar and vocabulary. Through the translation of the Bible and other Christian works, a great number of Greek words and Latinisms that had entered ecclesiastical Greek were transferred to the common lexicon of the Slavonic world. Obvious examples in Russian are *episkop, ikona, lampada* (the lamp that lit the icon), *ladan* "incense," from Greek *ladanon*, the mastic tree, cultivated for its perfumed resin, and *melodiya*. They also gained abstract concepts like *istoriya* and *filosofiya*. The presence of such words has enabled neologisms of the scientific age to be assimilated with very little difficulty.

The schism between the eastern and western forms of Christianity caused a conspicuous division of the Slavonic languages into those that use the Cyrillic alphabet and those that use the Roman. Although the influence of Byzantium reached the Czechs of Moravia and even the Poles, the western Slavs were pulled into the orbit of Rome, as were the Slovenes and Croats. Serbo-Croat exists in two written forms, the Cyrillic of the Orthodox Serbs and the Roman used by Catholic Slovenes and Croats. Cyrillic has, on the whole, lost ground to the more widespread Latin alphabet, notably in Romania, which adopted the Roman form during the nineteenth century. In the constituent republics of the former USSR Cyrillic extended its realms to provide a means of writing for Turkic and other Asiatic languages.

THE CYRILLIC ALPHABET

The uncial or "curved" Greek alphabet of the ninth century AD provided the model on which the Cyrillic alphabet, national script of the Russians and some other Slavs, is based. It was devised by the eponymous St Cyril from the Orthodox Church of Byzantium – he and his brother Methodius were known as "The Apostles of the Slavs.." Cyrillic enabled the written form of the Slavonic languages to represent a greater variety of sounds better than either the Greek or the Roman alphabets. It came to be adopted wherever the Christianity of the Orthodox Church took root in Russia, Ukraine, Bulgaria and Serbia. Among Slavonic languages which retained the Roman alphabet, Czech acquired diacritics ("accents") to embrace the additional phonetic values of Slavonic. They were introduced by Jan Hus (1367–1415) and later spread to other languages. Russian Christianity dates from the Ukrainian/Viking Prince Vladimir of Kiev (*c.* 956–1015). A violent and colorful figure, Vladimir carried out "market research" before choosing the Eastern Orthodox Church.

А а	Б б	В в
a as in father, but shorter	b as in back	v as in victor
Г г	Д д	Е е
g as in goat	d as in dig	ye as in yet
Ё ё	Ж ж	З з
yo as in yonder	zh s as in measure	z as in zoo
И и	Й й	К к
ee as in feet	y as in boy	k as in kite

Л л — l as in bottle

М м — m as in master

Н н — n as in now

О о — o as in for

П п — p as in peach

Р р — r as in rat

С с — s as in sat

Т т — t as in tired

У у — oo as in boot

Ф ф — f as in feather

Х х — ch as in (Scots) loch

Ц ц — ts as in bits

Ч ч — ch as in church

Ш ш — sh as in shirt

Щ щ — shch as in posh children

Ы ы — y as in physics

Э э — e as in let

Ю ю — yu as in yule

Я я — ya as in yak

THE THREE RUSSIANS

The language known to most people simply as "Russian" is usually referred to by linguists as "Great Russian." The epithet, although still appropriate in the post-Tsarist age, is now used chiefly to distinguish it from other varieties of Russian: Belarusian (White Russian) and Little Russian, better known as Ukrainian.

The three together make up the eastern branch of the Slavonic family and are so closely related that many prefer to consider them dialects of the same language. This they undoubtedly were throughout the Middle Ages and, even today, speakers of the three "Russians" understand each other with little difficulty. Since the break-up of the Soviet Union, both Belarus and Ukraine have asserted their independence by defining their languages as Belarusian and Ukrainian. Great "Moscow" Russian remains in use, as it does in other former Soviet republics which make up the Commonwealth of Independent States.

Great Russian evolved from the dialect of the Muscovite principality of the late Middle Ages, but Moscow was not the first great capital of a Russian state. In the ninth century, this honor belonged to Kiev, strategically placed on the Dnieper, the most important of the rivers that were Old Russia's principal means of communication. The first people to exploit the rivers fully for the purposes of trade were not the Russians but the Varangians, Norse Vikings who sailed their longships (and carried them where necessary past rapids and narrows) down a hazardous system of waterways to the Black Sea and Byzantium.

Although tradition has it that the dynasty of the Grand Princes of Kiev was founded by

THE SLAVONIC FAMILY

With Italic and Germanic, Slavonic is one of three dominant language groups in Europe. Separated from a heartland in western Russia/Ukraine by Scythian tribes, Slavonic speakers expanded during the early centuries AD, westward to the Elbe, northward at the expense of Finnic tribes, south-west into the Balkans, and eastward and south-east to the Volga and the Black Sea. From the common tongue came the modern Slavonic languages: an eastern branch, the "Three Russians," Russian, Belarusian and Ukrainian; a western branch, Polish, Czech and Slovak; and (ultimately cut off by the Magyar invasion of the Danube plain) a southern branch, now Slovene, Serbo-Croat, Macedonian and Bulgarian. The expansion of Great Russian across northern Asia was the result of much later Tsarist imperial conquest.

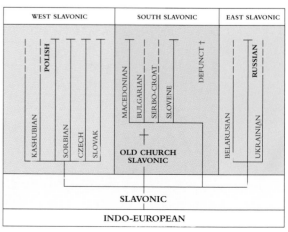

Rurik, a Dane from Jutland, Soviet historians play down the role of the alien Vikings in the foundation of Russia, assigning to them the role of nautical advisers and bodyguards. Nevertheless, the earliest form of the word Russia *Rus* is thought to share a common source with the Finnish *Ruotsi* "Sweden." Old Russian texts reveal a sprinkling of Norse loan-words related to navigation but *yakor* "anchor" is the only one in common use today. A more sinister legacy of the Varangians was the *knut* "knout," the notorious whip used for flogging criminals. The Old Norse form *knutr* survives in Icelandic.

The first mention of the state of Rus is in a trading agreement between the Byzantines and Oleg, Prince of Kiev, at the beginning of the tenth century, although the terms of the treaty have come down only in a later copy of an already much later chronicle. The goods transported from the Baltic and the forests of the north included amber, wax and furs. *Sobol*, one of the most prized of pelts, passed into medieval Latin as *sabelum*, giving French and English "sable."

As communications with the Byzantines increased, missionaries, following the example of St Cyril's preaching to the Slavs, reached Kiev in greater numbers. Their triumph came in 988 AD when Prince Vladimir was converted to the Orthodox faith and in the following century, with the introduction of monasticism, Christianity took firm hold of the Russian soul. There were soon seventeen monasteries in Kiev alone, where the principal occupation of the monks was the translation and copying of religious works. As no written form of the local speech existed, the language used was Old Church Slavonic, but many monks had no way of knowing what sounds some of the Cyrillic letters represented, so in reading aloud they would use Russian forms rather than Old Slavonic, a tendency compounded by the errors of later copyists. At the same time the influence of the language of worship on the devout Russians was immense, and over the centuries Russian has borrowed from Church Slavonic as freely as the Romance languages have borrowed from the Latin.

The East Slavs had now been separated from their western and southern fellows long enough for their language to have diverged in a number of ways, but the first major changes were in pronunciation. The sounds *l* and *r* in combination with a vowel were particularly unstable in Slavonic languages. An example is shown by the Germanic name Karl, which after Charlemagne became the Slavs' generic word for "king." In Polish it emerged as *krol*, in Czechoslovakian *kral*, while in Russian it is *korol*. The same process with *l* allows the word "milk" to be recognized in *miloko*, the two words being descended from the common European stock.

Gorod (as in Novgorod) means "town," *grad* (as in Leningrad) means "city" but the two are really the same word, doublets like *chose* and *cause* in French. As the Russian vocabulary stabilized, the Russian word kept its primary meaning while its Slavonic counterpart took on a general or metaphoric sense; thus *golova* means head while *glava* means "chapter" or "head" in the sense of "chief."

Twelfth-century manuscripts, the lives of

saints and chronicles of the early history of Kiev, take on more of a Russian character but writing was still dominated by ecclesiastical Slavonic. The flourishing cultural tradition was now faced with the crudest and most violent of interruptions, the invasion of the Mongols, which began in 1237. The Mongol-Tatar "Golden Horde" held Russia in thrall for two

centuries, destroying the power and influence of Kiev. While the eastern lands paid tribute to the Mongols, large areas of White Russia and the Ukraine fell beneath the rule of the expanding Lithuanian kingdom. It was during this violent period that the three branches of eastern Slavonic began to drift apart.

Later, when Poland and Lithuania united in

A fantasy in architecture, the cathedral of St Basil, Patriarch of the Eastern Orthodox Church, in the heart of Moscow. Basil founded eastern monasticism; his followers carried Christianity and the language of Old Church Slavonic into an area greater than the rest of Europe.

the sixteenth century, Ukrainian and Belarusian absorbed a considerable amount of the Polish vocabulary but for the moment the individuality of the languages, discernible in the oral tradition of folk songs and tales, was not reflected to any great extent in writing, for this remained altogether the province of the monks. As might be expected in troubled times, monasteries flourished throughout Russia.

It was the city of Moscow that gained most advantage from this period of adversity, its prestige increasing enormously when the principal archiepiscopal see was transferred there from Kiev. When the "Mongol Yoke" was finally thrown off at the end of the fifteenth century, the glory and the territorial spoils fell to the Muscovite Grand Prince, Ivan III.

The Turkic-Tatar language of the Mongols never had any great influence on Russian but at various times a number of words were borrowed from the Turkic-speaking nomads of central Asia. These usually refer to their opportunistic way of life on the open *steppe* (a word purely Russian in origin). Turkic words that Russian has transmitted to the west usually have fairly bloodcurdling connotations: Cossack, from *Kazak*, which originally applied to any kind of lawless freebooter and, less obviously, "horde." This word reached Europe by way of the Polish form *horda* rather than the Russian *orda*. Russian itself has borrowed and retained other less formidable words, including those for "horse" and "ass," *loshad* and *ishak*.

As the threat from the Asiatic hordes receded, their place was taken by the Cossacks, adventurers who adopted the lifestyle of the

former enemies of Russia. It was their allegiance, particularly of those who lived in the region of the River Don, that enabled the small principality of Moscow to expand to the south and east, laying the foundations of its future empire. The first ruler to be given officially the title of *tsar* was Ivan IV "The Terrible" who promptly did his best to discredit the name of *Caesar*, borrowed by the early Slavs from the German *Kaiser*.

The seventeenth century saw vast social changes in Russia, the establishment of serfdom, the growth of trade with the west and the end of the primacy of the monasteries as custodians of culture. A new administrative and commercial language appeared, the property of the rising middle class, far more colloquial in style than any contemporary literature, which still smacked of archaic Slavonicism. The recognition that there were two written forms of Russian finally led to the adoption in 1708, by decree of Peter the Great, of a new "civil alphabet." One of Peter's many reforms aimed at modernizing his country; the alphabet was still fairly conservative, but it lasted until the downfall of the Romanovs, being brought up to date after the Revolution of 1917.

The modernization of Russia is clearly reflected in the plethora of new words reaching the language, first by way of trade through Poland and Germany, then through deliberate borrowing from German, Dutch, English and, above all, French. To the first category belong German words like *yarmarka* "fair," from *Jahrmarkt*, and *passazhir* from *Passagier* "passenger." Travel for the purpose of pleasure or instruction was still a novelty when Peter himself visited England and Holland to study possible models for a Russian navy, because he needed to hold the Sea of Azov from the Crimean Tatars. In addition to the technical knowledge and methods of organization he borrowed, Russian sailors have inherited an extraordinary selection of foreign nautical vocabulary. *"Rul"* from Dutch *roer* a "rudder," seems a reasonable acquisition, but the English loans include such oddities as *gondek* "gun-deck," and *michman* from "midshipman." In the modern Russian Navy a *michman* is a warrant officer. Even more fantastic is the history of the "pea-jacket" worn by English sailors, and the *piijakker* of the Dutch mariner. Seafarers have always been notable bearers of useful terms; the first western ship to anchor in the St Petersburg roads after the city was founded by Peter the Great was a Dutchman, the second was English. Today, not only does every Russian sailor have his *pidzhak*, every man in Russia has one; it has become the everyday word for "jacket."

Western fashions in dress, furnishings and food must have seemed monstrous to many conservative Russians, so perhaps it is not surprising that they kept their outlandish names. Civilization at that time was judged to have reached its highest point in France, so the aristocrat in eighteenth-century St Petersburg wore a *pal'to* (from *paletot* "overcoat"), or a *syurtuk* ("frock-coat," from *surtout*) and would dine off a *serviz* beneath a *lyustra* ("chandelier," from *lustre*). After starting with *sup*, he might finish the meal with *plombir*, a dish of ice-cream and crystallized fruit, its name derived from the French spa of *Plombières*. *Polites*

decreed that he should pay a lady a *kompliment*, but do nothing to damage her *reputatsiya*. All these examples have remained in the language, but in the second half of the century, when fashion had convinced many Russians that their own language was some kind of aberration, Gallomania reached absurd proportions.

In the end, the effect of all this borrowing was negligible. Foreign nouns were assimilated and soon sprouted native prefixes and suffixes. Simple examples of the use of the most familiar Russian suffix *-nik* illustrate the process. The word *klass* has produced many offspring, including *odnoklassnik* "classmate," while *kofe* (borrowed from English) is poured naturally from a *kofeinik*. Russian has never refused a useful loanword: reaction to the Francophiles was directed more against their wholesale translation of idiomatic French phrases. When the language of the ruling classes was subject to these excesses of fashion, it is small wonder that eighteenth-century writers failed to create a language that could serve as a literary standard for posterity. Fortunately, the Napoleonic Wars, which caused people to view France in a very different light, coincided with a movement that was rediscovering the popular idiom of Russian as preserved in its rich folk-tradition. National pride was extended to incorporate pride in a national language to rival that of any other European country. The successful fusion of two traditions, the Old Slavonic and the popular Russian, had taken a long time, but the great writers of the nineteenth century, in particular the novelists, managed in a very short time to create a splendid literary heritage.

The last of the Tsars: Nicholas II and his Tsarina Alexandra. Divorced from the condition of his subjects by a ruling class for whom the language of prestige

was French rather than "barbarous" Russian, the last Tsar and his family were put to death at Ekaterinburg (now Sverdlovsk) in 1918.

Ukrainian and Belarusian

The nineteenth century was also marked by a flourishing of Ukrainian literature in "Little Russian." After the first partition of Poland in 1772, the majority of Ukrainians found themselves subjects of the Tsar, but in the mid-nineteenth century the spirit of independence in their writings provoked repressive measures against the language. First its use in schools was forbidden, then in 1876 all works printed in the new language were banned. Nevertheless it continued to thrive in Galicia, the Austrian portion in the division of Poland, which had a large population of Ukrainian-speakers.

Compared to Russian, Ukrainian preserves very few Old Slavonic forms, being based largely on popular oral tradition. One word that has gained international currency, and is Ukrainian in origin rather than Great Russian, is *caviar*, in fact a Turkic word supplied by the nomads of the southern Ukraine. The feelings of the Belarusians and White Russians towards the Tsar were very similar to those of the Ukrainians, but they did not proclaim their independence through their language until the beginning of this century.

Once Russian had come of age in the last century, discovering the richness and subtle nuances of its own vocabulary, it had nothing more to fear from excessive foreign influence. If, therefore, a name is needed for some new invention, Russian does not bother to construct a compound word from its own roots in the manner of German, even though it has the means to do this. Thus, the modern farmer drives a *kombain* or a *traktor*, the pilot flies an *aeroplan* (now *samolyot*), the soldier fights from a *tank*, the typist uses a *mashinka* and everybody watches a *televizor*. Occasionally words borrowed from the west are not so easily recognized – one curious example from the last century being the Russian for "railway station" *vokzal*, said to derive from the London district of Vauxhall.

Words that western Europe has accepted in return for these loans are predictably few, usually describing objects that belong specifically to Russian culture, like *samovar* or *troika*. One exception, in that the word has taken on a new function, particularly in English, is *mammoth*, although the original loan belongs to the seventeenth century, when the defrosted bones of the beasts first attracted scientific curiosity.

The only words to have caught the world's imagination on a similar scale in recent times are *Bolshevik*, *Soviet* and *Sputnik* and, most recently, *glasnost* and *perestroika,* words which introduced the break-up of a super-power. The vocabulary of political and scientific progress, and of the *intelligentsiya* in Russia is almost entirely borrowed from the Greek and Latin neologisms of French and English.

POLISH: LANGUAGE OF SOLIDARITY

Polish is the one major Slavonic language to have been heavily influenced by the languages of western Europe throughout its history. The geographical position of Poland at the westernmost edges of the Slavonic realms and the steadfast adherence of its population to the Roman Catholic faith were important factors in the strength of this influence, the latter particularly; the events of the early 1980s demonstrated just how strong the ties with the western Church remained.

While the more adventurous western Slavonic tribes such as the Wends pressed on across the north German plain, Poland was occupied by a large number of scattered tribes, inheritors of territory once occupied by the migrant Germanic Goths. It was not the friendliest area in which to settle, with extensive forests and marshes and the constant threat of raids from the Baltic people. It was the tribe that possessed the best of the environment, the *Polianie*, the "people of the plains" in the Poznan region, who were the first to make their mark on history, giving their name first to their own territory, "Great Poland," then to the area around Cracow, known as "Little Poland," and to the language of the nation that emerged.

Christianity reached Poland from Moravia in the tenth century and was the one stable factor in the fluctuating fortunes of the young nation. The most constant threats were that of being swamped by the medieval migration eastward of an expansive German peasantry seeking new lands, and the ambitions of the Order of Teutonic Knights; but all this must have seemed trivial to the Poles when their country was laid waste by the Tatars flooding out of Asia.

All writing during these hazardous times was in Latin, but the words that passed into Polish from the language of their now secure religion had a Czech-Germanic flavor; the Poles had usually learned their Latin from the Czechs, who had learned theirs from the Germans. *Kosciól* "church" and *klasztor* "cloister" or "monastery" came from Latin through Czech *kostel* and *kláster; mnich* "monk" had the same form in both Czech and Polish, and *pacierz* "prayer" is a rendering of Old Czech *pater* (from paternoster).

Direct German influence made its mark on everyday life during the later Middle Ages after the ebb of the Tatar tide. The standard small Polish coin was the *grosz* (from *Groschen*) which was used to pay "rent" *czynsz* (from *Zins*) and later to settle a bill *rachunek* (derived from the German *Rechnung*).

The German immigrants during the Middle Ages were often skilled craftsmen, and the Poles came to adopt the German *Meister* "master" as *mistrz*, and jobs for which the Poles took German names at an early date were *garbarz* "tanner" from *Gerber*, and *bednarz* "cooper" from *Binder*, as in *Fassbinder.* These were joined later by *malarz* "painter," from *Mahler.*

The Polish kingdom that flourished between the fourteenth and seventeenth centuries was highly cosmopolitan. As well as Germans there were large numbers of Jews who continued to speak Yiddish rather than adopt the language of their new country, and when Poland united with Lithuania in the

A Polish word the world has come to know – *Solidarność* "Solidarity," a Latin-based word with a Slavonic ending.

sixteenth century, many White Russians and Ukrainians became subjects of an empire that stretched to the Tatar steppes. Surprisingly, some Turkic-Tatar words have had a more fertile life in Polish than in Russian. *Bohater* "hero" (from *bahadur*) has produced offspring including *bohaterski* "heroism." The language that has had most influence on Polish was not one of these living languages, but the Latin of the Church, disseminated from Poland's great center of learning, the University of Cracow. As one Renaissance observer said, there were "more Latinists in Poland than ever there were in Latium."

The spirit of Humanism, imported from Italy, was the inspiration for the Golden Age of Polish literature in the sixteenth century. The language might have been expected to crumble under the weight of abstract Latinisms like *cyrcumstancja* and *dyferencya*, but it adapted readily to the load, incorporating many verbs as well as nouns, arriving chiefly through the all-pervading French of the seventeenth and eighteenth centuries. Being Catholic, Poland did not have the thesaurus of Church Slavonic from which to develop a native learned vocabulary. The effect produced was very similar to that of Latinisms in English. As in Russian, the frequency of borrowings from French was exaggerated, *fatygować* "to fatigue" or "tire" being an example.

The influence of Italian was felt for a time during the Renaissance, Polish importing the recently arrived "tomato" as *pomodor* (from *pomodoro*) and helping itself to *salata* at the same time. The Italian-derived *kuradent* "toothpick" proved useful to remove the tomato seeds, but most words relating to the social graces were later borrowings from French, including *bukiet* "bouquet" and many abstract concepts like *honor, fawor* and *kondolencja*.

Polish proved itself adept in providing Slavonic suffixes to form a whole group of related words from a single foreign source word, and one word that achieved world-wide celebrity in the 1980s did so through the activities of the Polish trades union, *Solidarnosc* "Solidarity," the Latin-derived word with its characteristic Slavonic ending. The suffix *-nosc* already had a distinguished history in the cultural and political movements of Poland; in the nineteenth century, when Poland had been erased from the political map of Europe, the writings of *Romantycznosc* kept alive the national identity of her people.

The troubled history of Poland in recent times has led to considerable emigration, particularly to the United States, where there are six million people of Polish descent who, among themselves, keep alive some of their old European customs. There are sizeable colonies too in France and Britain, in Canada and Brazil. The annexation by the Soviet Union of parts of eastern Poland after the Second World War left one and a half million Poles on the wrong side of the border, but the expulsion of Germans from western Poland allowed room for three million Poles, who had fled or had been deported during the war years, to return. They rebuilt their nation and re-named cities like Szczecin (Stettin) and Wroclaw (Breslau), the latter being an impossible pronunciation in

its Roman spelling for anyone but a Pole.

Trapped in a danger spot where the Germanic world overlapped with that of the Slavs, Kashubian, a group of Slavonic dialects, is still to be heard along the Baltic coast to the west of Gdynia. Once part of the Polish corridor to the sea, it has for long been influenced by German but, since 1945, has reverted to Poland and Polish for its literary language.

Wendish in Germany

The last survivors of the first great migration of Slavonic speakers to the west live in Lusatia in Germany. The few thousand remaining speak Wendish or Sorbian but conduct most of their daily business in German, and although all are bilingual, great efforts are made to preserve the language, which has a considerable literary tradition. Lusatian exists in two distinct dialects, for the "Upper" and "Lower" Lusatians have long been separated from each other by Germans. Echoing the way in which "High" and "Low" German reflect the landscape rather than any quality, Upper Lusatian or Sorbian is centerd on Bautzen in the south, and Lower Lusatian is centerd around Cottbus in the north. The language is an extremely conservative form of western Slavonic, despite its reliance on German for all new vocabulary. Its closest relation is Slovak rather than Czech (the province belonged to the Bohemian crown for 300 years), which has undergone radical changes in the course of its evolution. The Lower Lusatians refer to the Upper Lusatians as "Hajak," from *haj*, their word for "yes," a Slavonic parallel to the name *Langue d'oc.*

CZECH AND SLOVAK

The forms of western Slavonic in the Czech Republic and Slovakia have so much in common that, during the brief life of Czechoslovakia (1918–91), attempts were made to declare the official language "Czechoslovak." Differences in grammar and pronunciation and, above all, the spirit of Romantic nationalism in the nineteenth-century revival of the two languages, made it a difficult task. The separation of the two nations in 1991 repeated what was taking place in the former Soviet Union; the old linguistic "fault lines" appeared as in some sort of earthquake. Czech became the language of the new Czech Republic and the new republic of Slovakia was once again able to identify itself with the historic realms of the Slovak language.

Czech has a more distinguished history than Slovak, with a literary tradition that goes back to the late Middle Ages. Although Bohemia was always, in theory, a vassal of the Holy Roman Emperor, during the thirteenth and fourteenth centuries it was the most powerful kingdom of central Europe. As in Poland, the earliest writings were in Latin, but by the fourteenth century Czech had a flourishing literature, the first in any living Slavonic language. The influence of Latin (often in rather Germanic form) is very marked in Old Czech manuscripts, which dealt predominantly with religious subjects. Many of these Latin borrowings were transmitted to Polish, where writing in the vernacular was slower to emerge into common use.

It was Bohemia's subsequent role in the reform of the Catholic Church that inspired much of the literature of the Golden Age of Czech, but, in the end, this also brought about the downfall both of the kingdom and of the language. A leading figure in this crucial chapter in Czech history was Jan Hus, who adopted many of the revolutionary ideas of John Wycliffe and was burnt at the stake for heresy in 1415.

Not the least of his achievements was the introduction of order into the hitherto chaotic spelling of Czech. In its essentials, Hus's system is still in use today. Instead of *cz*, Hus wrote *c* with a dot on top. His dots were later replaced by hooks or chevrons, the letters *š*, *č*, *ž*, giving the language its characteristic appearance on the printed page. There is also the notorious *ř*, which causes so much embarrassment in the pronunciation of the name *Dvořák*. Without these diacritic marks the rendering of Slavonic sounds in the Roman alphabet is a cumbersome business, as can be seen in the daunting accumulations of consonants in written Polish.

The immediate consequence of Hus's martyrdom was the first in a long series of religious wars, which brought Bohemia into 200 years of continual conflict with Austria, until, in 1620 at the beginning of the Thirty Years' War, the precarious independence of the Czechs came to an end with the Battle of the White Mountain. In the period of repression that followed, the Bohemian Brethren, the most influential Protestant sect, were expelled from the country. Their translation of the Bible had been the high point in the development of literary Czech.

The language of the Kralice Bible, as it is called, is still revered in the same way as is that of the Authorized Version in England. But henceforth "Bohemians" would be better known in the rest of Europe for their supposedly unconventional lifestyle in exile. In Bohemia and Moravia German replaced Czech as the language of education and culture, and the habit of writing in Czech virtually died out. The Czechs now found themselves in a similar position to that of the Slovaks, who had long been under the rule of Hungary. Czech and Slovak histories were brought together with the creation of the modern republic in 1918, but within its boundaries there remained a large German population, the Sudetens, who were expelled or fled, en masse, in 1945.

German has always been the chief foreign source of Czech vocabulary. Given the nature of relations with the Germans, many early loans were military words, like *rytíř* "knight," from *Reiter*, and *hejtman* from *Hauptmann*, although this word became more widely known in its Polish form *hetman*, the leader of a troop of soldiers. There also arose a tendency to borrow from German by means of translation. In Old Czech the word *zámek* means "lock," but it took on the second sense of "castle," following the example of German *Schloss*, which had both meanings. This urge to translate or "calque" German words and phrases became very strong during the long period of Austrian rule. It is presumably less painful than using the actual words of their rulers. Even directly borrowed words are often disguised by Czech endings, as in *knoflík* "button" and *knedlík* "dumpling" from *Knopf* and *Knödel*, or in adjectives like *bizární* and *vágni*, from French *bizarre* and *vague*.

Despite the sorry state of the Czech language in the eighteenth century, it was a Czech, Josef Dobrovsky, whose scholarship (even though he wrote in German) earned him the unofficial title of "Patriarch of Slavonic philology." He encouraged Czech writers to revive the language of the Kralice Bible and rid the language of German influence. At the same time the Slovaks were regaining national consciousness through their writing. One reason for their unwillingness to accept Czech as a common written language was that they were predominantly Catholic, another that literary Czech is based on the speech of Prague, the dialect furthest removed from Slovak, which stands much closer to the form of Czech spoken in Moravia. The Slovaks nevertheless felt free to borrow from Czech in establishing their written language; the Czechs continued, where possible, to avoid foreign words, preferring to translate, even if, in doing so, they were in fact imitating the Germans. Many international words found in the other Slavonic languages are absent from Czech. History, for example, is *dějiny*, a translation of Latin *gesta* "deeds," while theatre is *divadlo*, derived from the verb "to see." This process continues in the twentieth century, a recent example being *letadlo*, the Czech for "aeroplane" derived from the verb "to fly."

Among Czech words which have come into universal use, robot (from *robota* "work") has a sinister as well as a practical connotation. And there is a smell of the powder keg around others, such as the small pistol (*pist'ala*), the Czech/British "Bren" Brno/Enfield machine gun and the howitzer (*houfnice* "stone sling").

THE SOUTHERN SLAVS

The Slovenes, Serbs and Croats, uneasy neighbors for the greater part of their history, are descendants of the south Slavonic Slovene, Srbi and Hvrati, who broke south from their amorphous homelands in eastern Europe into the Balkan peninsula in the sixth century. They enveloped the almost mystical land of Illyria, and overran Macedonia and much of Greece. By the eighth century, the embryo kingdoms of Serbia, Croatia and Bulgaria had begun to take shape; the Bulgars, south Slavs, were ruled for a while by Asiatic Bulgars whose name became theirs.

The south Slavonic of Serb and Croat were close enough to each other to be brought together at a linguistic conference in Vienna (1851). Serbo-Croat, as the common language came to be called, became the major language of the short-lived monarchy, then republic, of Yugoslavia, until its break-up in internecine warfare in the 1990s. The ancient linguistic distinction between Serb and Croat, never wide, has once again appeared, though much of it is in pettifogging detail. Serb and Croat speakers cannot misunderstand each other.

The principal variants of Serbo-Croat, which do not correspond exactly to old boundaries between Serbians and Croatians, are classified by the three different words used to say "what?," *što*, *kaj* and *ča*. It was a version of the *što* dialect, the most widespread, that was chosen as the most suitable standard.

The one obvious difficulty in establishing Serbo-Croat was the fact that Serbs and Croats wrote in different alphabets. While Serbia was still an independent kingdom before the arrival of the Turks in the Balkans, Croatia had become subject to the Republic of Venice. This meant that the Serbians belonged to the Orthodox Church, the Croatians to the Roman Catholic. As a result Serbians have always used a Cyrillic alphabet and Croatians, although they persisted for some time in using the ancient Glagolitic script for their ecclesiastical writings, have been accustomed to the Roman alphabet too long for them to change their ways.

Despite this apparent handicap, the spelling of Serbo-Croat, whichever alphabet it is written in, is more consistent phonetically than any other Slavonic language. The great common factor, which made the union of Serbian and Croatian possible, is the intonation found in both forms of the language. The pronunciation of individual syllables may vary enormously from dialect to dialect, but the tune of the word does not. Vocabulary, too, is subject to enormous local variations, especially in the names of the objects of everyday life, foodstuffs for example. The influence of German is still strong in Croatia, which was for a long time part of the Austro-Hungarian Empire. In many places butter is still *puter* and ham *šunka* (from *Schinken*). In other areas Italian loans survive, like *pršuta* from *prosciutto*, but in Serbia the principal foreign influence was Turkish. However, as in Bulgaria, the Turkish element has been eliminated wherever possible, out of nationalistic pride. Russian had considerable influence on educated Serbian in the eighteenth century, when Russian teachers and priests attempted to inspire a Slavonic revival. The resulting Russianized Serbian was such an unnatural hybrid that nineteenth-century writers did their best to erase its memory. In the young nations of the former Yugoslavia, the language still tends to borrow from western sources rather than from Russian or other Slavonic languages.

Slovenian

The Slovenes, who have their own independent republic centerd on the city of Ljubljana, have enjoyed a more peaceful history than their fellow south Slavs. The stability of their lifestyle in their mountain valleys is reflected in their current prosperity and in the great variety of dialects in their highly conservative language. Similarities between Slovenian and Slovak indicate the route taken by the Slavs in their expansion to the south west, but the arrival of the Magyars cut off the Slovenes from their fellow Slavs to the north. To the south, the frontier of the language is not clearly marked, as there are several intermediate dialects between Slovenian and Croatian.

As subjects first of Venice, then of the Austro-Hungarian Empire, the Slovenes gave their rulers little cause for concern, except at the time of the Reformation, when the anti-Protestant zeal of the Austrians caused all books written in Slovenian to be burnt. Chief among the works that suffered this fate were the translations of the Bible which had been the first important examples of written Slovenian. The language, however, was not eclipsed by these setbacks to the same extent as contemporary Czech. Slovenian uses the Roman alphabet modified by some of the diacritic signs first employed in Czech. The establishing of a modern standard for the

language has not been easy because of the existence of so many dialects. In the past the only significant foreign influence on Slovenian has been German, but words borrowed later almost always came by way of Serbo-Croat.

Macedonian

Macedonian is the official language of the republic of Macedonia, which declared independence from Yugoslavia in 1991.

A region where, in antiquity, Greek met Illyrian and Thracian, Macedonia became part of the Slavonic-speaking world when it was overrun, like most of the Balkans, by tribes from central Europe in the sixth century. It was ruled in turn by Bulgarians, Byzantines and Turks (for 500 years) until 1918 when the greater part was incorporated into the embryo state of Yugoslavia.

Macedonian is seen by most linguists as close to Bulgarian, and by the Bulgarians simply as a dialect of their speech; whatever the argument, it has an important claim to fame as a cradle of literary or "Church" Slavonic and was thus influential wherever the Eastern Orthodox Church flourished.

With a substantial minority of Albanian speakers (the last of the Illyrians?), Macedonia became a center of controversy when it gained independence, above all because it shared its name with the greater part of northern Greece. Greek Macedonia had become hellenized long before its renowned son, Alexander the Great, built his huge empire; the choice of the new republic's name seemed to the Greeks to amount almost to a territorial claim to part of their birthright.

Bulgarian

With about eight million speakers, Bulgarian hardly ranks among the major languages of the modern world, yet from an historical point of view, it can be considered to have had a wider linguistic influence than any other member of the Slavonic family, including Russian. It played a leading role, not only in the creation of Old Slavonic, which in turn played a critical part in the development of Russian, but also in its contribution to languages, notably Romanian and, to a lesser extent, Hungarian, a language outside the European family.

After reaching the height of its independent power at the beginning of the tenth century, Bulgaria had to submit to the rule of the Byzantine Empire. This helped maintain the prestige of the country as the center for ecclesiastical writing in Old Slavonic. At that time the Bulgarians were the only Slav people to have an Orthodox Patriarch, something the Russians lacked until the sixteenth century.

From the Middle Ages onward Bulgaria was lavish in passing words to the lexicons of its neighbors, and Bulgarian words make up more than half the vocabulary of modern Romanian. Even the independent Magyars could not escape the influence of the numerically superior Slavs. One of their borrowings, *medve* "bear," belongs to Slavonic prehistory, when to name the animal directly was taboo and it was therefore called "honey eater," in Old Slavonic *medvedi* (in *med* "honey" one sees English "mead"). The Turks, too, treated the bear with respect − they have a proverb: "Until you have crossed the bridge, keep calling the bear 'uncle.'"

The divergence of spoken Bulgarian from the language of the Orthodox Church was already far advanced when the Ottoman Turks reached the Balkans in the fourteenth century. Bulgaria was the first area of Europe to be incorporated in their empire, even before the fall of Constantinople. Five centuries of Turkish domination could not fail to leave its mark on the language, especially in military and financial matters, the areas in which the Bulgarians felt the hand of their conquerors most strongly. A system whereby one in four Christian youths were taken to Istanbul, converted to Islam and trained to serve as administrators or fight as janissaries (in Bulgarian *iničerin*) allowed the early Ottoman Empire to keep a firm hold on the Balkans.

In the nineteenth century, the Bulgarians followed the Greeks and the Serbians in attempting to throw off Turkish rule and once this was accomplished in 1878, they became involved in the Balkan power struggle between Austria and Russia. History eventually took Bulgaria into the orbit of Russia, and in the revival of Bulgarian as a written language, Russian has been the obvious model to consult. The spelling reforms of 1945 gave Bulgarian an alphabet very like that of Russian, and the language borrows most of its new words from the modern center of Slavonic culture. Borrowings from Turkish, formerly in general use, have been consciously avoided. It would not do for the new state to use the Turkish word *bajrák* for the symbol of its independence, so instead it has borrowed from Russian the equally foreign, but more acceptable, *flag*.

CHAPTER NINE

The Baltic tongues

Lithuanian and Latvian are the surviving forms of Baltic, one of the smallest of the independent branches of the Indo-European family. History was for long content to regard them simply as forms of Slavonic, or coupled them into a single entity known as Balto-Slavonic. It is now known that the marked similarities between the branches are the result of contact between them stretching back into prehistory rather than being signs of their having a parent in common.

The dialects of Baltic peoples other than the Lithuanians and Latvians, or Letts, have vanished from history. They were Old Prussian, the language of the Baltic Prussians or Borussians who occupied the coastal belt from the River Vistula to the Memel, and the more easterly Curonian, which gave way to Lithuanian and Latvian in the sixteenth century.

The Borussians came under pressure from the Teutonic knights in the thirteenth century and their lands were settled by German peasants. From this time onwards, "Prussian" became more of a German than an independently Baltic concept. Baltic Prussian probably became extinct in the seventeenth century, surviving only in a few tracts, including a translation of Luther's Catechism in a bilingual edition.

The Lithuanians first enter history in the eleventh century. Remote in a corner of Europe bypassed by the great migrations and campaigns that had marked the Dark Ages, they were Europe's last pagans, in whose domestic rites small green snakes played a part (Herodotus referred to them as Neuri, and remarked upon their folklore, which tells of a plague of snakes driving them from their homes). The domestic snakes did not survive Christianization, when incoming Germans seized them and burnt them on huge bonfires.

The long isolation of the Lithuanians from Europe's main political and religious developments insulated their language from others that might have influenced it. The result was that Lithuanian retained family characteristics that were evidently far more ancient than those of any other language in Europe. It was sometimes said that a Lithuanian peasant could understand simple sentences in Sanskrit, but the claim is now taken with a pinch of salt. However, the Lithuanian vocabulary is replete with words that demonstrate its family origins and relationships with other European tongues; Lithuanian *mirtis* "death," Sanskrit *mrtis*, with the shifted English meaning in "murder"; Lithuanian *vyras* "man," Latin *vir*; Lithuanian *senas* "old," Sanskrit *sanas*, Latin *senex*.

The antiquity of its language and the relatively small size of modern Lithuania conceal a history as energetic as that of many larger nations. From the twelfth century onwards, the Lithuanians, led by their grand dukes, were among the most ambitious powers in eastern Europe, building an empire that included White Russia (then White Ruthenia) and much of Ukraine. They defeated the Mongols and captured Kiev, but became

THE BALTIC FAMILY		
Old Prussian	Lithuanian	Latvian

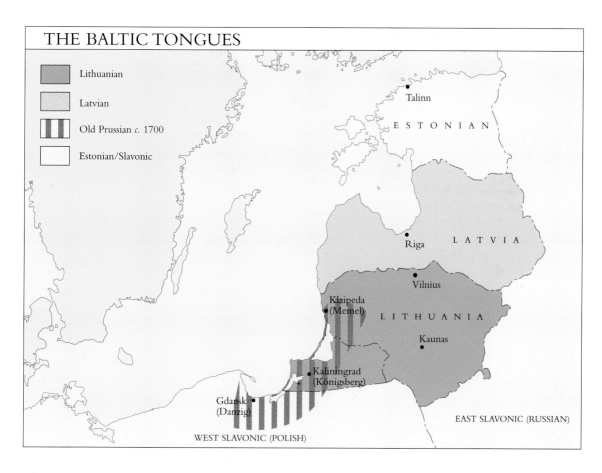

THE BALTIC TONGUES

- Lithuanian
- Latvian
- Old Prussian *c.* 1700
- Estonian/Slavonic

Talinn

ESTONIAN

Riga

LATVIA

Vilnius

Klaipeda
(Memel)

LITHUANIA

Kaunas

Kaliningrad
(Königsberg)

Gdansk
(Danzig)

EAST SLAVONIC (RUSSIAN)

WEST SLAVONIC (POLISH)

Christian only after union with Catholic Poland in 1386.

The Grand Duchy of Lithuania finally disappeared, along with its small northern neighbor Latvia, and Poland, into the Russian Empire in 1795. All regained their independence in 1918, but Lithuania and Latvia were annexed by the Soviet Union in 1940. Both regained their freedom in 1991.

Sometimes called Lettish, Latvian has been referred to as "Lithuanian in the mouths of foreigners," the "foreigners" being the Livonians of Finnic origin in the north-eastern Baltic lands, whose language lives on in Estonia.

Latvia did not achieve an identity of its own until the sixteenth century, when its first literature, a Catholic Catechism, appeared. Like the languages of many of the smaller European nations, Latvian flourished during the nineteenth century, at the end of which a standard form emerged, now the official language of the independent republic.

CHAPTER TEN

The outsiders

Only three European states have national languages that are not offshoots of the Indo-European linguistic stem. The outsiders, Finnish/Estonian and Hungarian, are members of the same family, the Finno-Ugric branch of the Uralic languages, but they are as distantly related and as mutually unintelligible as, say, Portuguese and Polish. The discovery of their common origins was the work of travellers and scholars in the eighteenth century.

Twelve other languages belonging to the group are still spoken in Russia on both sides of the Urals, some by a mere handful of people, others by up to a million and more. The first people to detach themselves from the family were the Samoyeds, who moved north-eastwards into Siberia; the remaining Uralic languages are all classed as Finno-Ugric. There are several Finnic tongues with enough speakers to be officially recognized within Russia, notably the Mordvinians (the "man-eaters") and the Cheremisses (the "Dark Cloaks") or Mari, who were among the first northern tribes to enter history in the writings of Herodotus (fifth century BC). Their present homeland marks an ancient course of gradual migration towards the Baltic where Estonian, closely akin to Finnish, is the official language of the Republic of Estonia along the southern shore of the Gulf of Finland.

The prehistoric movements of the peoples of the Ugric branch are more difficult to trace. They are thought to have separated from the Finnic group as long ago as 3,000–4,000 BC (some scholars argue a far earlier date, about 8,000 BC). The closest related languages to Hungarian are Ostyak and Vogul of the Siberian lands beyond the Urals, around the River Ob. At some time in the first millennium BC, perhaps later, the speakers of the Ugric language must have divided. The ancestors of the Ostyaks began to move towards their present homes while another group, who were to carry a form of the language to present-day Hungary, moved southward. The Ugric speakers at first led a wandering existence as hunters and fishermen, later becoming nomadic herdsmen through contact with Turkic peoples. Many words relating to animal husbandry and agriculture were picked up in the process. It is the presence of these Turkic loans in Hungarian that partly accounts for the belief of some scholars that Finno-Ugric can be linked to the Altaic languages, which include Turkish and many languages of central Asia – with which, it is speculated, even the Japanese and their tongue may have some remote prehistoric affinity.

The Hungarians' own name for themselves, Magyar, in its earlier form *Megeri* contained the Turkish suffix *-eri*, meaning man, and when they first came to the notice of the Byzantine Empire, they were confused with their frequent companions, the Bulgar Turks. It was from the word *onogur*, literally "ten arrows," an alliance of ten tribes, some Magyar, some Turkish, that medieval Greek and Latin produced the name by which the people and the language have since been known outside their own country.

It was not until the end of the ninth century that the Magyars reached the Danubian plain beyond the Carpathian Mountains and started to settle in the area of modern Hungary, but they swiftly informed Europe of their arrival, marauding or exacting protection money wherever they could. Superb horsemen, their raids reaching into Germany and Italy, they swept through much of France before their final defeat at Lechfeld, near Augsburg, in 955. Their flair as cavalrymen, however, outlived their early depredations, and in modern times Hungarian has given most western languages the words *huszar* "hussar" and *szablya* "sabre."

Their initial behavior in Europe did not eliminate people's natural tendency to confuse them with the quite unrelated Huns. However, with the adoption of Christianity by King Stephen in 1001, Hungary became a relatively well-regulated medieval feudal kingdom and an important center for trans-European trade. The Magyars borrowed significantly from the Slavonic peoples around them, especially words that betokened a more sedentary way of life, like *asztal* a "table," from the Slavonic *stolu*, and many agricultural terms. Their own language had a lesser effect on their neighbors, with the exception of the Romanians of Transylvania, which was part of the Hungarian kingdom. The one noteworthy invention that the Magyars introduced to the rest of Europe in the late Middle Ages was the novel form of transport used in the town of Kocs. The fame of the place may have been forgotten, but its name has travelled far, giving German *Kutsche*, French *coche* and ultimately English "coach."

The medieval kingdom was much larger than the modern state of Hungary (nearly two million Hungarian-speakers live inside the borders of Romania). Hungarian independence came to an end in 1526, when Hungary was defeated by the Turks at the Battle of Mohács.

Ottoman rule gave way to Austrian rule in 1686, and this continued until the collapse of the Austro-Hungarian Empire at the end of the First World War. Through their use as languages of administration, both Turkish and German lent a number of words to Hungarian, but foreign rule only added to the Magyars' strong sense of national identity.

At the same time Hungarian was developing an impressive literary tradition, inspired both by patriotic pride and by the extraordinary lyrical qualities of the language. Although Hungarian revolutions tend to result in heroic failure (1848 and 1956 being the prime examples), the indomitable spirit of the people is still enshrined in the language they set off with from the Urals some 2,500 years ago, which they have managed to preserve against considerable odds. Hungarian now has many more speakers than any other Uralic language. Its alien characteristics have naturally limited the number of words to be borrowed by other European languages. At least one is known to every housewife with an international cookbook, *goulash*, which derives from *gulyás*, a "herdsman." The old Magyar horsemen carried their meat across the plains as they did their language. As the meat cannot have been at all fresh when it came to the time to cook it, a liberal sprinkling of *paprika* was necessary to disguise the taste.

Finnish and Estonian

The arrival of the Finns, and their neighbors and relations, the Estonians, in north-east Europe was less spectacular than that of the Magyars. Writing in the first century AD,

Tacitus mentions the Fenni, a distant northern tribe, but there is no knowing how far north the informants of his sources had travelled. The word "Finn" is Germanic; the Finns themselves call their country Suomi. Tacitus may have been referring to the Lapps, some of whom at that time were living in southern Finland while others, with their unique ability to extract a living from the semi-frozen wasteland, were well established further north.

Lappish belongs to the Finno-Ugric family, but it is very different from Finnish, and it is thought to have arrived in Scandinavia first. It is also possible, however, that the Lapps borrowed their language from Finnish at an early date, since when their different way of life has adapted it to their own needs. The Lapps today inhabit the north of Norway, Sweden, Finland and northern Russia, and, although they number 35,000 in all, there are six separate languages, each possessing several distinct dialects. Their one important loan to other languages, transmitted through Russian, is *tundra*, their word for the Arctic region that until recently they have been the only Europeans to exploit.

Archaeological evidence does point to a new culture having reached Finland about the time Tacitus was writing, but the Finns did not arrive there all together as one people. In the modern dialects of Finnish there are still marked differences between the Hämäläinen, who originally crossed by sea from Estonia, and the Karelians, who arrived from the east overland. Many of the latter are recent arrivals from Finnish Karelia, who did not wish to stay under Soviet rule when large areas of eastern Finland were annexed in 1940 and 1944. Finland itself has only existed as an independent state since 1917, having been subject throughout most of its history to Sweden and then, from the early nineteenth century, to Russia.

A small proportion (about seven per cent) of the population are Swedish speakers and a large number of foreign loans in Finnish are of Old Norse or Swedish origin, or have reached Finland via Sweden. Often these have been difficult to reconcile to the phonetic structure of the Finnish language, such as its distaste (shared with Hungarian) for more than one initial consonant. Thus the Old Germanic word *strond* (English and German *strand*) was adopted as *ranta*. Like Lithuanian and Latvian, Finnish and Estonian are written in the Roman alphabet.

Writing in Finnish only began after the Reformation in the sixteenth century and grew markedly in strength with the rise of national consciousness in the nineteenth century. The system of spelling, although disconcerting to other European eyes, is perfectly regular. Double consonants have a definite value, as for example in Italian, and this convention also applies to vowels. A long vowel is simply written twice. When a Finn writes *Eurooppa*, he is not having trouble with his electric typewriter, but giving an exact phonetic account of how the word is pronounced. By virtue of the climate, the Finnish lifestyle has always been rather specialized but in the twentieth century at least one feature of their culture, the *sauna*, has gained international popularity.

The '"coach" began its travels through the languages of
the west from the small town of Kocs in Hungary, where
its full name was *kocsi szeker*, the "Kocs cart."

CHAPTER ELEVEN

Europe's national languages

Since the first century AD, the population of Europe has increased more than twenty-fold, from about thirty million to upwards of 650 million people. In that time, three major linguistic groups of antiquity – Italic, Germanic and Slavonic – have spawned dozens of languages, ranging from the official tongues of powerful nations to local varieties heard only in a handful of villages, and among old people. The descendants of other once-powerful parent tongues, like Celtic, barely survive (only Irish, of all the old Celtic tongues, is the official language of a nation); others, Illyrian and Thraco-Phrygian, have vanished apart from genetic traces in Albanian and Armenian.

The status of the surviving languages varies considerably. Some countries, notably Belgium and Switzerland, have three or more official languages, while others, such as France, have up to eight minority forms and afford them little or no official recognition.

The political upheavals of the twentieth century's last years brought significant changes to the linguistic map of eastern Europe. Where once Russian ruled throughout the former Soviet community, new nations from the Baltic to the Black Sea have asserted their own local tongues as national, however slight the difference between, say, Ukrainian or Belarusian and Russian: neither is sufficiently distinct to regard Russian as a foreign language. Much the same argument applies to the Serbo-Croat of Serbia, Bosnia and Croatia (the former Yugoslavia), although local purists will claim a difference.

The summary of European languages on the following pages gives a broad indication of what is spoken where in Europe, country by country. The boundaries indicating the range of each language are of necessity imprecise; languages are indifferent to frontiers or regional borders of any sort.

NORWAY, SWEDEN AND ICELAND

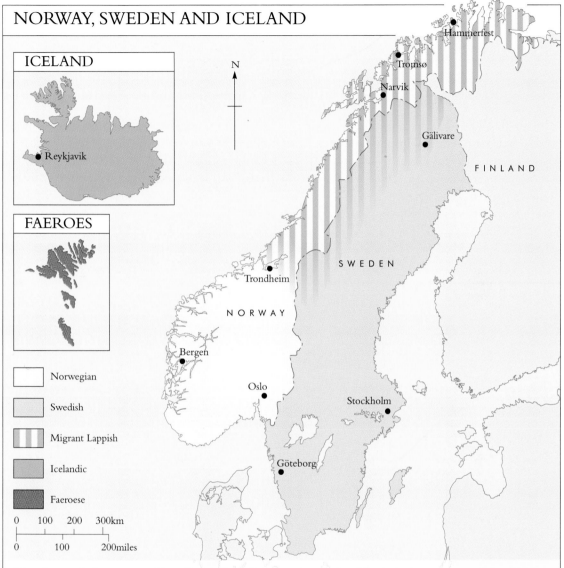

ICELAND

Reykjavik

FAEROES

☐ Norwegian

▨ Swedish

▥ Migrant Lappish

▨ Icelandic

▨ Faeroese

0   100   200   300km

0   100   200miles

N

Hammerfest

Tromsø

Narvik

Gälivare

FINLAND

SWEDEN

Trondheim

NORWAY

Bergen

Oslo

Stockholm

Göteborg

The Germanic languages of Scandinavia and Iceland are spoken over an area three times larger than the British Isles by a combined population of little more than a third of that of Britain. Norway (population 4.3 million) has two forms of **Norwegian**: *Bokmål* 'Book Language' and *Nynorsk* 'New Norwegian'. The first reflects Denmark's suzerainty over Norway until the nineteenth century; it is the commonly written and spoken form. *Nynorsk*, reconstructed from dialects in the nineteenth century, is taught in all schools but is little used beyond rural districts. **Swedish** is the sole official language of Sweden (popula-

tion 8.75 million). Both Norway and Sweden possess a small population of Lapps (both sedentary and migratory and mostly bilingual) speaking **Lappish** *(see Finland)*.

Icelandic, the most conservative of Germanic languages, became the official language of the island when it achieved independence from Denmark in 1944. **Danish** remains the Icelanders' second tongue. Midway between Iceland and its erstwhile ruler Denmark lie the Faeroe Islands which are still part of the Danish Crown. **Faeroese**, the language of about 40,000 people, is official in the islands.

DENMARK

Danish is spoken by the 5.2 million population of Denmark and is taught in the schools of Iceland, the Faeroe Islands and in Greenland where, however, most of the small population speaks **Greenlandic**, a form of Inuktitut 'manspeech' (Eskimo). Once the most influential of the Scandinavian languages, Danish has to a small extent given way to **German** on the southern border of the country, where German has some local standing; conversely, Danish is heard in German Sleswig, but both communities are bilingual.

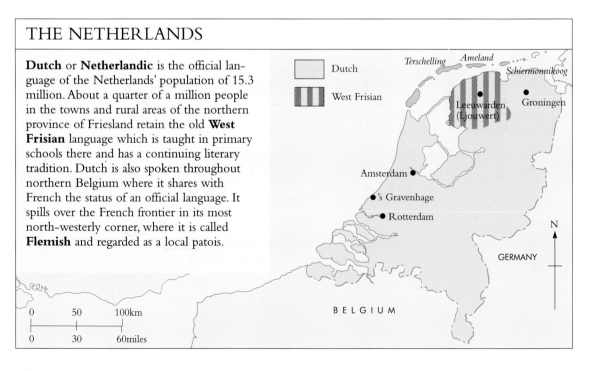

THE NETHERLANDS

Dutch or **Netherlandic** is the official language of the Netherlands' population of 15.3 million. About a quarter of a million people in the towns and rural areas of the northern province of Friesland retain the old **West Frisian** language which is taught in primary schools there and has a continuing literary tradition. Dutch is also spoken throughout northern Belgium where it shares with French the status of an official language. It spills over the French frontier in its most north-westerly corner, where it is called **Flemish** and regarded as a local patois.

UNITED KINGDOM AND IRELAND
(The British Isles)

The official language of the United Kingdom (England, Wales, Scotland and Northern Ireland, total population 58 million) is **English**. It is the official language also in the Republic of Ireland, where it gives formal precedence to **Irish Gaelic** but is the everyday vernacular of most people. **Welsh** and **Scottish Gaelic** are spoken on the British mainland in Wales and in the Western Isles of Scotland. Welsh is the most successful survivor of the old Celtic languages and is heard customarily in the country districts of Wales, particularly in the north. The language is fostered in all the Welsh schools, but almost all Welsh speakers are bilingual.

Scottish Gaelic, a 'colonial' form of Irish Gaelic, maintains a foothold in the north-west of Scotland and the Hebrides, but almost all its speakers are bilingual. Irish itself, although the first official language of Ireland, is closer to extinction than other surviving Celtic languages; of Ireland's 3.5 million population, less than one per cent speak Irish habitually, mostly in the westernmost counties. Irish continues to be promoted by successive governments; it is taught in schools, and official literature and notices appear in both Irish and English.

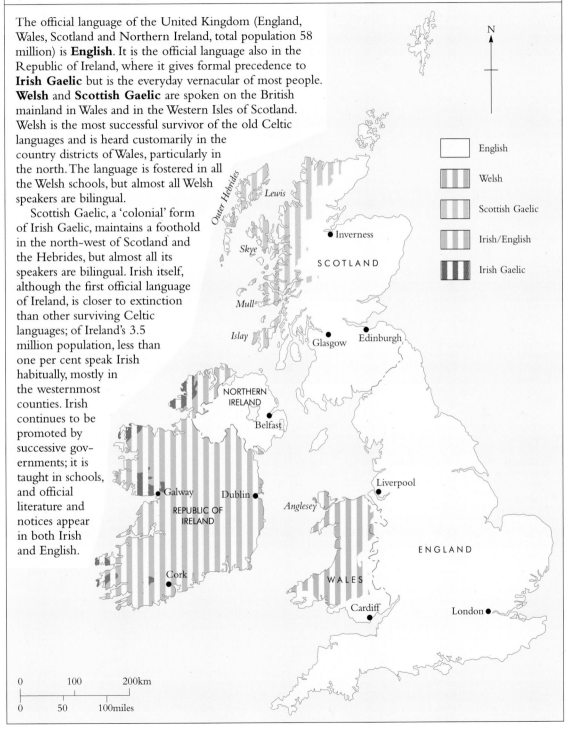

English

Welsh

Scottish Gaelic

Irish/English

Irish Gaelic

BELGIUM AND LUXEMBOURG

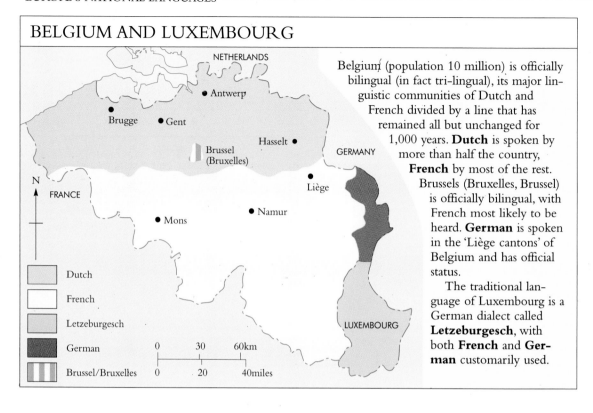

Belgium (population 10 million) is officially bilingual (in fact tri-lingual), its major linguistic communities of Dutch and French divided by a line that has remained all but unchanged for 1,000 years. **Dutch** is spoken by more than half the country, **French** by most of the rest. Brussels (Bruxelles, Brussel) is officially bilingual, with French most likely to be heard. **German** is spoken in the 'Liège cantons' of Belgium and has official status.

The traditional language of Luxembourg is a German dialect called **Letzeburgesch**, with both **French** and **German** customarily used.

FRANCE

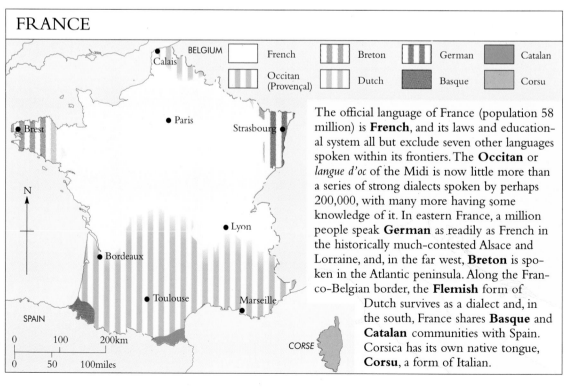

The official language of France (population 58 million) is **French**, and its laws and educational system all but exclude seven other languages spoken within its frontiers. The **Occitan** or *langue d'oc* of the Midi is now little more than a series of strong dialects spoken by perhaps 200,000, with many more having some knowledge of it. In eastern France, a million people speak **German** as readily as French in the historically much-contested Alsace and Lorraine, and, in the far west, **Breton** is spoken in the Atlantic peninsula. Along the Franco-Belgian border, the **Flemish** form of Dutch survives as a dialect and, in the south, France shares **Basque** and **Catalan** communities with Spain. Corsica has its own native tongue, **Corsu**, a form of Italian.

GERMANY

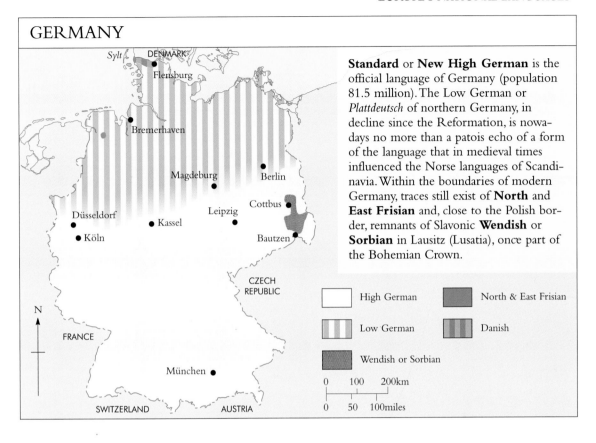

Standard or **New High German** is the official language of Germany (population 81.5 million). The Low German or *Plattdeutsch* of northern Germany, in decline since the Reformation, is nowadays no more than a patois echo of a form of the language that in medieval times influenced the Norse languages of Scandinavia. Within the boundaries of modern Germany, traces still exist of **North** and **East Frisian** and, close to the Polish border, remnants of Slavonic **Wendish** or **Sorbian** in Lausitz (Lusatia), once part of the Bohemian Crown.

□ High German	▨ North & East Frisian	
▥ Low German	▤ Danish	
▨ Wendish or Sorbian		

0   100   200km

0   50   100miles

AUSTRIA

Contested for by Germans, Magyars and Slavs during its early history, Austria (population 8 million) has been **German** speaking for the greater part of the past 1,000 years, but the German of Vienna is as different from that of Berlin as New York's English is from that of London. Speakers of minority tongues in Austria make up little more than one per cent of the total population, with some **Serbo-Croat** and **Hungarian** in the east. There are speakers of **Slovenian** in Carinthia, while **Czech** and **Slovak** are heard on the Austrian side of the frontier which has the two republics to the north.

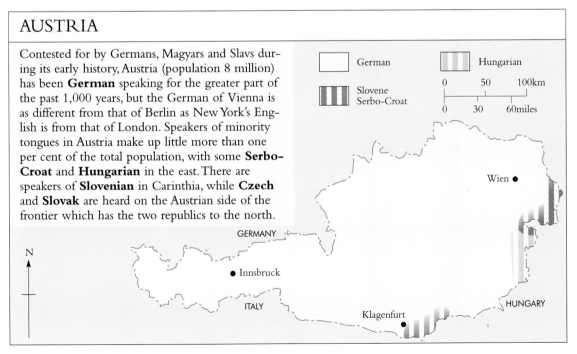

□ German	▥ Hungarian
▤ Slovene Serbo-Croat	

0   50   100km

0   30   60miles

SPAIN AND PORTUGAL

The dominant language of Spain since its speakers led the recovery of the peninsula from the Moors, Castilian **Spanish** is the official language of the country (population 39 million). Another million-plus Spanish speakers live in the Canary Islands, and Spanish is, of course, the official language of most of the Latin-American countries. As one of the world's major colonizing languages, Spanish is spoken by about six times as many people beyond Spain as in it. **Catalan**, a Romance language in its own right with as distinguished a history as Castilian, is still spoken by five million people in the northern Mediterranean provinces of Spain. There are

Catalan speakers also in France (Roussillon); and, with French, Catalan is the official language of Andorra.

Once on a footing with Castilian, **Galician** is now little more than a local dialect in Atlantic Spain, although it provided the basis for **Portuguese**. There are no competing languages in Portugal (population, including Madeira and the Azores, 9.3 million). The most vocal minority in the Iberian peninsula is the **Basque** population, whose language has no known relatives. Although Spanish Basques number about two million, only a quarter use their unique language, mostly in the rural areas.

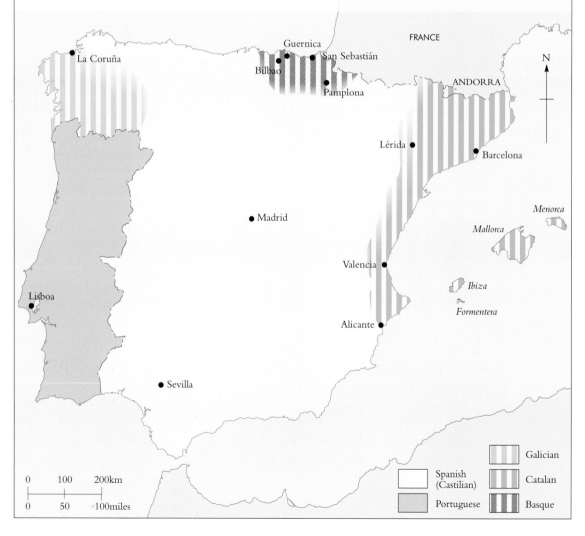

SWITZERLAND

Switzerland (population 7.2 million) has three official languages, **German**, **French** and **Italian**. A fourth, **Romansch,** is treated as a 'national' rather than an official language. Far and away the most widely used is German; almost two-thirds of the population speak it in nineteen of the twenty-five cantons, while French is used in four cantons and Italian in one (Ticino). Romansch, which is part of the Rhaeto-Romance group of Latin languages, along with the Friulian and Ladin of Italy, is spoken and used for official purposes in the Grisons (Ger. *Graubünden*).

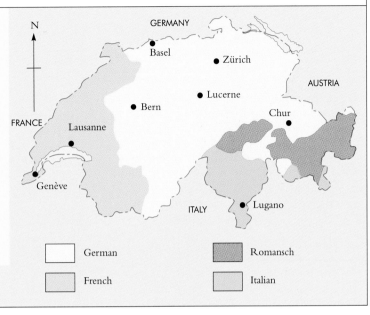

☐ German		▨ Romansch	
▨ French		☐ Italian	

```
0        50        100km
0        30        60miles
```

ITALY

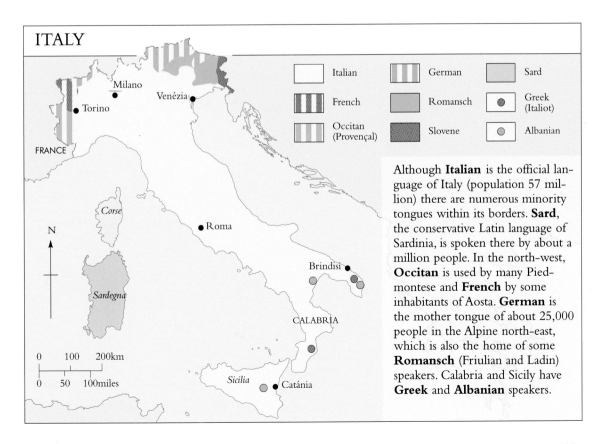

☐ Italian		▦ German		☐ Sard
▦ French		▨ Romansch		◉ Greek (Italiot)
▦ Occitan (Provençal)		▨ Slovene		◉ Albanian

Although **Italian** is the official language of Italy (population 57 million) there are numerous minority tongues within its borders. **Sard**, the conservative Latin language of Sardinia, is spoken there by about a million people. In the north-west, **Occitan** is used by many Piedmontese and **French** by some inhabitants of Aosta. **German** is the mother tongue of about 25,000 people in the Alpine north-east, which is also the home of some **Romansch** (Friulian and Ladin) speakers. Calabria and Sicily have **Greek** and **Albanian** speakers.

```
0      100     200km
0      50      100miles
```

GREECE

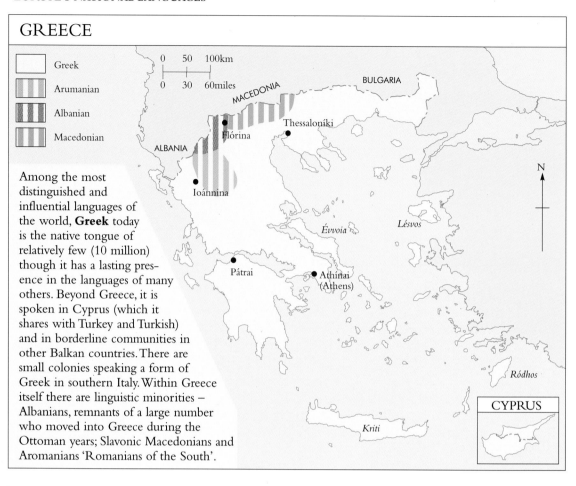

Greek

Arumanian

Albanian

Macedonian

0   50   100km

0   30   60miles

BULGARIA

MACEDONIA

Thessaloníki

ALBANIA

Flórina

Ioánnina

N

Évvoia

Lésvos

Pátrai

Athínai
(Athens)

Ródhos

CYPRUS

Kríti

Among the most distinguished and influential languages of the world, **Greek** today is the native tongue of relatively few (10 million) though it has a lasting presence in the languages of many others. Beyond Greece, it is spoken in Cyprus (which it shares with Turkey and Turkish) and in borderline communities in other Balkan countries. There are small colonies speaking a form of Greek in southern Italy. Within Greece itself there are linguistic minorities – Albanians, remnants of a large number who moved into Greece during the Ottoman years; Slavonic Macedonians and Aromanians 'Romanians of the South'.

ALBANIA

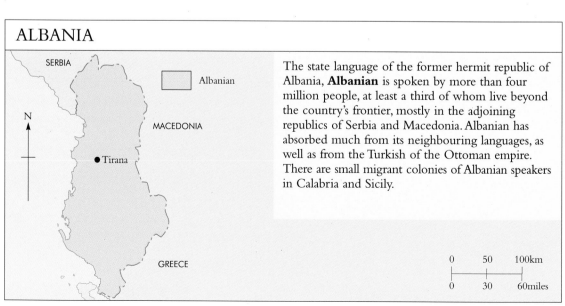

SERBIA

N

MACEDONIA

Tirana

GREECE

Albanian

The state language of the former hermit republic of Albania, **Albanian** is spoken by more than four million people, at least a third of whom live beyond the country's frontier, mostly in the adjoining republics of Serbia and Macedonia. Albanian has absorbed much from its neighbouring languages, as well as from the Turkish of the Ottoman empire. There are small migrant colonies of Albanian speakers in Calabria and Sicily.

0   50   100km

0   30   60miles

FINLAND

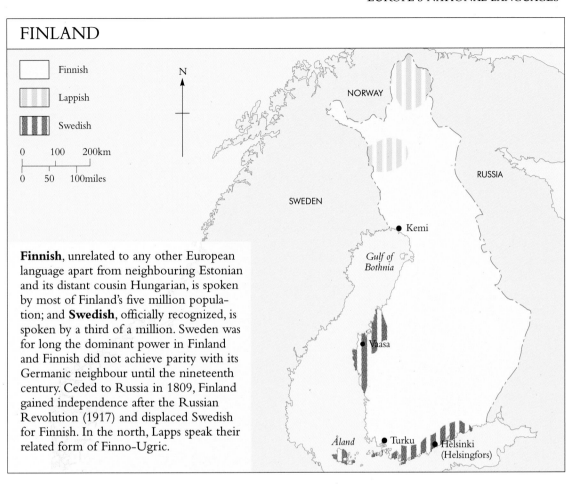

Finnish

Lappish

Swedish

0   100   200km

0   50   100miles

Finnish, unrelated to any other European language apart from neighbouring Estonian and its distant cousin Hungarian, is spoken by most of Finland's five million population; and **Swedish**, officially recognized, is spoken by a third of a million. Sweden was for long the dominant power in Finland and Finnish did not achieve parity with its Germanic neighbour until the nineteenth century. Ceded to Russia in 1809, Finland gained independence after the Russian Revolution (1917) and displaced Swedish for Finnish. In the north, Lapps speak their related form of Finno-Ugric.

HUNGARY

Hungarian, or **Magyar,** is spoken by most of Hungary's 10.3 million population which includes minority communities of **German**, **Slovak** and **Romany** speakers, together totalling less than a million. Hungarian is also spoken in the Ukraine, Romania, Slovakia, Serbia and Austria. Hungarian has no affinity with any of its surrounding Germanic, Slavonic or Romance languages, possessing as its only relatives in Europe the Finnic tongues of Finland, Estonia and northern Russia.

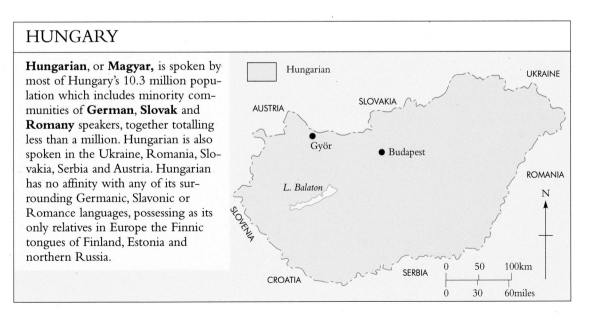

Hungarian

0   50   100km

0   30   60miles

POLAND

Having 'ceased to exist' twice during the last two hundred years, Poland (population 38 million, national language **Polish**) has been more homogeneous linguistically since 1945 than at any time in its modern history. As a result of the Second World War, the national boundaries of Poland shifted dramatically westward to the Oder-Neisse line, displacing traditional **German** speakers while surrendering much of its eastern territory to the USSR. Some German speakers remain in areas occupied by them since the Middle Ages, while **Belarusian** and **Ukrainian** communities remain in the east. **Kashubian** (a West Slavonic language like Polish, Czech and Slovakian) exists on the Baltic coast, though it is now no more than a local patois.

Polish		Belarusian	
Kashubian		Former German-speaking areas (pre-1945)	
Ukrainian			

CZECH REPUBLIC AND SLOVAKIA

Created as an independent nation in 1918, Czechoslovakia's brief existence came to an end in 1991 when it separated into two sovereign states, the Czech Republic (population 10.3 million) and Slovakia (population 5.3 million).

The national languages, **Czech** and **Slovak**, both West Slavonic, are closely related but distinct, the Czech language being influenced by the German of its neighbours in Germany and Austria.

After its role as the junior of the two languages in the former Czechoslovakia, Slovak has asserted its linguistic distinctiveness since independence, limiting the use of minority languages, notably **Hungarian**, in the south of the country.

Czech	
Slovak	
Hungarian	

RUSSIAN FEDERATION: UKRAINE, BELARUS, LATVIA, LITHUANIA, MOLDOVA, ARMENIA

'Great Russian' or simply **Russian**, was the official language of the former USSR; it is now the state language of the Russian Federation which, in addition to its dominant Russian population (148 million), has more than a dozen minorities, the largest being **Tatar** (3.5 per cent), a relic of the medieval Golden Horde. Russian is still in use in the former Soviet, now independent, republics of Ukraine, Belarus, Latvia and, to a lesser extent, Lithuania.

Ukrainian is the official language of the Ukraine (population 51.5 million) and **Belarusian** is the official language of Belarus (population 10.25 million), both languages being closely related to Russian. The Baltic languages, **Latvian** and **Lithuanian**, have been re-established by their two countries (populations 2.5 and 3.75 million respectively), and **Estonian**, a Finno-Ugric language, has been re-established in Estonia (population 1.5 million). There are substantial minorities of Russian speakers in Latvia and Estonia.

In the far south-west of the old USSR, the republic of Moldova (population 4.4 million) has adopted **Moldovan** (Romanian written in the Latin script) as its national language. In the far south, beyond the new Russian Federation frontier, the languages of the Caucasus include Georgian, Azerbaijani (Turkic) and **Armenian**, the European language that wandered eastward. Russian remains in use in the former Soviet republics of south-central Asia, notably in Kyrgyzstan, where for many purposes it remains on a footing with Turkic Kyrgyz.

N

FINLAND

RUSSIA

Baltic Sea

● Tallinn
ESTONIA

Riga
LATVIA

● Moskva
(Moscow)

LITHUANIA
Vilnius

● Minsk

POLAND

BELARUS

● Kiyev
(Kiev)

UKRAINE

MOLDOVA ● Odessa
Chisinau
(Kiskinev)

ROMANIA

Caspian Sea

GEORGIA ● Baku
Black Sea   T'bilis ● AZERBAIJAN
● Yerevan
BULGARIA   ARMENIA

TURKEY

	Russian		Belarusian
	Ukrainian		Lithuanian
	Romanian		Latvian

| 0 | 300 | 600km |
| 0 | 150 | 300miles |

SLOVENIA, CROATIA, BOSNIA-HERZEGOVINA, SERBIA AND MACEDONIA

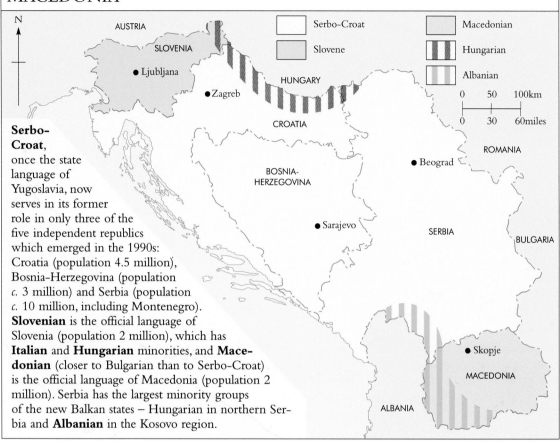

Serbo-Croat, once the state language of Yugoslavia, now serves in its former role in only three of the five independent republics which emerged in the 1990s: Croatia (population 4.5 million), Bosnia-Herzegovina (population *c.* 3 million) and Serbia (population *c.* 10 million, including Montenegro). **Slovenian** is the official language of Slovenia (population 2 million), which has **Italian** and **Hungarian** minorities, and **Macedonian** (closer to Bulgarian than to Serbo-Croat) is the official language of Macedonia (population 2 million). Serbia has the largest minority groups of the new Balkan states – Hungarian in northern Serbia and **Albanian** in the Kosovo region.

BULGARIA

A small but distinguished member of the Slavonic family and closely related to Macedonian, **Bulgarian** is the national language of Bulgaria (population 8.5 million). For long part of the Ottoman Empire, Bulgaria did not achieve independence until 1885. There are some small minorities within its borders, chiefly Turkish speakers from the 'Turkey in Europe' foothold north of the Bosporus, and gypsy **Romany** speakers.

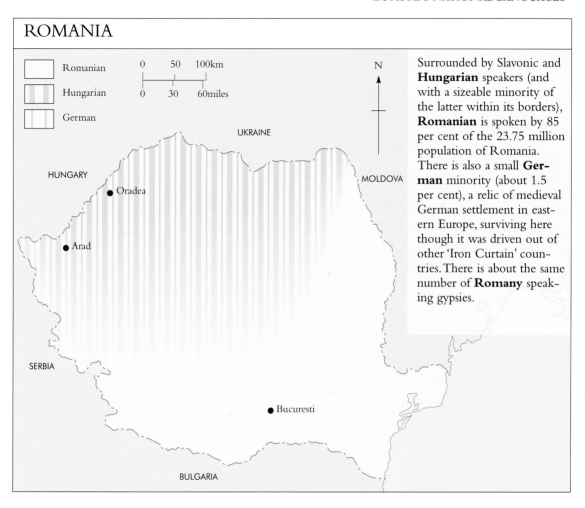

ROMANIA

Romanian
Hungarian
German

0   50   100km
0   30   60miles

N

UKRAINE

HUNGARY

● Oradea

● Arad

SERBIA

MOLDOVA

● Bucuresti

BULGARIA

Surrounded by Slavonic and **Hungarian** speakers (and with a sizeable minority of the latter within its borders), **Romanian** is spoken by 85 per cent of the 23.75 million population of Romania. There is also a small **German** minority (about 1.5 per cent), a relic of medieval German settlement in eastern Europe, surviving here though it was driven out of other 'Iron Curtain' countries. There is about the same number of **Romany** speaking gypsies.

Turkish in Europe

Turkish qualifies as a language of Europe by reason of its toehold on the continent, that part known as 'Turkey in Europe' north of the Sea of Marmara and including Istanbul. Turkish is unrelated to the Indo-European family of languages. It is a member of the Turkic family (part of a much wider grouping, the Altaic languages) spoken by Kazakh, Kirghis, Turkmen Uzbek and other people throughout central Asia.

For much of modern history, Turkish was the language of the 'master race' in southeastern Europe, the Ottoman Turks. For a while, the scimitars threatened even more of

Europe when their armies besieged Vienna until defeated in 1683. Traces of Turkish exist in all the Balkan languages of the people who were for centuries part of the Ottoman Empire.

Maltese

The native language of the Maltese has been a form of Arabic since the ninth century; before that time, it is believed, the language of the island was the Punic (Phoenician) of Carthage. Until the island was taken over by Britain in 1800, Italian was the islanders' second tongue, but today most Maltese speak English in addition to their own language, although the island became independent in 1964.

Glossary

As with all sciences, linguistics has its own vocabulary, that is to say, terms rarely met with beyond the science itself. WORDS has consciously avoided the use of these terms, keeping as far as possible to those to which the non-expert reader is accustomed. It may, however, assist the lay reader if even these more commonplace terms are defined, as each may have several meanings. (The entries here are in philological progression rather than in alphabetical order.)

language "The whole body of words and ways of combining them common to a people or race."

language family Those languages that can be shown to descend from a common parent (the Indo-European family of languages).

standard language That form of a language that is accepted and used by its speakers as a whole (standard English, standard German).

dialect From the Greek "way of speaking;" a variety of speech differing from the standard. A language in its entirety may be described as a dialect of the parent from which it descends.

patois Old French for "rough speech;" an unwritten form of a language used within a limited area.

creole Creole languages are those Romance tongues – Portuguese, Spanish and French – as they were, or are, spoken by African slaves and their descendants in the countries to which they were taken.

pidgin Pidgin describes a primitive form of creole, but the word "pidgin" itself is a Chinese corruption of the English word "business."

lingua franca Literally "Frankish tongue," a mixed jargon used for inter-communication by people speaking different native tongues. Its origins are in the Mediterranean where it came into being among sailors to the Levant.

philology The science of words and language. Philologists are men who "chase a panting syllable through time and space, start it at home and hunt it through the dark, to Gaul, to Greece, and into Noah's Ark" (William Cowper 1731-1800).

Further reading

Aitken, A. J. and T. McArthur *Languages of Scotland* W. & R. Chambers 1979

Atkinson, B. F. C. *The Greek Language* Faber & Faber 1931

Bacon, W. *Finland* Hale 1970

Baugh, A. C. *A History of the English Language* Routledge & Kegan Paul 1976

Bodmer, F. *Loom of Language* Allen & Unwin 1943

Boorstin, D. *The Americans: The Colonial Experience* Pelican 1965

Borrow, G. Romano *Lavo-lil* John Murray 1888

Browning, R. *Medieval and Modern Greek* Hutchinson 1969

Bynon, T. *Historical Linguistics* Cambridge University Press 1977

Clark, J. *Early English* Andre Deutsch 1967

Da Silva Neto, S. *Historia da Língua Portuguêsa* Rio de Janeiro 1957

De Bray, R. G. A. *Guide to the Slavonic Languages* Dent 1969

Devoto, G. *Il Linguaggio D'Italia* Rizzoli 1974

Dickens, A. G. *Martin Luther and the Reformation* English Universities Press 1967

Diringer, D. *A History of the Alphabet* Unwin Brothers 1977

Ekwall, E. *Concise Oxford Dictionary of English Placenames* Clarendon Press 1980

Elcock, W. D. *The Romance Languages* Faber & Faber 1960

Entwistle, W. J. *The Spanish Language, together with Portuguese, Catalan and Basque* Faber & Faber 1950

Entwistle, W. J. and W. A. Morison *Russian and the Slavonic Languages* Faber & Faber 1964

Ewert, A. *The French Language* Faber & Faber 1966

Gallop, R. *The Book of the Basques* Macmillan 1939

García de Diego, V. *Diccionario Etimologico Españole Hispanico* Madrid 1923

Gili, J. *Introductory Catalan Grammar* Dolphin 1967

Graur, A. *The Romance Character of Romanian* The Publishing house of the Academy of the Socialist Republic of Romania 1967

Greene, D. *The Irish Language* Published for the Cultural Relations Committee of Ireland at The Three Candles, Dublin 1966

Haarhoff, T. J. *Afrikaans: Its Origin and Development* Clarendon Press 1936

Haugen, E. *The Scandinavian Languages* Mouton 1972

Jespersen, O. *Language* Allen & Unwin 1922

Littré, M. P. E. *Dictionnaire de la Langue Française* Paris 1863-72

Lockwood, W. B. A. *Panorama of Indo-European Languages* Hutchinson University Library 1972

Lockwood, W. B. *An Informal History of the German Language* Andre Deutsch 1976

Lockwood, W. B. *Languages of the British Isles, Past and Present* Andre Deutsch 1975

Mallory, J. P. *In Search of the Indo-Europeans* Thames and Hudson 1994

Mann, Stuart E. *Czech Historical Grammar* Athlone Press 1957

Marckwardt, A. H. and J. L. Dillard *American English* Oxford University Press 1980

McEvedy, C. and R. Jones *Atlas of World Population History* Penguin 1978

Mencken, H. L. *The American Language* Jonathan Cape 1922

Menéndez Pidal, R. *Orígenes Del Español* Madrid 1950

Migliorini, B. *The Italian Language* Faber & Faber 1966

Muirithe, D. O. *The English Language in Ireland* Mercier Press 1977

Munson, D. *The Guid Scots Tongue* William Blackwood 1977

Nash, E. G. *The Hansa* The Bodley Head 1929

O'Connell Walshe, M. *Introduction to the Scandinavian Languages* Andre Deutsch 1965

Palmer, L. R. *The Latin Language* Faber & Faber 1954

Pamlényi E. *A History of Hungary* Collet's 1975

Partridge, E. *A World of Words* Routledge & Sons 1938

Pinker, S. *The Language Instinct* Penguin 1994

Priebsch, R. and W. E. Collinson *The German Language* Faber & Faber 1934

Pulgram, E. *The Tongues of Italy* Harvard University Press 1958

Read, J. *The Catalans* Faber & Faber 1979

Renfrew, Colin *Archaeology and Language* Penguin 1987

Rickard, P. A. *History of the French Language* Hutchinson 1974

Rosten L. *Hooray for Yiddish* Elm Tree Books 1983

Salverda de Grave, J. J. *L'Influence de la Langue Française en Hollande d'Apres Les Mots Empruntes* Paris 1913

Smith, L. P. *Words and Idioms* Constable 1925

Stephens, M. *Linguistic Minorities in Western Europe* Gomer Press 1978

Tagliavini C. *Le Origini Delle Lingue Neolatine* Bologna 1952

Thomson, G. D. *The Greek Language* W. Heffer & Sons 1960

Turner, G. W. *The English Language in Australia and New Zealand* Longman 1966

Unbegaun, B. O. *Selected Papers on Russian and Slavonic Philology* Clarendon Press 1969

van der Merwe, H. J. J. M. *An Introduction to Afrikaans* A. A. Balkema 1951

Van Haeringen, C. B. *Netherlandic Language Research* E. J. Brill 1954

Vasmer, M. *Russisches Etymologisches Wörterbuch* Indogermanische Bibliothek 1950-58

Velleman, A. *Dicziunari Scurznieu da la Lingua Ladina* Samaden l929

Vinokur, G. O. *La Langue Russe* Biblioteque Russe de L'Institut d' Etudes Slaves 1947

Index

Entries in **bold** type indicate words whose origins are discussed in the text. Page references in *italic* type indicate information in captions and charts, and/or illustrations.

Acknowledgements

The author wishes to renew his thanks to the collaborators and advisers of the first edition: Neil Fairbairn; William McDonald; W.M. Lockwood; R.H. Robins; and Dr A. Angelou.

PICTURE CREDITS

T=TOP B= BELOW L = LEFT R=RIGHT
Mary Evans Picture Library 12; Ancient Art & Architecture 13; Michael Holford 21; Homer Sykes 25; E.T Archive 29; Bruce Coleman Ltd 31; Zefa 33; The Mansell Collection 34; Ephesus Museum, Turkey/Bridgeman Art Library 40; Zefa 45; Ancient Art & Architecture 48; The Royal Geographical Society/Chile Boundary Commission 50; Woolf-Greenham Collection 51; Susan Griggs Agency 52, 53; Mick Sharp Photography 54; Bruce Coleman Ltd 57; Trip/Helene Rogers 59; Ancient Art & Architecture 68; Michael Holford 71; Mary Evans Picture Library 72; Zefa 75; Hulton Picture Library 76; Bruce Coleman Ltd 77; Susan Griggs Agency 81T; Bodleian Library, Oxford 81B; Susan Griggs Agency 83; Bruce Coleman Ltd 85, 89; Michael Holford 93; E.T Archive 100T; Ancient Art & Architecture 100B; Susan Griggs Agency 103, 107; Uppsala Universitetsbibliotek 110; Susan Griggs Agency 112; Bruce Coleman Ltd 115, 118; The Mansell Collection 120, 122, 123; Zefa 124; The National

Gallery 129; Mary Evans Picture Library 131; Trip 133; E.T Archive 137L; Topham Picture Library 137R; E.T Archive 138; Mary Evans Picture Library 139; E.T Archive 140; The Graves Art Gallery 143; Hulton Picture Library 145; Zefa 148, 153; Ancient Art & Architecture 154; Bruce Coleman Ltd/Keith Gunnar 160; Mary Evans Picture Library 163; Camera Press 165; Topham Picture Library 177.

Whilst every care has been taken to trace copyright owners of the photographs appearing in this book, Eddison Sadd Editions would like to apologise to anyone whose copyright has been unknowingly infringed.

EDDISON•SADD EDITIONS

Editorial director	Ian Jackson
Editor	Vivienne Wells
Proof reader	Michele Turney
Indexer	Helen Smith
Art director	Nick Eddison
Mac designer	Brazzle Atkins
Map artwork	Hardlines
Picture researcher	Liz Eddison
Production director	Charles James